NTC POCKET REFERENCES

Dictionary of
Quotations

Dictionary of
Quotations

NTC Publishing Group
Lincolnwood, Illinois USA

**Cataloging in Publication Data
is available from the United States Library of Congress**

© 1997 by NTC Publishing Group, 4255 West Touhy Avenue,
Lincolnwood (Chicago), Illinois 60646-1975 U.S.A.
Manufactured in the United Kingdom.

Compiler
Jennifer Speake

Editorial director
Michael Upshall

Text editors
Avril Cridlan
Helen McCurdy
Martin Noble
Catherine Thompson

Production
Tony Ballsdon

A

Aalto Alvar (Hugo Alvar Henrik) 1898–1976. Finnish architect and designer.

It is the task of the architect to give life a gentler structure.
Connoisseur June 1987

Acheson Dean (Gooderham) 1893–1971. US politician.

Great Britain has lost an empire and has not yet found a role.
Speech at the Military Academy, West Point, 5 Dec 1962

The first requirement of a statesman is that he be dull.   2
This is not always easy to achieve.
Observer 21 June 1970

Acton John Emerich Edward Dalberg-Acton, 1st Baron Acton
1834–1902. English historian and Liberal politician.

Power tends to corrupt and absolute power corrupts absolutely.
Letter to Mandell Creighton April 1887

Adams Henry Brooks 1838–1918. US historian and novelist.

Politics, as a practice, whatever its professions, has always been
the systematic organization of hatreds.
Education of Henry Adams ch 1

A friend in power is a friend lost.   2
Education of Henry Adams ch 7

One friend in a lifetime is much; two are many; three are hardly   3
possible.
Education of Henry Adams ch 20

Addison Joseph 1672–1719. English poet, playwright and essayist.

There is nothing more requisite in business than dispatch.
Ancient Medals

The woman that deliberates is lost.

Cato IV. i

Content thyself to be obscurely good. / When vice prevails, / and impious men bear sway, / The post of honour is a private station.

Cato IV. iv

From hence, let fierce contending nations know / What dire effects from civil discord flow.

Cato V. iv

Music, the greatest good that mortals know, / And all of heaven we have below.

'Song for St Cecilia's Day'

A perfect Tragedy is the noblest Production of human Nature.

Spectator no 39

We have in England a particular bashfulness in every thing that regards religion.

Spectator no 458

Adenauer Konrad 1876–1967. German politician.

A thick skin is a gift from God.

New York Times 30 Dec 1959

Adler Alfred 1870–1937. Austrian psychologist.

Whenever a child lies you will always find a severe parent. A lie would have no sense unless the truth were felt to be dangerous.

New York Times 1949

Aeschylus *c*. 525–*c*. 456 BC. Athenian dramatist.

Every ruler is harsh whose rule is new.

Prometheus Bound

Agar Herbert 1897–1980. US poet and writer.

The truth which makes men free is for the most part the truth which men prefer not to hear.

Time for Greatness

Agate James Evershed 1877–1947. English essayist and theatre critic.

I am not interested in what anybody else thinks.My mind is not a bed to be made and remade.

Ego

Albee Edward 1928– . US dramatist.

I have a fine sense of the ridiculous, but no sense of humour.
Who's Afraid of Virginia Woolf?

Alcuin (Flaccus Albinus Alcuinus) 735–804. English scholar.

The voice of the people is the voice of God.
Letter to the Emperor Charlemagne, AD 800

Aldington Richard 1892–1962. English Imagist poet, novelist, and critic.

Patriotism is a lively sense of collective responsibility.
Nationalism is a silly cock crowing on its own dunghill.
Colonel's Daughter

Aldrich Henry 1648–1710. English scholar.

If all be true that I do think, / There are five reasons we should drink; / Good wine—a friend—or being dry / Or lest we should be by and by / Or any other reason why.
'Reasons for Drinking'

Alexander II 1818–1881. Tsar of Russia 1855–81.

It is better to abolish serfdom from above than to wait for it to abolish itself from below.
Speech to the Moscow nobility March 1856

Alexander the Great 356–323 BC. King of Macedonia.

I will not steal a victory.
Remark on refusing to attack the Persian army before
the Battle of Gaugamela 331 BC, quoted in Plutarch *Lives*

Alexander Cecil Frances 1818–1895. Irish poet and hymn writer.

All things bright and beautiful, / All creatures great and small, / All things wise and wonderful, / The Lord God made them all.
'All Things Bright and Beautiful'

Alfonso XIII of Spain 1885–1941. King of Spain.

Assassination—an accident of my trade.
Remark after an attempt on his life May 1906

Ali Muhammad (Cassius Clay) 1942– . US world heavyweight champion boxer.

Float like a butterfly, sting like a bee.
Catch-phrase

Allen Woody. Adopted name of Allen Stewart Konigsberg 1935– . US film writer, director, and actor.

If only God would give me some clear sign! Like making a large deposit in my name at a Swiss bank.
New Yorker 5 Nov 1973

Bisexuality immediately doubles your chances of a date on Saturday night.   2
New York Herald Tribune 1975

It's not that I'm afraid to die. I just don't want to be there when it happens.   3
Death

Money is better than poverty, if only for financial reasons.   4
Without Feathers

Allston Washington 1779–1843. US painter.

The love of gain has never made a painter, but it has marred many.
Lectures on Art

Alva or Alba Ferdinand Alvarez de Toledo, duke of 1508–1582. Spanish politician and general.

I have tamed men of iron and why then shall I not be able to tame these men of butter?
Reply to King Philip II of Spain on being appointed governor general of the Netherlands 1567

Amiel Henri Frédéric 1821–1881. Swiss philosopher and writer.

Truth is not only violated by falsehood; it may be outraged by silence.

Journal in Time

Amis Kingsley 1922– . English novelist and poet.

I was never an Angry Young Man. I am angry only when I hit my thumb with a hammer.

On the labelling of authors as *Angry Young Men*, *Eton College Chronicle*

It was no wonder that people were so horrible when they started   *2* life as children.

Lucky Jim

Anderson Sherwood 1876–1941. US writer.

I found it impossible to work with security staring me in the face.

To his publisher, on declining a weekly cheque.

Andrewes Lancelot 1555–1626. Church of England bishop.

The nearer the Church the further from God.

'Sermon on the Nativity' 1622

Anonymous

Know thyself.

Saying written on the wall of the ancient temple of Delphi

Anouilh Jean 1910–1987. French dramatist.

Tragedy is restful and the reason is that hope, that foul, deceitful thing, has no part in it.

Antigone

Anstey Christopher 1724–1805. English poet.

How he welcomes at once all the world and his wife, /And how civil to folk he ne'er saw in his life.

The New Bath Guide

Anthony Susan B(rownell) 1820–1906. US campaigner for women's rights.

> The true Republic: men, their rights and nothing more; women, their rights and nothing less.
>
> Motto of her newspaper *Revolution*

Antiphanes fl. 360 BC. Greek comic poet.

> Idly inquisitive tribe of grammarians, / who dig up the poetry of others / By the roots ... Get away, bugs, / that bite secretly at the eloquent.
>
> Greek Anthology

Apocrypha appendix to Old Testament of the Bible.

> He that toucheth pitch shall be defiled therewith.
>
> Ecclesiasticus 13:1

> Let us now praise famous men, and our fathers that begat us.   *2*
>
> Ecclesiasticus 44:1

> Their bodies are buried in peace: but their name liveth for   *3*
> evermore.
>
> Ecclesiasticus 44:14

Appleton Thomas Gold 1812–1884. US writer.

> A Boston man is the east wind made flesh.
>
> Attributed remark

> Good Americans, when they die, go to Paris.   *2*
> Quoted in O W Holmes *Autocrat of the Breakfast Table*

Aragon Louis 1897–1982. French poet and novelist.

> The function of genius is to furnish cretins with ideas twenty years later.
>
> *Traité du Style* 'Le Porte-Plume'

Arbuthnot John 1667–1735. Scottish writer and physician.

> Law is a bottomless pit.
>
> *The History of John Bull*

Archimedes *c.* 287–212 BC. Greek mathematician.

Eureka! I have found it!
>> Remark, quoted in Vitruvius Pollio *De Architectura* IX

Aristotle 384–322 BC. Greek philosopher.

Man by nature is a political animal.
>> *Politics*

Armistead Lewis Addison 1817–1863. US army officer.

Give them the cold steel, boys!
>> Attributed remark during American Civil War

Armstrong Louis (*Satchmo*) 1901–1971. US jazz musician and singer.

A lot of cats copy the Mona Lisa, but people still line up to see the original.
>> Reply when asked whether he objected
>> to people copying his style

Arnold Matthew 1822–1888. English poet and critic.

The men of culture are the true apostles of equality.
>> *Culture and Anarchy*

The pursuit of perfection, then, is the pursuit of sweetness and light ...   2
>> *Culture and Anarchy*

The sea of faith / Was once, too, at the full, and round earth's   3
shore / Lay like the folds of a bright girdle furl'd; / But now I
only hear / Its melancholy, long, withdrawing roar.
>> 'Dover Beach'

And we are here as on a darkling plain / Swept with confused   4
alarms of struggle and flight, / Where ignorant armies clash by
night.
>> 'Dover Beach'

Home of lost causes, and forsaken beliefs, and unpopular   5
names, and impossible loyalties!
>> Of Oxford, in *Essays in Criticism First Series,* preface

The unplumb'd, salt, estranging sea.   *6*
                                   'Isolation, or To Marguerite'

Culture, the acquainting ourselves with the best that has been   *7*
known and said in the world, and thus with the history of the
human spirit.
                    Literature and Dogma preface to 1873 edition

Strew on her roses, roses, / And never a spray of yew. / In quiet *8*
she reposes: / Ah! would that I did too.
                                                     'Requiescat'

All the live murmur of a summer's day.   *9*
                                              The Scholar-Gipsy

This strange disease of modern life.   *10*
                                              The Scholar-Gipsy

And that sweet City with her dreaming spires, / She needs not   *11*
June for beauty's heightening.
                                                          Thyrsis

Arnold Thomas 1795–1842. English schoolmaster.

My object will be, if possible, to form Christian men, for
Christian boys I can scarcely hope to make.
                  Letter, on appointment to headmastership of Rugby

Asaf George 1880–1951. British songwriter.

What's the use of worrying? / It never was worth while, / So,
pack up your troubles in your old kit-bag, / And smile, smile,
smile.
                       'Pack Up Your Troubles In Your Old Kit-Bag'

Ascham Roger *c*. 1515–1568. English scholar and royal tutor.

He that will write well in any tongue must follow the counsel of
Aristotle: to speak as the common people do, to think as wise
men do.
                                                       Toxophilus

Ashford Daisy 1881–1972. English author, age nine years.

My life will be sour grapes and ashes without you.
Young Visiters ch 8

Oh I see said the Earl but my own idear is that these things are   2
piffle before the wind.
Young Visiters ch 5

I am not quite a gentleman but you would hardly notice it but   3
can't be helped anyhow.
Young Visiters ch 1

Asimov Isaac 1920–1992. Russian-born US author of science fiction
and nonfiction.

If my doctor told me I only had six months to live, I wouldn't
brood. I'd type a little faster.
Life

Asquith Herbert Henry, 1st Earl of Oxford and Asquith 1852–1928.
British Liberal politician, prime minister 1908–16.

Youth would be an ideal state if it came a little later in life.
Observer 15 Apr 1923

One to mislead the public, another to mislead the Cabinet, and   2
the third to mislead itself.
Of the War Office's sets of figures, quoted in
Alistair Horne *Price of Glory*

Asquith Margot 1865–1945. Second wife of Herbert Asquith.

He can't see a belt without hitting below it.
Of Lloyd George, *Listener* 11 June 1953

Lord Birkenhead is very clever but sometimes his brains go to   2
his head.
Listener 11 June 1953

Astaire Fred. Adopted name of Frederick Austerlitz 1899–1987. US
dancer, actor, singer, and choreographer.

I have no desire to prove anything by dancing ... I just dance.
Remark

Astley Jacob 1579–1652. English Royalist general.

O Lord! thou knowest how busy I must be this day: / if I
forget thee, do not thou forget me.
Prayer before the Battle of Edgehill,
quoted in Sir Philip Warwick Memoires

Astor Nancy, Lady Astor (Nancy Witcher Langhorne) 1879–1964.
US-born British politician.

One reason why I don't drink is because I wish to know when
I am having a good time.
Christian Herald June 1960

I married beneath me, all women do.   2
Dictionary of National Biography 1961–1970

Atatürk (Mustafa) Kemal 1881–1938. Turkish president.

I don't act for public opinion. I act for the nation and for my own
satisfaction.
Quoted in Lord Kinross Atatürk

Atkinson Brooks 1894–1984.

After each war there is a little less democracy to save.
Once Around the Sun

Attenborough David 1926–   . English traveller and zoologist.

Anyone who spends any time watching animals has to conclude
that the overriding purpose of an individual's existence is to
pass on some part of it to the next generation.
The Trials of Life

Attlee Clement (Richard), 1st Earl 1883–1967. English Labour
politician.

I should be a sad subject for any publicity expert. I have none of
the qualities which create publicity.
Quoted in Harold Nicolson, Diary 14 Jan 1949

I think the British have the distinction above all other nations of   2
being able to put new wine into old bottles without bursting them.
Hansard 24 Oct 1950

Democracy means government by discussion, but it is only *3*
effective if you can stop people talking.
                          Speech at Oxford, 14 June 1957

I must remind the Right Honourable Gentleman that *4*
a monologue is not a decision.
                          Remark addressed to Winston Churchill,
                          in F. Williams *Prime Minister Remembers*

Auden W(ystan) H(ugh) 1907–1973. English-born US poet.

A poet's hope: to be, / like some valley cheese, / local, but
prized elsewhere.
                                        Collected Poems

One cannot review a bad book without showing off. *2*
                          Dyer's Hand, 'Reading'

Some books are undeservedly forgotten; none are undeservedly *3*
remembered.
                          Dyer's Hand, 'Reading'

When he laughed, respectable senators burst with laughter, / *4*
And when he cried the little children died in the streets.
                                        'Epitaph on a Tyrant'

To us he is no more a person / Now but a whole climate of opinion. *5*
                          'In Memory of Sigmund Freud'

She survived whatever happened; she forgave; she became. *6*
                                        'The Model'

To the man-in-the-street, who, I'm sorry to say, / Is a keen *7*
observer of life, / The word 'Intellectual' suggests straight
away / A man who's untrue to his wife.
                                        New Year Letter note

We must love one another or die. *8*
                                        'September 1, 1939'

My Dear One is mine as mirrors are lonely. *9*
                          'The Sea and the Mirror' – 'Miranda'

Was he free? Was he happy? The question is absurd: / Had
anything been wrong, we should certainly have heard. *10*
> 'The Unknown Citizen'

My face looks like a wedding-cake left out in the rain. *12*
> Quoted in H Carpenter *W H Auden* pt 2, ch 6

Augier Émile 1820–1889. French dramatist.

Longing to be back in the mud.
> *Le Mariage d'Olympe*

Augustine of Hippo St 354–430 Christian theologian.

Give me chastity and continency, but do not give it yet.
> *Confessions*

Love and do what you will. *2*
> Treatise on the Joannine Epistles.

Austen Jane 1775–1817. English novelist.

One half of the world cannot understand the pleasures of the other.
> *Emma*

There certainly are not so many men of large fortune in the *2*
world, as there are pretty women to deserve them.
> *Mansfield Park* ch 1

Let other pens dwell on guilt and misery. *3*
> *Mansfield Park* ch 48

It is a truth universally acknowledged, that a single man in *4*
possession of a good fortune, must be in want of a wife.
> *Pride and Prejudice* ch 1

For what do we live, but to make sport for our neighbours, and *5*
laugh at them in our turn?
> *Pride and Prejudice* ch 57

Austin Alfred 1835–1913. English poet.

I dare not alter these things, they come to me from above.
> Rejecting the accusation of writing ungrammatical verse

Averroës 1126–1198. Arabian philosopher (Arabic *Ibn Rushd*).

Philosophy is the friend and milk-sister of the Law.
The Decisive Treatise

Ayckbourn Alan 1939–   . English dramatist.

Few women care to be laughed at and men not at all, except for
large sums of money.
The Norman Conquests

Ayer A(lfred) J(ules) 1910–1989. English philosopher.

If I had been someone not very clever, I would have done an
easier job like publishing. That's the easiest job I can think of.
Remark

Aytoun William Edmondstoune 1813–1865. Scottish poet.

The earth is all the home I have, / The heavens my wide roof-
tree.
The Wandering Jew

B

Bacon Francis 1561–1626. English politician, philosopher, and essayist.

If a man will begin with certainties, he shall end in doubts; but if he will be content to begin with doubts, he shall end in certainties.

Advancement of Learning bk I

Time, which is the author of authors. *2*

Advancement of Learning bk I

A man must make his opportunity, as oft as find it. *3*

Advancement of Learning bk II

Man seeketh in society comfort, use, and protection. *4*

Advancement of Learning bk II

They are ill discoverers that think there is no land, when they *5* can see nothing but sea.

Advancement of Learning bk II

Hope is a good breakfast, but it is a bad supper. *6*

Apothegms

Envy never makes holiday. *7*

De Augmentis Scientiarum

Silence is the virtue of fools. *8*

De Augmentis Scientiarum

I do not believe that any man fears to be dead, but only the *9* stroke of death.

An Essay on Death

A little philosophy inclineth man's mind to atheism, but depth *10* in philosophy bringeth men's minds about to religion.

Essays, 'Atheism'

If a man be gracious and courteous to strangers, it shows he is a citizen of the world. *11*
Essays, 'Goodness, and Goodness of Nature'

Virtue is like a rich stone, best plain set. *12*
Essays, 'Of Beauty'

Nothing doth more hurt in a state than that cunning men pass for wise. *13*
Essays, 'Of cunning'

Men fear death as children fear to go in the dark. *14*
Essays, 'Of Death'

Riches are for spending. *15*
Essays, 'Of Expense'

There is little friendship in the world, and least of all between equals. *16*
Essays, 'Of Followers and Friends'

God Almighty first planted a garden; and, indeed, it is the purest of human pleasures. *17*
Essays, 'Of Gardens'

All rising to great place is by a winding stair.*1* *18*
Essays, 'Of Great Place'

Men in great place are thrice servants: servants of the sovereign or state, servants of fame, and servants of business. *19*
Essays, 'Of Great Place'

He that hath wife and children hath given hostages to fortune. *20*
Essays, 'Of Marriage and the Single Life'

Wives are young men's mistresses, companions for middle age, and old men's nurses. *21*
Essays, 'Of Marriage and the Single Life'

Children sweeten labours, but they make misfortunes more bitter. *22*
Essays, 'Of Parents and Children'

Fame is like a river, that beareth up things light and swollen, and drowns things weighty and solid. *23*
Essays, 'Of Praise'

Revenge is a kind of wild justice. *24*
Essays, 'Of Revenge'

Money is like muck, not good except it be spread. *25*
Essays, 'Of Seditions and Troubles'

The remedy is worse than the disease. *26*
Essays, 'Of Seditions and Troubles'

Reading maketh a full man; conference a ready man and *27*
writing an exact man.
Essays, 'Of Studies'

Some books are to be tasted, others to be swallowed, and some *28*
few to be chewed and digested.
Essays, 'Of Studies'

There is a superstition in avoiding superstition. *29*
Essays, 'Of Superstition'

Suspicions amongst thoughts are like bats amongst birds, they *30*
ever fly by twilight.
Essays, 'Of Suspicion'

There is nothing makes a man suspect much, more than to *31*
know little.
Essays, 'Of Suspicion'

What is truth? said jesting Pilate; and would not stay for an answer. *32*
Essays, 'Of Truth'

I have taken all knowledge to be my province. *33*
Letter to Lord Burleigh 1592

Opportunity makes a thief. *34*
Letter to the Earl of Essex 1598

Books must follow sciences, and not sciences books. *35*
Proposition touching Amendment of Laws

Baden-Powell Robert 1857–1941. Founder of the Boy Scout
movement.

A Scout smiles and whistles under all circumstances.
Scouting for Boys

Baez Joan 1941–   . US folk singer and pacifist activist.

I've never had a humble opinion. If you've got an opinion,
why be humble about it?

Remark

Bagehot Walter 1826–1877. English writer and economist.

Royalty is a government in which the attention of the nation is
concentrated on one person doing interesting actions. A
Republic is a government in which that attention is divided
between many, who are all doing uninteresting actions.

The English Constitution

One of the greatest pains to human nature is the pain of a new   2
idea.

Physics and Politics

The most melancholy of human reflections, perhaps, is that, on   3
the whole, it is a question whether the benevolence of mankind
does most good or harm.

Physics and Politics

Bairnsfather Bruce 1888–1959. British artist/cartoonist.

Well, if you knows of a better 'ole, go to it.

Fragments from France

Baker Janet 1933–   . English opera singer.

Singing lieder is like putting a piece of music under a microscope.

Opera News July 1977

Baldwin James 1924–1987. US writer and civil-rights activist.

It comes as a great shock to see Gary Cooper killing off the
Indians and, although you are rooting for Gary Cooper, that the
Indians are you.

Speech at Cambridge University 17 Feb 1965

Money, it turned out, was exactly like sex, you thought of nothing   2
else if you didn't have it and thought of other things if you did.

'Black Boy looks at the White Boy'

Anyone who has ever struggled with poverty knows how extremely expensive it is to be poor.

Nobody Knows My Name, 'Fifth Avenue, Uptown: a letter from Harlem'

3

Freedom is not something that anybody can be given; freedom is something people take and people are as free as they want to be.

Nobody Knows My Name, 'Notes for a Hypothetical Novel'

4

Baldwin Stanley, 1st Earl Baldwin of Bewdley 1867–1947. English politician, prime minister 1923–24.

A platitude is simply a truth repeated until people get tired of hearing it.

Hansard 29 May 1924

'Safety first' does not mean a smug self-satisfaction with everything as it is. It is a warning to all persons who are going to cross a road in dangerous circumstances.

The Times 21 May 1929

2

I think it is well also for the man in the street to realize that there is no power on earth that can protect him from being bombed. Whatever people may tell him, the bomber will always get through. The only defence is in offence, which means that you have to kill more women and children more quickly than the enemy if you want to save yourselves.

Hansard 10 Nov 1932

3

The intelligent are to the intelligentsia what a gentleman is to a gent.

Quoted in G M Young *Stanley Baldwin*

4

Balfour Arthur James, 1st Earl of Balfour 1848–1930. Scottish politician, prime minister 1902–05.

It is unfortunate, considering that enthusiasm moves the world, that so few enthusiasts can be trusted to speak the truth.

Letter to Mrs Drew, May 1891

Biography should be written by an acute enemy.

Observer 30 Jan 1927

2

I never forgive but I always forget.   *3*
                        Quoted by R Blake *Conservative Party*

Balzac Honoré de 1799–1850. French novelist.

Equality may perhaps be a right, but no power on earth can
turn it into a fact.
                                        La Duchesse de Langeais

Bankhead Tallulah 1903–1968. US actress.

I'm as pure as the driven slush.
                                        Saturday Evening Post 12 Apr 1947

There is less in this than meets the eye.   *2*
                        Of Maeterlinck's play *Aglavaine and Selysette*, in
                        Alexander Woollcott *Shouts and Murmurs*

Baraka (Imamu) Amiri. Born LeRoi Jones 1934–   . US poet, dramatist
and black activist.

A rich man told me recently that a liberal is a man who tells
other people what to do with their money.
                                        Kulchur Spring 1962 'Tokenism'

God has been replaced, as he has all over the West, with   *2*
respectability and airconditioning.
                                        Midstream

Barbellion W N P. Pen name of Bruce Frederick Cummings 1889–1919.
English diarist.

Give me the man who will surrender the whole world for a
moss or a caterpillar, and impracticable visions for a simple
human delight.
Enjoying Life and Other Literary Remains 'Crying for the Moon'

Barker Ronnie 1929–   . English comic actor and writer.

The marvellous thing about a joke with a double meaning is
that it can only mean one thing.
                                        Sauce, 'Daddie's Sauce'

Barnes Clive 1927– . US writer

The kind of show to give pornography a dirty name.
            Of *Oh, Calcutta!*, *New York Times* 18 June 1969

Barnes Julian 1946– . English novelist.

Do not imagine that Art is something which is designed to give gentle uplift and self-confidence. Art is not a *brassière*. At least, not in the English sense. But do not forget that *brassière* is the French for life-jacket.
                                    Flaubert's Parrot

Barnum P(hineas) T(aylor) 1810–1891. US showman.

How were the receipts today in Madison Square Garden?
                                    Last words

Barrie J(ames) M(atthew) 1860–1937. Scottish dramatist and novelist.

Never ascribe to an opponent motives meaner than your own.
            Address at St Andrew's 3 May 1922

His lordship may compel us to be equal upstairs, but there will   2
never be equality in the servants' hall.
                        The Admirable Crichton I

I'm a second eleven sort of chap.   3
                        The Admirable Crichton III

It's grand, and you canna expect to be baith grand and comfortable.   4
                        The Little Minister

Every time a child says 'I don't believe in fairies' there is a   5
little fairy somewhere that falls down dead.
                                    Peter Pan I

To die will be an awfully big adventure.   6
                                    Peter Pan III

Do you believe in fairies? ... If you believe, clap your hands!   7
                                    Peter Pan IV

That is ever the way. 'Tis all jealousy to the bride and good   8
wishes to the corpse.
                                    Quality Street

The printing press is either the greatest blessing or the greatest   **9**
curse of modern times, one sometimes forgets which.
Sentimental Tommy

There are few more impressive sights in the world than a   **10**
Scotsman on the make.
What Every Woman Knows

Baruch Bernard (Mannes) 1870–1965. US financier.

Let us not be deceived—we are today in the midst of a cold war.
Speech to South Carolina Legislature 16 Apr 1947

To me old age is always fifteen years older than I am.   **2**
Newsweek 29 Aug 1955

Bashkirtseff Marie 1860–1884. Russian diarist and painter.

If I had been born a man, I would have conquered Europe.
As I was born a woman, I exhausted my energy in tirades
against fate, and in eccentricities.
Journal June 1884

Basil *St* c. 330–379. Cappadocian monk.

Teaching a Christian how he ought to live does not call so
much for words as for daily example.
Oration

Bateman Edgar 19th century–   . English songwriter.

Wiv a ladder and some glasses, / You could see to 'Ackney
Marshes, / If it wasn't for the 'ouses in between.
If It Wasn't For The 'Ouses In Between

Baudelaire Charles Pierre 1821–1867. French poet.

But the real travellers are only those who leave / For the sake
of leaving.
'The Voyage'

Baum L(yman) Frank 1856–1919. US writer, children's author.

'The road to the City of Emeralds is paved with yellow brick,'
said the Witch, 'so you cannot miss it.'
The Wonderful Wizard of Oz

Bayly Thomas Haynes 1797–1839. English writer.

Absence makes the heart grow fonder.

Isle of Beauty

Béjart Maurice 1927– . French ballet director and choreographer.

The last refuge in our world where a man can discover the exact measure of his own soul.

Of the stage, in *Dynamic Tradition* in *Ballet and Modern Dance*

Beatty David, 1st Earl 1871–1936. English admiral in World War I.

There's something wrong with our bloody ships to-day, Chatfield.

Remark during the Battle of Jutland 1916

Beaumont and Fletcher Francis 1584–1616 and Fletcher John 1579–1625 English dramatists.

You are no better than you should be.

The Coxcomb

Death hath so many doors to let out life.   *2*

The Customs of the Country

But what is past my help, is past my care.   *3*

The Double Marriage

It is always good / When a man has two irons in the fire.   *4*

The Faithful Friends

Let's meet, and either do, or die.   *5*

The Island Princess

I find the medicine worse than the malady.   *6*

The Lover's Progress

I'll put a spoke among your wheels.   *7*

The Mad Lover

'Tis virtue, and not birth that makes us noble: / Great actions speak great minds.   *8*

The Prophetess

Kiss till the cow come home.   *9*

The Scornful Lady

Whistle and she'll come to you.   *10*
Wit Without Money

Beauvoir Simone de 1908–1986. French socialist, feminist, and writer.

One is not born a woman. One becomes one.
The Second Sex

Beaverbrook (William) Max(well) Aitken, 1st Baron Beaverbrook 1879–1964. Canadian-born British financier, newspaper proprietor, and politician.

The Daily Express declares that Great Britain will not be involved in a European war this year or next year either.
Daily Express 19 Sept 1938

He did not seem to care which way he travelled providing he   *2*
was in the driver's seat. With the publication of his Private
Papers in 1952, he committed suicide 25 years after his death.
Of Earl Haig *Men and Power* 1956

Beckett Samuel 1906–1989. Irish novelist and dramatist.

Vladimir: That passed the time.
Estragon: It would have passed in any case.
Vladimir: Yes, but not so rapidly.
Waiting for Godot

Becon Thomas 1512–1567. English Protestant divine.

For when the wine is in, the wit is out.
Catechism

Bee Barnard Elliott 1824–1861. US soldier.

Let us determine to die here, and we will conquer. There is Jackson standing like a stone wall. Rally behind the Virginians.
Said at the first Battle of Bull Run

Beecham Thomas 1879–1961. English orchestral conductor.

The English may not like music, but they absolutely love the noise it makes.
New York Herald Tribune 1961

There are two golden rules for an orchestra: start together and finish together. The public doesn't give a damn what goes on in between. *2*

Beecham Stories

At a rehearsal I let the orchestra play as they like. At the concert I make them play as I like. *3*

N Cardus *Sir Thomas Beecham*

Beerbohm Max 1872–1956. English caricaturist and author.

There is always something rather absurd about the past.

1880

I have known no man of genius who had not to pay, in some affliction or defect either physical or spiritual, for what the gods had given him. *2*

And Even Now

Mankind is divisible into two great classes: hosts and guests. *3*
Hosts and Guests

The dullard's envy of brilliant men is always assuaged by the suspicion that they will come to a bad end. *4*

Zuleika Dobson

Beers Ethel Lynn 1827–1879. US poet.

All quiet along the Potomac to-night.
All Quiet along the Potomac

Behan Brendan 1923–1964. Irish dramatist.

He was born an Englishman and remained one for years.
Hostage

I'm a secret policeman, and I don't care who knows it! *2*
The Hostage

There's no such thing as bad publicity except your own obituary. *3*
Dominic Behan *My Brother Brendan*

Behn Aphra 1640–1689. English female novelist and playwright.

Love ceases to be a pleasure, when it ceases to be a secret.
The Lover's Watch, 'Four o'clock'

Faith, Sir, we are here to day, and gone to morrow.   **2**
The Lucky Chance IV

Variety is the soul of pleasure.   **3**
The Rover, Part II, I

Come away; poverty's catching.   **4**
The Rover, Part II III.i

Money speaks sense in a language all nations understand.   **5**
The Rover, Part II III. i

Behrens Peter 1868–1940. German architect.

Architecture comprises two ideas: the mastery of the practical, and the art of the beautiful.
Architectural Press 1981

Bell Alexander Graham 1847–1922. Scottish-born US scientist and inventor of the telephone.

Mr Watson, come here; I want you.
First complete sentence spoken over the telephone March 1876

Belloc (Joseph) Hilaire Pierre 1870–1953. French-born English writer and politician.

Gentlemen, I am a Catholic. As far as possible, I go to Mass every day. This is a rosary. As far as possible, I kneel down and tell these beads every day. If you reject me on account of my religion, I shall thank God that He has spared me the indignity of being your representative.
Speech to voters of South Salford 1906

Your little hands were made to take / The better things and leave the worse ones: / They also may be used to shake / The massive paws of elder persons.   **2**
Bad Child's Book of Beasts dedication

I shoot the Hippopotamus / With bullets made of platinum, / Because if I use leaden ones / His hide is sure to flatten 'em.   **3**
The Bad Child's Book of Beasts, 'Hippopotamus'

The chief defect of Henry King / Was chewing little bits of string. **4**
Cautionary Tales, 'Henry King'

Physicians of the Utmost Fame / Were called at once; but **5**
when they came / They answered, as they took their Fees, /
'There is no Cure for this Disease.'
Cautionary Tales, 'Henry King'

And always keep a-hold of Nurse / For fear of finding **6**
something worse.
Cautionary Tales, 'Jim'

In my opinion, Butlers ought / To know their place, and not to **7**
play / The Old Retainer night and day.
Cautionary Tales, 'Lord Lundy'

Lord Lundy from his earliest years / Was far too freely moved **8**
to tears.
Cautionary Tales, 'Lord Lundy'

Matilda told such Dreadful Lies, / It made one Gasp and **9**
Stretch one's Eyes; / Her Aunt, who, from her Earliest Youth, /
Had kept a Strict Regard for Truth, / Attempted to Believe
Matilda: / The effort very nearly killed her.
Cautionary Tales, 'Matilda'

Of Courtesy, it is much less / Than Courage of Heart or **10**
Holiness, / Yet in my Walks it seems to me / That the Grace of
God is in Courtesy.
'Courtesy'

Carthage had not desired to create, but only to enjoy: therefore **11**
she left us nothing.
Esto Perpetua

I'm tired of Love: I'm still more tired of Rhyme. / But Money **12**
gives me pleasure all the time.
'Fatigued'

Whatever happens we have got / The Maxim Gun, and they **13**
have not.
Modern Traveller

The accursed power which stands on Privilege / (And goes with   *14*
Women, and Champagne, and Bridge) / Broke – and
Democracy resumed her reign: / (Which goes with Bridge, and
Women and Champagne).

'On a Great Election'

When I am dead, I hope it may be said: / 'His sins were scarlet,   *15*
but his books were read.'

'On His Books'

I am a sundial, and I make a botch / Of what is done much   *16*
better by a watch.

'On a Sundial'

Bellow Saul 1915– . Canadian-born US novelist.

Death is the dark backing a mirror needs if we are to see
anything.

Observer Dec 1983

Benchley Robert 1889–1945. US humorist, actor, and drama critic.

My only solution for the problem of habitual accidents and, so
far, nobody has asked me for my solution, is to stay in bed all
day. Even then, there is always the chance that you will fall out.
Chips off the old Benchley, 'Safety Second'

The surest way to make a monkey of a man is to quote him.   *2*
My Ten Years in a Quandary

In America there are two classes of travel – first class, and with   *3*
children.

Pluck and Luck

Benda Julien 1867–1956. French writer and philosopher.

La trahison des clercs. The treason of the intellectuals.

Book title

Benét Stephen Vincent 1898–1943. US writer.

Bury my heart at Wounded Knee.

Yale Review (1927) vol 17, 'American Names'

Bennett Alan 1934– . English dramatist, screenwriter, and actor.

Life is rather like a tin of sardines – we're all of us looking for the key.

Beyond the Fringe

I have never understood this liking for war. It panders to instincts already catered for within the scope of any respectable domestic establishment.   2

Forty Years On I

We started off trying to set up a small anarchist community, but people wouldn't obey the rules.   3

Getting On I

We were put to Dickens as children but it never quite took. That unremitting humanity soon had me cheesed off.   4

Old Country II

Bennett Arnold 1867–1931. English novelist

'Ye can call it influenza if ye like...There was no influenza in my young days. We called a cold a cold.'

The Card ch 8

'And yet ...what's he done? Has he ever done a day's work in his life? What great cause is he identified with?' 'He's identified,' said the first speaker, 'with the great cause of cheering us all up.'   2

The Card ch 12

The price of justice is eternal publicity.   3

Things that have Interested Me, 'Secret Trials'

Pessimism, when you get used to it, is just as agreeable as optimism.   4

Things that have Interested Me, 'Slump in Pessimism'

Being a husband is a whole-time job.   5

The Title I

Journalists say a thing that they know isn't true, in the hope that if they keep on saying it long enough it will be true.   6

The Title II

Benson A C 1862–1925. English writer.

I don't like authority, at least I don't like other people's authority.
Excerpts from Letters to M. E. A.

Land of Hope and Glory, Mother of the Free, / How shall we   *2*
extol thee, who are born of thee?
'Land of Hope and Glory'

Bentham Jeremy 1748–1832. English philosopher and legal reformer.

All punishment is mischief: all punishment in itself is evil.
Principles of Morals and Legislation

Bentley Edmund Clerihew 1875–1956. English writer.

What I like about Clive / Is that he is no longer alive. / There's
a great deal to be said / For being dead.
Biography for Beginners 'Clive'

The Art of Biography / Is different from Geography. /   *2*
Geography is about Maps, / But Biography is about Chaps.
Biography for Beginners, introduction

Sir Christopher Wren / Said, 'I am going to dine with some men.   *3*
/ If anybody calls / Say I am designing St Paul's.'
Biography for Beginners, 'Sir Christopher Wren'

Sir Humphrey Davy / Abominated gravy. / He lived in the   *4*
odium / Of having discovered Sodium.
Biography for Beginners, 'Sir Humphrey Davy'

George the Third / Ought never to have occurred. / One can   *5*
only wonder / At so grotesque a blunder.
More Biography, 'George the Third'

Ben-Gurion David 1886–1973. Israeli politician, prime minister
1948–53, 1955–63.

In Israel, in order to be a realist, you must believe in miracles.
Comment on television 5 Oct 1956

Bergman Ingrid 1917–1982. Swedish-born actress.

Keep it simple. Make a blank face and the music and the story
will fill it in.

Advice on film acting

Bergson Henri 1859–1941. French philosopher.

La fonction essentielle de l'univers, qui est une machine à faire
des dieux. The essential function of the universe, which is a
machine for making gods.
Les Deux sources de la morale et de la religion

Berkeley George 1685–1753. Irish philosopher and cleric.

I do know that I, who am a spirit or thinking substance, exist
as certainly as I know my ideas exist.
Three Dialogues between Hylas and Philonous

Berlin Irving. Adopted name of Israel Baline 1888–1989. Russian-
born US songwriter.

God bless America, Land that I love.

'God Bless America'

Oh! how I hate to get up in the morning, / Oh! how I'd love to   2
remain in bed.

'Oh! How I Hate to Get Up in the Morning'

I'm dreaming of a white Christmas, / Just like the ones I used   3
to know, / Where the tree-tops glisten / And children listen / To
hear sleigh bells in the snow.

'White Christmas'

The song is ended (but the melody lingers on).   4

Song title

There's no business like show business.   5

Song title

Berlin Isaiah 1909–   . Latvian-born British philosopher.

Liberty is liberty, not equality or fairness or justice or human
happiness or a quiet conscience.
Two Concepts of Liberty

Berlioz (Louis) Hector 1803–1869. French romantic composer.

Time is a great teacher, but unfortunately it kills all its pupils.
Almanach des lettres françaises

Bernanos Georges 1888–1948. French author.

Hell, ... is to love no more.
Journal d' un curé de campagne (Diary of a Country Priest) ch 2

The wish for prayer is itself a prayer.   *2*
Diary of a Country Priest ch 2

Berne Eric 1910–1970. US psychiatrist

Games people play.

Book title

Betjeman John 1906–1984. English poet and essayist.

One cannot assess in terms of cash or exports and imports an imponderable thing like the turn of a lane or an inn or a church tower or a familiar skyline.
Observer 1969

Phone for the fish-knives, Norman / As Cook is a little unnerved;   *2*
You kiddies have crumpled the serviettes / And I must have things daintily served.
'How to get on in Society'

Think of what our Nation stands for, / Books from Boots' and   *3*
country lanes, / Free speech, free passes, class distinction.
'In Westminster Abbey'

Come, friendly bombs, and fall on Slough! / It isn't fit for   *4*
humans now, / There isn't grass to graze a cow.
'Slough'

Ghastly good taste, or a depressing story of the rise and fall of   *5*
English architecture.
Book title

Bevan Aneurin (Nye) 1897–1960. Welsh Labour politician.

This island is made mainly of coal and surrounded by fish. Only an organizing genius could produce a shortage of coal and fish at the same time.
Speech at Blackpool 24 May 1945

We know what happens to people who stay in the middle of the road. They get run down. 2
>*Observer* 6 Dec 1953

If we complain about the tune, there is no reason to attack the monkey when the organ grinder is present. 3
>*Hansard* 16 May 1957

Damn it all, you can't have the crown of thorns and the thirty pieces of silver. 4
>Michael Foot *Aneurin Bevan*

Bevin Ernest 1881–1951. English Labour politician.

My [foreign] policy is to be able to take a ticket at Victoria Station and go anywhere I damn well please.
>*The Spectator* April 1951

Bible The sacred book of the Jewish and Christian religions.

In the beginning God created the heaven and the earth.
>Genesis 1:1

And God saw that it was good. 2
>Genesis 1:10

Male and female created he them. 3
>Genesis 1:27

And the Lord God planted a garden eastward in Eden. 4
>Genesis 2:7

But of the tree of the knowledge of good and evil, thou shalt not eat of it. 5
>Genesis 2:17

the serpent was more subtil than any beast of the field. 6
>Genes is 3:1

A land flowing with milk and honey. 7
>On the land of Canaan, Exodus 3:8

For dust thou art, and unto dust thou shalt return. 8
>Genesis 3:19

Am I my brother's keeper?   *9*

                                    Genesis 4:1

His hand will be against every man, and every man's hand   *10*
against him.

                                    Genesis 16:12

Old and well stricken in age.   *11*

                                    Genesis 18:11

Mizpah; for he said, The Lord watch between me and thee,   *12*
when we are absent one from another.

                                    Genesis 31:49

I will not let thee go, except thou bless me.   *13*

                                    Genesis 32:26

A coat of many colours.   *14*

                                    Genesis 37:3

Bring down my grey hairs with sorrow to the grave.   *15*

                                    Genesis 42:38

I AM THAT I AM.   *16*

                                    Exodus 3:14

Eye for eye, tooth for tooth, hand for hand, foot for foot.   *17*

                                    Exodus 21:23

A stiff-necked people   *18*

                                    Exodus 33:3

The Lord bless thee, and keep thee: / The Lord make his face   *19*
to shine upon thee, and be gracious unto thee: / The Lord lift
up his countenance upon thee, and give thee peace.

                                    Numbers 6:24

Man doth not live by bread only, but by every word that   *20*
proceedeth out of the mouth of the Lord doth man live.

                                    Deuteronomy 8:3

Underneath are the everlasting arms.   *21*

                                    Deuteronomy 33:27

Hewers of wood and drawers of water.   *22*

                                    Joshua 9:21

The stars in their courses fought against Sisera. 23

Judges 5:20

She brought forth butter in a lordly dish. 24

Judges 5:25

Intreat me not to leave thee, or to return from following after 25
thee: for whither thou goest, I will go; and where thou lodgest, I
will lodge: thy people shall be my people, and thy God my God.

Ruth 1:16

Saul and Jonathan were lovely and pleasant in their lives, and 26
in their death they were not divided.

2 Samuel 1:23

How the mighty are fallen in the midst of the battle! 27

2 Samuel 1:25

The half was not told me. 28

1 Kings 10:7

There ariseth a little cloud out of the sea, like a man's hand. 29

1 Kings 18:44

After the fire a still small voice. 30

1 Kings 19:11

Let not him that girdeth on his harness boast himself as he that 31
putteth it off.

1 Kings 20:11

And a certain man drew a bow at a venture. 32

1 Kings 22:34

The driving is like the driving of Jehu, the son of Nimshi: for 33
he driveth furiously.

2 Kings 9:20

The Lord gave, and the Lord hath taken away; blessed be the 34
name of the Lord.

Job 1:21

Curse God, and die. 35

Job 2:9

Man is born unto trouble, as the sparks fly upward.   *36*
                                                 Job 5:7

I know that my redeemer liveth, and that he shall stand at the   *37*
latter day upon the earth: / And though after my skin worms
destroy this body, yet in my flesh shall I see God.
                                                 Job 19:25

The price of wisdom is above rubies.   *38*
                                                 Job 28:18

Who is this that darkeneth counsel by words without knowledge?   *39*
                                                 Job 38:2

Wisdom is the principal thing; therefore get wisdom; and with   *40*
all thy getting get understanding.
                                                 Proverbs 4:7

Go to the ant, thou sluggard; consider her ways, and be wise.   *41*
                                                 Proverbs 6:6

Yet a little sleep, a little slumber, a little folding of the hands   *42*
to sleep.
                                                 Proverbs 6:10

So shall thy poverty come as one that travelleth, and thy want   *43*
as an armed man.
                                                 Proverbs 6:11

A wise son maketh a glad father: but a foolish son is the   *44*
heaviness of his mother.
                                                 Proverbs 10:1

In the multitude of counsellors there is safety.   *45*
                                                 Proverbs 11:14

As a jewel of gold in a swine's snout, so is a fair woman which   *46*
is without discretion.
                                                 Proverbs 11:22

Hope deferred maketh the heart sick.   *47*
                                                 Proverbs 13:12

He that spareth his rod hateth his son.   *48*
                                                 Proverbs 13:24

A soft answer turneth away wrath. *49*

Proverbs 15:1

There is a friend that sticketh closer than a brother. *50*

Proverbs 18:24

Wine is a mocker, strong drink is raging. *51*

Proverbs 20:1

Confidence in an unfaithful man in time of trouble is like a *52*
broken tooth, and a foot out of joint.

Proverbs 25:19

As a dog returneth to his vomit, so a fool returneth to his folly. *53*

Proverbs 26:11

Who can find a virtuous woman? for her price is above rubies. *54*

Proverbs 31:10

Vanity of vanities, saith the Preacher, vanity of vanities; all is *55*
vanity.

Ecclesiastes 1:2

To every thing there is a season, and a time to every purpose *56*
under the heaven: / A time to be born, and a time to die.

Ecclesiastes 3:1

The race is not to the swift, nor the battle to the strong. *57*

Ecclesiastes 9:11

Cast thy bread upon the water: for thou shalt find it after many *58*
days.

Ecclesiastes 11:1

Man goeth to his long home, and the mourners go about the *59*
streets: / Or ever the silver cord be loosed, or the golden bowl
be broken, or pitcher be broken at the fountain, or the wheel
broken at the cistern. / Then shall the dust return to the earth as
it was: and the spirit shall return unto God who gave it.

Ecclesiastes 12:5

Let him kiss me with the kisses of his mouth: for thy love is *60*
better than wine.

Song of Solomon 1:2

Stay me with flagons, comfort me with apples: for I am sick of   *61*
love.
                                            Song of Solomon 2:5

Rise up, my love, my fair one, and come away. / For, lo! the   *62*
winter is past, the rain is over and gone; / The flowers appear on
the earth: the time of the singing of birds is come, and the voice
of the turtle is heard in our land.
                                            Song of Solomon 2:10

Set me as a seal upon thine heart, as a seal upon thine arm: for   *63*
love is strong as death; jealousy is cruel as the grave.
                                            Song of Solomon 8:6

Many waters cannot quench love.   *64*
                                            Song of Solomon 8:7

A garden inclosed is my sister, my spouse.   *65*
                                            Song of Solomon 12:4

They shall beat their swords into plowshares, and their spears   *66*
into pruninghooks.
                                            Isaiah 2:4

The people that walked in darkness have seen a great light: they   *67*
that dwell in the land of the shadow of death, upon them hath
the light shined.
                                            Isaiah 9:2

The wolf also shall dwell with the lamb, and the leopard shall   *68*
lie down with the kid.
                                            Isaiah 11:7

Watchman, what of the night?   *69*
                                            Isaiah 21:11

The voice of him that crieth in the wilderness, Prepare ye the   *70*
way of the Lord, make straight in the desert a highway for our
God. Every valley shall be exalted, and every mountain and
hill shall be made low: and the crooked shall be made straight,
and the rough places plain.
                                            Isaiah 43:3

There is no peace, saith the Lord, unto the wicked.   *71*
> Isaiah 48:22

Man of sorrows, and acquainted with grief.   *72*
> Isaiah 53:2

Peace to him that is far off, and to him that is near.   *73*
> Isaiah 57:19

Saying, Peace, peace; when there is no peace.   *74*
> Jeremiah 6:14

Can the Ethiopian change his skin, or the leopard his spots?   *75*
> Jeremiah 13:23

Your old men shall dream dreams, your young men shall see visions.   *76*
> Joel 2:28

Blesssed are the meek: for they shall inherit the earth.   *77*
> Matthew 5:5

Ye are the salt of the earth.   *78*
> Matthew 5:13

Let your light so shine before men, that they may see your good works.   *79*
> Matthew 5:16

Agree with thine adversary quickly, whiles thou art in the way with him.   *80*
> Matthew 5:25

Where your treasure is, there will your heart be also.   *81*
> Matthew 6:21

No man can serve two masters ... Ye cannot serve God and mammon.   *82*
> Matthew 6:24

Consider the lilies of the field, how they grow; they toil not, neither do they spin.   *83*
> Matthew 6:28

Neither cast ye your pearls before swine.   *84*
> Matthew 6:34

Sufficient unto the day is the evil thereof.   *85*
                                        Matthew 6:34

By their fruits ye shall know them.   *86*
                                        Matthew 7:20

Be ye therefore wise as serpents, and harmless as doves.   *87*
                                        Matthew 10:16

He that is not with me is against me.   *88*
                                        Matthew 12:30

A prophet is not without honour, save in his own country and   *89*
in his own house.
                                        Matthew 13:57

If the blind lead the blind, both shall fall into the ditch.   *90*
                                        Matthew 15:14

Get thee behind me, Satan.   *91*
                                        Matthew 16:23

What is a man profited, if he shall gain the whole world, and   *92*
lose his own soul.
                                        Matthew 16:26

Thou shalt love thy neighbour as thyself.   *93*
                                        Matthew 19:19

Render therefore unto Caesar the things which are Caesar's.   *94*
                                        Matthew 22:21

The spirit indeed is willing, but the flesh is weak.   *95*
                                        Matthew 26:41

All they that take the sword shall perish with the sword.   *96*
                                        Matthew 26:52

The sabbath was made for man, and not man for the sabbath.   *97*
                                        Mark 2:27

If a house be divided against itself, that house cannot stand.   *98*
                                        Mark 3:25

He that hath ears to hear, let him hear.   *99*
                                        Mark 4:9

Had suffered many things of many physicians, and had spent *100*
all that she had, and was nothing better but rather grew worse.
Mark 5:26

Suffer the little children to come unto me. *101*
Mark 10:14

To give light to them that sit in darkness and in the shadow of *102*
death, to guide our feet into the way of peace.
Luke 1:79

Lord, now lettest thou thy servant depart in peace, according *103*
to thy word.
Luke 2:29

Physician, heal thyself. *104*
Luke 4:23

For the labourer is worthy of his hire. *105*
Luke 10:7

But Martha was cumbered about much serving. *106*
Luke 10:40

Wasted his substance with riotous living. *107*
Luke 15:13

Bring hither the fatted calf, and kill it. *108*
Luke 15:23

In the beginning was the Word, and the Word was with God, *109*
and the Word was God.
John 1:1

There is no truth in him. *110*
John 8:44

The poor always ye have with you. *111*
John 12:8

Greater love hath no man than this, that a man lay down his life *112*
for his friends.
John 15:13

Silver and gold have I none; but such as I have give I thee.   *113*
                                                           Acts 3:6

It is more blessed to give than to receive.   *114*
                                                         Acts 20:35

A citizen of no mean city.   *115*
                                                         Acts 21:39

Much learning, doth make thee mad.   *116*
                                                         Acts 26:24

The wages of sin is death.   *117*
                                                       Romans 6:23

Vengeance is mine; I will repay, saith the Lord.   *118*
                                                      Romans 12:19

It is better to marry than to burn.   *119*
                                                 1 Corinthians 6:9

Though I speak with tongues of men and of angels, and have   *120*
not charity, I am become as sounding brass, or a tinkling cymbal.
                                                 1 Corinthians 13:1

Charity never faileth.   *121*
                                                 1 Corinthians 13:8

When I was a child, I spake as a child, I understood as a child,   *122*
thought as a child; but when I became a man, I put away
childish things.
                                                1 Corinthians 13:11

And now abideth faith, hope, charity, these three; but the   *123*
greatest of these is charity.
                                                1 Corinthians 13:13

The last enemy that shall be destroyed is death.   *124*
                                                1 Corinthians 15:26

Behold, I shew you a mystery; We shall not all sleep but we   *125*
shall all be changed, / In a moment, in the twinkling of an eye,
at the last trump.
                                                1 Corinthians 15:51

O death, where is thy sting? O grave, where is thy victory.   ***126***
                                        1 Corinthians 15:55

God loveth a cheerful giver.   ***127***
                                        2 Corinthians 9:7

Let not the sun go down upon your wrath.   ***128***
                                        Ephesians 4:26

The love of money is the root of all evil.   ***129***
                                        1 Timothy 6:10

Be not forgetful to entertain strangers: for thereby some have ***130***
entertained angels unawares.
                                        Hebrews 13:1

All flesh is as grass, and all the glory of man as the flower of ***131***
grass. The grass withereth, and the flower thereof falleth away.
                                        Peter 1:24

Charity shall cover the multitude of sins.   ***132***
                                        Peter 4:8

I am Alpha and Omega, the beginning and the ending, saith the   ***133***
Lord.
                                        Revelation 1:7

And I looked, and behold a pale horse: and his name that sat   ***134***
on him was Death.
                                        Revelation 6:8

And I saw a new heaven and a new earth: for the first time   ***135***
heaven and the first earth were passed away; and there was no
more sea.
                                        Revelation 21:1

Bidault Georges 1899–1983. French politician, prime minister 1946,
1949–50.

The weak have one weapon: the errors of those who think they
are strong.

                                        Observer July 1962

Bierce Ambrose (Gwinett) 1842–*c*. 1914. US writer.

Admiration, *n*. Our polite recognition of another's resemblance
to ourselves.

Cynic's Word Book

Bore, *n*. A person who talks when you wish him to listen.   2
Cynic's Word Book

Cynic, *n*. A blackguard whose faulty vision sees things as they   3
are, not as they ought to be.

Cynic's Word Book

Education, *n*. That which discloses to the wise and disguises   4
from the foolish their lack of understanding.

Cynic's Word Book

History, *n*. An account, mostly false, of events, mostly   5
unimportant, which are brought about by rulers, mostly
knaves, and soldiers, mostly fools.

Cynic's Word Book

Noise, *n*. A stench in the ear... The chief product and   6
authenticating sign of civilization.

Devil's Dictionary

Abdication, *n*. the act whereby a sovereign attests his sense of   7
the high temperature of the throne.

Devil's Dictionary

Patience, *n*. A minor form of despair, disguised as a virtue.   8
Devil's Dictionary

Binyon Laurence 1869–1943. British poet.

They shall grow not old, as we that are left grow old: / Age
shall not weary them, nor the years condemn. / At the going
down of the sun and in the morning / We will remember them.
'Poem For the Fallen'

Birrell Augustine 1850–1933. English writer.

That great dust-heap called 'history'

Obiter Dicta 'Carlyle'

Bismarck 1815–1898. Prussian prime minister 1862–90.

Politics is not an exact science.
>Speech in Prussian Chamber 18 Dec 1863

Blood and iron. 2
>Speech in Prussian House of Deputies 28 Jan 1886

Blackstone William 1723–1780. English jurist.

That the king can do no wrong, is a necessary and fundamental principle of the English constitution.
>*Commentaries*

Blake William 1757–1827. English poet, artist, engraver, and visionary.

A Robin Redbreast in a Cage / Puts all Heaven in a Rage.
>*Auguries of Innocence*

The strongest poison ever known / Came from Cæsar's laurel crown. 2
>*Auguries of Innocence*

To see a World in a Grain of Sand, / And a Heaven in a Wild Flower, Hold Infinity in the palm of your hand, / And Eternity in an hour. 3
>*Auguries of Innocence*

Everything that lives, / Lives not alone, nor for itself. 4
>*Book of Thel* 2

Love seeketh not itself to please, / Nor for itself hath any care, / But for another gives its ease, / And builds a Heaven in Hell's despair. 5
>'The Clod and the Pebble'

Great things are done when men and mountains meet. 6
>*Gnomic Verses* 1

What is it men in women do require? / The lineaments of gratified desire. / What is it women do in men require? / The lineaments of gratified desire. 7
>*Gnomic Verses* 17

The road of excess leads to the palace of wisdom.   **8**
>   *Marriage of Heaven and Hell: The*
>   *Voice of the Devil*, 'Proverbs of Hell'

The tigers of wrath are wiser than the horses of instruction.   **9**
>   *Marriage of Heaven and Hell: The*
>   *Voice of the Devil*, 'Proverbs of Hell'

And did those feet in ancient time / Walk upon England's   **10**
mountains green? / And was the holy Lamb of God / On
England's pleasant pastures seen?
>   *Milton* preface

Never seek to tell thy love, / Love that never told can be.   **11**
>   'Never Seek to Tell Thy Love'

I was angry with my friend / I told my wrath, my wrath did end.   **12**
/ I was angry with my foe: / I told it not, my wrath did grow.
>   'A Poison Tree'

Tiger! Tiger! burning bright / In the forests of the night, / What   **13**
immortal hand or eye / Could frame thy fearful symmetry?
>   'The Tiger'

Blamey Thomas Albert 1884–1951. Australian field marshal.

The rabbit that runs away is the rabbit that gets shot.
>   Address to his troops

Bloomer Amelia Jenks 1818–1894. US campaigner for women's rights.

The costume of woman ... should conduce at once to her health,
comfort, and usefulness ... while it should not fail also to
conduce to her personal adornment, it should make that end of
secondary importance.
>   Letter June 1857

Blunden Edmund 1896–1974. English poet.

I am for the woods against the world, / But are the woods for me?
>   'The Kiss'

Cricket to us, like you, was more than play, / It was a worship   **2**
in the summer sun.
>   *Pride of the Village*

Blythe Ronald 1922– . English writer.

As for the British churchman, he goes to church as he goes to the bathroom, with the minimum of fuss and with no explanation if he can help it.

Age of Illusion

Bolívar Simón 1783–1830. S. American nationalist and revolutionary.

A people that loves freedom will in the end be free.

Letter from Jamaica

Bolingbroke Henry St John, Viscount Bolingbroke 1678–1751. English Tory politician and political philosopher.

Nations, like men, have their infancy.

On the Study of History

Bond Edward 1935– . English dramatist.

We have only one thing to keep us sane, pity; and the man without pity is mad.

Lear

Boorstin Daniel J 1914– . US writer.

The celebrity is a person who is known for his well-knownness.

The Image

Booth John Wilkes 1839–1865. US assassin of President Abraham Lincoln.

Tell mother – tell mother – I died for my country.
After having assassinated President Lincoln 1865

Borges Jorge Luis 1899–1986. Argentine poet and short-story writer.

The Falklands thing was a fight between two bald men over a comb.
Of the Falklands War 1982, *Time* 14 Feb 1983

Writing is nothing more than a guided dream.   2
Dr Brodie's Report

Borrow George Henry 1803–1881. English author and traveller.

A losing trade, I assure you, sir: literature is a drug.
Lavengro ch 30

Good ale, the true and proper drink of Englishmen.   2
Lavengro ch 48

Youth will be served, every dog has his day, and mine has been   3
a fine one.
Lavengro ch 92

Bosquet Maréchal 1810–1861. French marshal.

It is magnificent, but it is not war.
Remark on the Charge of the Light Brigade, 1854

Bossidy John Collins 1860–1928. US writer.

And this is good old Boston, / The home of the bean and the cod,
/ Where the Lowells talk to the Cabots, And the Cabots talk only
to God.

On the Aristocracy of Harvard

Bottomley Gordon 1874–1948. English poet and dramatist.

When you destroy a blade of grass / You poison England at her
roots: / Remember no man's foot can pass / Where evermore
no green life shoots.

'To Ironfounders and Others'

Bottomley Horatio 1860–1933. English newspaper editor.

I have not had your advantages. What poor education I have received
has been gained in the University of Life.
Speech at Oxford Union 2 Dec 1920

Bourne W St Hill 1846–1929.

The sower went forth sowing, / The seed in secret slept.
Church Bells, 'The Sower Went Forth Sowing'

Bowen Edward Ernest 1836–1901. English schoolmaster.

Forty years on, when afar and asunder / Parted are those who
are singing to-day.

'Harrow School Song', *Forty Years On*

Bowen Elizabeth 1899–1973. Irish novelist.

Experience isn't interesting till it begins to repeat itself—in fact, till it does that, it hardly is experience.

Death of the Heart

There is no end to the violations committed by children on children, quietly talking alone.

House in Paris pt 1, ch 2   *2*

Jealousy is no more than feeling alone against smiling enemies.

House in Paris pt 2, ch 8   *3*

No, it is not only our fate but our business to lose innocence, and once we have lost that, it is futile to attempt a picnic in Eden.

'Out of a Book'   *4*

Bowen George Ferguson 1821–1899. Colonial governor.

The rain it raineth on the just / And also on the unjust fella: / But chiefly on the just, because / The unjust steals the just's umbrella.

Sichel, *Sands of Time*

Bowra Maurice 1898–1971. English scholar and critic.

I'm a man more dined against than dining.

Quoted in Betjeman *Summoned by Bells*

Bradbury Malcolm 1932–   . English novelist and critic.

Marriage is the most advanced form of warfare in the modern world.

The History Man

Bradley Omar Nelson 1893–1981. US general in World War II.

In war there is no second prize for the runner up.

Military Review, Sept 1951

Braham John *c.* 1774–1856. English tenor singer.

England, home and beauty.

The Americans 'The Death of Nelson'

Braisted Harry 1834–1881. US Songwriter

If you want to win her hand, / Let the maiden understand / That she's not the only pebble on the beach.

'You're Not the Only Pebble on the Beach'

Brando Marlon 1924– . US actor.

An actor is a guy who, if you aren't talking about him, isn't listening.

Observer Jan 1956

Branson Richard 1950– . English entrepreneur.

Borrow fivers off everyone you meet.

Answer on being asked what is the
quickest way to become a millionaire

Braque Georges 1882–1963. French painter.

Art is meant to disturb, science reassures.

Pensées sur l'Art

La vérité existe; on n'invente que le mensonge. Truth exists;   **2**
only lies are invented.
Le Jour et la Nuit: Cahiers 1917–52 (Day and Night, Notebooks)

Brecht Bertolt 1898–1956. German dramatist and poet.

Food comes first, then morals.

Dreigroschenoper (Threepenny Opera)

Unhappy the land that is in need of heroes.   **2**
Leben des Galilei (Life of Galileo)

War always finds a way.   **3**
Mutter Courage (Mother Courage)

Brenan Gerald 1894–1987. English writer.

Those who have some means think that the most important thing in the world is love. The poor know that it is money.
Thoughts in a Dry Season

Brenner Sidney 1927– . South African scientist, one of the
pioneers of genetic research.

> Progress in science depends on new techniques, new
> discoveries and new ideas, probably in that order.
> > *Nature* May 1980

Breton *c.*1545–*c.*1626. English poet.

> We rise with the lark and go to bed with the lamb.
> > *The Court and Country*

> A Mad World, My Masters. 2
> > Dialogue title

Bright John 1811–1889. British Liberal politician.

> England is the mother of Parliaments.
> > Speech in House of Commons 1865

> Force is not a remedy. 2
> > Speech in Birmingham 1880

Brome Richard 17th century. English dramatist.

> I am a gentleman, though spoiled i' the breeding.... We came in
> with the Conqueror.
> > *English Moor*

Bronowski Jacob 1908–1974. Polish-born US historian and
mathematician.

> That is the essence of science: ask an impertinent question, and
> you are on the way to a pertinent answer.
> > *Ascent of Man*

> The wish to hurt, the momentary intoxication with pain, is the 2
> loophole through which the pervert climbs into the minds of
> ordinary men.
> > *Face of Violence* ch 5

> The world is made of people who never quite get into the first 3
> team and who just miss the prizes at the flower show.
> > *Face of Violence* ch 6

Brontë Anne 1820–1849. English novelist.

Because the road is rough and long, / Shall we despise the
skylark's song?

Views of Life

Brontë Charlotte 1816–1855. English novelist.

Reader, I married him.

Jane Eyre

Brontë Emily 1818–1848. English novelist and poet.

No coward soul is mine.

Last Lines

Vain are the thousand creeds / That move men's hearts: *2*
unutterably vain.

Last Lines

Brooke Rupert (Chawner) 1887–1915. English poet.

Stands the Church clock at ten to three? / And is there honey
still for tea?

The Old Vicarage, Grantchester

Unkempt about those hedges blows / An English unofficial rose.   *2*

The Old Vicarage, Grantchester

If I should die, think only this of me ... That there's some   *3*
corner of a foreign field / That is forever England.

'The Soldier'

Brookner Anita 1928–   . English novelist.

Good women always think it is their fault when someone else is
being offensive. Bad women never take the blame for anything.

Hotel du Lac

Brooks Mel. Stage name of Melvin Kaminsky 1926–   . US film
director and comedian.

That's it baby, when you got it, flaunt it.

The Producers

Brown Helen Gurley 1922–   . Founding editor of *Cosmopolitan* magazine.

Sex and the single girl.

Book title

Brown John Mason 1900–1969. US journalist.

Tallulah Bankhead barged down the Nile last night as Cleopatra – and sank.

New York Post 11 Nov 1937

Brown T E 1830–1897. English poet

A garden is a lovesome thing, God wot!

My Garden

Brown Thomas 1663–1704. English satirist.

I do not love you Dr. Fell, / But why I cannot tell; / But this I know, and know full well, / I do not love you, Dr. Fell.

The Works of Mr Thomas Brown

Browne Thomas 1605–1682. English author and physician.

All places, all airs make unto me one country; I am in England, everywhere, and under any meridian.

Religio Medici

No man can justly censure or condemn another, because indeed   2
no man truly knows another.

Religio Medici

Persecution is a bad and indirect way to plant religion.   3
Religio Medici

We all labour against our own cure; for death is the cure of all   4
diseases.

Religio Medici

We carry within us the wonders we seek without us. There is all   5
Africa, and her prodigies in us.

Religio Medici

The long habit of living indisposeth us for dying.   6
Urn Burial

Man is a noble animal, splendid in ashes, and pompous in the   7
grave.
                                                    Urn Burial

Old families last not three oaks.   8
                                                    Urn Burial

What song the Syrens sang, or what name Achilles assumed   9
when he hid himself among women.
                                                    Urn Burial

Browning Elizabeth Barrett 1806–1861. English poet.

How do I love thee? Let me count the ways.
                              Sonnets from the Portuguese

Browning Robert 1812–1889. English poet.

He said true things, but called them by wrong names.
                                   Bishop Blougram's Apology

Boot, saddle, to horse, and away!   2
                              Cavalier Tunes, 'Boot and Saddle'

Oh, to be in England / Now that April's there.   3
                                   Home Thoughts from Abroad

That's the wise thrush; he sings each song twice over, / Lest   4
you should think he never could recapture / The first fine
careless rapture!
                                   Home Thoughts from Abroad

Just for a handful of silver he left us, / Just for a riband to stick 5
in his coat.
                                               The Lost Leader

Never glad confident morning again!   6
                                               The Lost Leader

We that had loved him so, followed him, honoured him, / Lived   7
in his mild and magnificent eye, / Learned his great language,
caught his clear accents, / Made him our pattern to live and to die!
                                   The Lost Leader of Wordsworth

Ah, did you once see Shelley plain, / And did he stop and speak **8**
to you / And did you speak to him again?

Memorabilia

Truth is within ourselves. **9**

Paracelsus

It was roses, roses, all the way. **10**

The Patriot

The year's at the spring, / And day's at the morn; / Morning's **11**
at seven; / The hill-side's dew-pearled; / The lark's on the
wing; / The snail's on the thorn: / God's in his heaven – / All's
right with the world!

Pippa Passes

Grow old along with me! / The best is yet to be, / The last of **12**
life, for which the first was made.

Rabbi ben Ezra

One who never turned his back but marched breast forward, / **13**
Never doubted clouds would break, / Never dreamed, though
right were worsted, wrong would triumph.

Summun Bonum

What's become of Waring / Since he gave us all the slip? **14**

Waring

Brummell Beau (George Bryan) 1778–1840. English dandy.

Who's your fat friend?

Referring to the Prince Regent, in Gronow, *Reminiscences*

Bryant Anita 1940– . Former Miss America.

If homosexuality were the normal way, God would have made
Adam and Bruce.

New York Times 5 June 1977

Buchan John, Baron Tweedsmuir 1875–1940. Scottish politician and
author.

To live for a time close to great minds is the best kind of
education.

Memory Hold-the-Door

'It's a great life if you don't weaken.'   *2*

Mr Standfast

Buffon Comte de (George-Louis Leclerc) 1707–1778. French
naturalist.

Genius is only a great aptitude for patience.

Attributed remark

Style is the man himself.   *2*

Discourse on Style

Bukharin Nikolai Ivanovich 1888–1938. Soviet politician and theorist.

We might have a two-party system, but one of the two parties
would be in office and the other in prison.

Attributed remark

Buñuel 1900–1983. Spanish film director.

The discreet charm of the bourgeoisie.

Film title

Bunn Alfred 'Poet' *c* 1796–1860. English poet and theatre manager.

I dreamt that I dwelt in marble halls.

'I Dreamt That I Dwelt'

Bunyan John 1628–1688. English author.

A castle, called Doubting-Castle, the owner whereof was
Giant Despair.

Pilgrim's Progress

He that is down needs fear no fall, / He that is low no pride.   *2*

Pilgrim's Progress

It beareth the name of Vanity-Fair, because the town where 'tis   *3*
kept, is lighter than vanity.

Pilgrim's Progress

The name of the slough was Despond.   *4*

Pilgrim's Progress

An ornament to her profession.   *5*

Pilgrim's Progress

Sleep is sweet to the labouring man. **6**

Pilgrim's Progress

So he passed over, and all the trumpets sounded for him on the **7** other side.

Pilgrim's Progress

Who would true valour see, / Let him come hither; / One here **8** will constant be, / Come wind, come weather. / There's no discouragement / Shall make him once relent / His first avow'd intent / To be a pilgrim.

Pilgrim's Progress

Burgess Anthony 1917–1993. English novelist and literary critic.

A work of fiction should be, for its author, a journey into the unknown, and the prose should convey the difficulties of the journey.

Homage to Qwert Yuiop

Burgon 1813–1888. English divine.

A rose-red city – half as old as Time!

Petra

Burke Edmund 1729–1797. Irish Whig politician and political theorist.

The greater the power, the more dangerous the abuse.

Speech on the Middlesex Election 1771

It is the nature of all greatness not to be exact. **2**

Speech on American Taxation 1774

To tax and to please, no more than to love and to be wise, is not **3** given to men.

Speech on American Taxation 1774

I do not know the method of drawing up an indictment against **4** an whole people.

Speech on Conciliation with America 1775

Magnanimity in politics is not seldom the truest wisdom; and a **5** great empire and little minds go ill together.

Speech on Conciliation with America 1775

The use of force alone is but *temporary*. It may subdue for a   **6**
moment; but it does not remove the necessity of subduing again:
and a nation is not governed, which is perpetually to be
conquered.
> Speech on Conciliation with America 1775

The people are the masters.   **7**
> Speech on the Economical Reform 1780

An event has happened, upon which it is difficult to speak, and   **8**
impossible to be silent.
> Speech on the Impeachment of Warren Hastings 1789

It is a general popular error to imagine the loudest complainers   **9**
for the public to be the most anxious for its welfare.
> *Observation on a Publication, 'The present state of the nation'*

Not merely a chip of the old 'block', but the old block itself.   **10**
> On Pitt's First Speech

Custom reconciles us to everything.   **11**
> *On the Sublime and Beautiful*

The age of chivalry is gone. That of sophisters, economists,   **12**
and calculators, has succeeded; and the glory of Europe is
extinguished for ever.
> *Reflections on the Revolution in France*

People will not look forward to posterity, who never look   **13**
backward to their ancestors.
> *Reflections on the Revolution in France*

A state without the means of some change is without the means   **14**
of its conservation.
> *Reflections on the Revolution in France*

Superstition is the religion of feeble minds.   **15**
> *Reflections on the Revolution in France*

Burke Johnny 1908–1964. US songwriter.

Every time it rains, it rains / Pennies from heaven.
> 'Pennies from Heaven'

Burney Frances (Fanny) 1752–1840. English novelist and diarist.

Travelling is the ruin of all happiness! There's no looking at a
building here after seeing Italy.

Cecilia

Burns Robert 1759–1796. Scottish poet.

But to see her was to love her, / Love but her, and love for ever.
'Bonnie Lesley'

'A⸰ Fond Kiss' Should auld acquaintance be forgot, / And   *2*
ⁱever brought to mind?
'Auld Lang Syne'

We'll tak a cup o' kindness yet, / For auld lang syne.   *3*
'Auld Lang Syne'

Gin a body meet a body / Coming through the rye; /   *4*
Gin a body kiss a body. / Need a body cry?
'Coming through the Rye'

A man's a man for a' that.   *5*
'For a' that and a' that'

Green grow the rashes O.   *6*
'Green Grow the Rashes'

Man's inhumanity to man / Makes countless thousands mourn!   *7*
'Man was made to Mourn'

My heart's in the Highlands, my heart is not here; / My heart's in   *8*
the Highlands a-chasing the deer; / Chasing the wild deer, and
following the roe, / My heart's in the Highlands, wherever I go.
'My Heart's in the Highlands'

O, my Luve's like a red red rose / That's newly sprung in June.   *9*
'My Love is like a Red Red Rose'

Liberty's in every blow! / Let us do or die!   *10*
'Scots, Wha Hae'

Some hae meat, and canna eat, / And some wad eat that want it;   *11*
/ But we hae meat and we can eat, / And sae the Lord be thankit.
'The Selkirk Grace, as attributed to Burns'

The best laid schemes o' mice an' men / Gang aft a-gley.   *12*
'To a Mouse'

Wee, sleekit, cow'rin, tim'rous beastie, / O what a panic's in   *13*
thy breastie!
'To a Mouse'

What can a young lassie do wi' an auld man?   *14*
'What can a Young Lassie'

O whistle, and I'll come to you, my lad.   *15*
'Whistle, and I'll come to you, my Lad'

Ye banks and braes o' bonny Doon, / How can ye bloom sae   *16*
fresh and fair?
'Ye Banks and Braes o' Bonny Doon'

Burroughs Edgar Rice 1875–1950. US novelist.
Me Tarzan, you Jane.

Tarzan of the Apes

Burt Benjamin Hapgood 1880–1950. US lyricist and composer.
When you're all dressed up and no place to go.

Song title

Burton Robert 1577–1640. English philosopher.
All poets are mad.

Anatomy of Melancholy

Cookery is become an art, a noble science.   *2*
Anatomy of Melancholy

One religion is as true as another.   *3*
Anatomy of Melancholy

One was never married, and that's his hell; another is, and   *4*
that's his plague.
Anatomy of Melancholy

They lard their lean books with the fat of others' works.   *5*
Anatomy of Melancholy

Bush George 1924–   . 41st president of the USA 1989–93, a Republican.

Read my lips—no new taxes.
> *Promise made during 1988 US presidential campaign*

Butler Samuel 1835–1902. English writer.

Life is like playing a violin solo in public and learning the instrument as one goes on.
> *Speech at the Somerville Club 27 Feb 1895*

It has been said that though God cannot alter the past,   *2*
historians can; it is perhaps because they can be useful to Him
in this respect that He tolerates their existence.
> *Erewhon Revisited*

Conscience is thoroughly well-bred and soon leaves off talking   *3*
to those who do not wish to hear it.
> *Further Extracts from Notebooks*

The three most important things a man has are, briefly, his   *4*
private parts, his money, and his religious opinions.
> *Further Extracts from Notebooks*

An apology for the Devil: It must be remembered that we have   *5*
only heard one side of the case. God has written all the books.
> *Notebooks ch 14*

The great pleasure of a dog is that you may make a fool of   *6*
yourself with him and not only will he not scold you, but he will
make a fool of himself too.
> *Notebooks ch 14*

The history of art is the history of revivals.   *7*
> *Notebooks,* 'Handel and Music'

All progress is based upon a universal innate desire on the part   *8*
of every organism to live beyond its income.
> *Notebooks,* 'Life'

Oh God! Oh Montreal!   *9*
> 'Psalm of Montreal'

They would have been equally horrified at hearing the   *10*
Christian religion doubted, and at seeing it practised.
> *The Way of All Flesh* ch 15

All animals, except man, know that the principal business of   *11*
life is to enjoy it— and they do enjoy it as much as man and other
circumstances will allow.
> *The Way of All Flesh* ch 19

The advantage of doing one's praising for oneself is that one   *12*
can lay it on so thick and exactly in the right places.
> *The Way of All Flesh* ch 34

His instinct told him that the best liar is he who makes the   *13*
smallest amount of lying go the longest way.
> *The Way of All Flesh* ch 39

'Tis better to have loved and lost, than never to have lost at all.   *14*
> *The Way of All Flesh* ch 77

Butler William 1535–1618. English physician.

Doubtless God could have made a better berry but doubtless
God never did.
> Of the strawberry, in Izaak Walton, *Compleat Angler*

Byron George Gordon, 6th Baron Byron 1788–1824. English poet.

The self-torturing sophist, wild Rousseau.
> *Childe Harold* II. 77

Years steal / Fire from the mind as vigour from the limb; / And   *2*
life's enchanted cup but sparkles near the brim.
> *Childe Harold* III. 8

And all went merry as a marriage bell.   *3*
> *Childe Harold* III. 21

There was a sound of revelry by night, / And Belgium's capital   *4*
had gather'd then / Her beauty and her chivalry, and bright /
The lamps shone o'er fair women and brave men;
> *Childe Harold* III. 21

I love not man the less, but Nature more.   *5*

> *Childe Harold* IV. 178

The Assyrian came down like a wolf on the fold, / And his   *6*
cohorts were gleaming in purple and gold; / And the sheen of
their spears was like stars on the sea, When the blue wave rolls
nightly on deep Galilee.

> *Destruction of Sennacherib*

What men call gallantry, and gods adultery, / Is much more   *7*
common where the climate's sultry.

> *Don Juan* I. 63

Man's love is of man's life a thing apart, / 'Tis woman's whole   *8*
existence.

> *Don Juan* I. 194

There's nought, no doubt, so much the spirit calms / As rum   *9*
and true religion.

> *Don Juan* II. 34

Think you, if Laura had been Petrarch's wife, He would have   *10*
written sonnets all his life?

> *Don Juan* III. 8

The isles of Greece, the isles of Greece! / Where burning   *11*
Sappho loved and sung, / Where grew the arts of war and peace,
/ Where Delos rose, and Phœbus sprung!

> *Don Juan* III. 86

The mountains look on Marathon – / And Marathon looks on   *12*
the sea; / And musing there an hour alone, / I dream'd that
Greece might still be free.

> *Don Juan* III. 86

And if I laugh at any mortal thing, / 'Tis that I may not weep.   *13*
> *Don Juan* IV. 4

There is a tide in the affairs of women, / Which, taken at the   *14*
flood, leads—God knows where.

> *Don Juan* VI. 2

Cervantes smiled Spain's chivalry away.   **15**
                                          Don Juan XIII, 11

Though women are angels, yet wedlock's the devil.   **16**
                                          Hours of Idleness. To Eliza

I awoke one morning and found myself famous.   **17**
                                          T Moore *Life of Byron* (referring to the
                                          instantaneous success of *Childe Harold*)

So, we'll go no more a roving / So late into the night,/ Though   **18**
the heart be still as loving, / And the moon be still as bright.
                                          'So, We'll Go No More a Roving'

C

Čapek Karel 1890–1938. Czech writer.

Man will never be enslaved by machinery if the man tending the machine be paid enough.

News Chronicle

Cabell James Branch 1879–1958. US novelist and journalist.

The optimist proclaims that we live in the best of all possible worlds; and the pessimist fears this is true.

The Silver Stallion

Caedmon 7th century. Earliest known English poet.

Light was first / Through the Lord's word / Named day: / Beauteous, bright creation.

'Creation. The First Day'.

Caesar Gaius Julius 100–40 BC. Roman statesman and general.

The die is cast.

At the crossing of the Rubicon

You also, Brutus? 2

Attributed remark on seeing his protégé
Brutus among the assassins attacking him

Veni, vidi, vici (I came, I saw, I conquered). 3

On his campaign in Pontus, quoted in
Suetonius, *Lives of the Caesars*, 'Julius Caesar'

Calderón de la Barca Pedro 1600–1681. Spanish dramatist.

Even in dreams good works are not wasted.

La Vida es Sueño

Camden William 1551–1623. English antiquary.

Betwixt the stirrup and the ground / Mercy I asked, mercy I found.

Remains, 'Epitaph for a Man Killed by Falling from His Horse'

Campbell Jane Montgomery 1817–1878. English hymn writer.

We plough the fields, and scatter / The good seed on the land.
'We Plough the Fields'

Campbell Kim 1947–   . Canadian politician, prime minister 1993.

Don't mess with me, I got tanks.
remark while defence minister

Campbell Mrs Patrick (born Beatrice Stella Tanner) 1865–1940. English actress.

It doesn't matter what you do in the bedroom as long as you don't do it in the street and frighten the horses.
D Fielding *Duchess of Jermyn Street*

Campbell Thomas 1777–1844. Scottish poet.

O leave this barren spot to me! / Spare, woodman, spare the beechen tree.
The Beech-Tree's Petition

Gentlemen, you must not mistake me. I admit that he is the
sworn foe of our nation, and, if you will, of the whole human
race. But, gentlemen, we must be just to our enemy. We must
not forget that he once shot a bookseller.
Of Napoleon, in G O Trevelyan *The
Life and Letters of Lord Macaulay*

Campion Thomas 1567–1620. English poet and musician.

There is a garden in her face, / Where roses and white lilies
grow; ... / There cherries grow, which none may buy / Till
'Cherry ripe' themselves do cry.
Book of Airs, 'There is a Garden in her Face'

Camus Albert 1913–1960. Algerian-born French writer.

You know what charm is: a way of getting the answer yes
without having asked any clear question.
The Fall

As a remedy to life in society I would suggest the big city.
Nowadays it is the only desert within our means.
Notebooks

An intellectual is someone whose mind watches itself. *3*

Notebooks

Every revolutionary ends as an oppressor or a heretic. *4*

The Rebel

What is a rebel? A man who says no. *5*

The Rebel

Canetti Elias 1905– . Bulgarian-born writer.

History portrays everything as if it could not have come otherwise. History is on the side of what happened.

The Human Province

Canning George 1770–1827. English Tory politician, prime minister 1827.

Save me, oh, save me from the candid friend.

New Morality

Capone Al(phonse) (*Scarface*) 1898–1947. US gangster.

I've been accused of every death except the casualty list of the World War.

Newspaper interview.

Capp Al (Alfred Gerard Caplin) 1909–1979. US cartoonist.

A product of the untalented, sold by the unprincipled to the utterly bewildered.

On abstract art, *National Observer* 1 July 1963

Carducci Giosuè 1835–1907. Italian poet.

Far better in one's work to forget than to seek to solve the vast riddles of the universe.

Idillio Maremmano

Carlyle Thomas 1795–1881. Scottish essayist and social historian.

Happy the people whose annals are blank in history-books!

Frederick the Great

The history of the world is but the biography of great men. *2*

Heroes and Hero-Worship

The seagreen Incorruptible.   **3**
> *History of the French Revolution* bk IV ch 4, of Robespierre

A whiff of grapeshot.   **4**
> *History of the French Revolution* bk V, ch 3

Captains of industry.   **5**
> *Past and Present*

Man is a tool-using animal. ... Without tools he is nothing, with   **6**
tools he is all.
> *Sartor Resartus* bk I, ch 5

The everlasting no.   **7**
> *Sartor Resartus* bk II, title of ch

Carnegie Dale 1888–1955. US author and teacher.

How to win friends and influence people.
> Book title

Carroll Lewis. Pen name of Charles Lutwidge Dodgson 1832–1898.
English writer.

'Beware the Jabberwock, my son!'
> *Alice Through the Looking-Glass* ch 1

'O frabjous day! Callooh! Callay!' / He chortled in his joy.   **2**
> *Alice Through the Looking-Glass* ch 1

'If seven maids with seven mops / Swept it for half a year, / Do   **3**
you suppose,' the Walrus said, / 'That they could get it clear?'
/ 'I doubt it,' said the Carpenter, / And shed a bitter tear.
> *Alice Through the Looking-Glass* ch 4

'Let's fight till six, and then have dinner,' said Tweedledum.   **4**
> *Alice Through the Looking-Glass* ch 4

The rule is, jam to-morrow and jam yesterday – but never jam   **5**
to-day.
> *Alice Through the Looking-Glass* ch 5

Why, sometimes I've believed as many as six impossible   **6**
things before breakfast.
> *Alice Through the Looking-Glass* ch 5

It's as large as life, and twice as natural!   **7**
> *Alice Through the Looking-Glass* ch 7

'Curiouser and curiouser!' cried Alice. **8**
Alice's Adventures in Wonderland ch 2

'You are old, Father William,' the young man said, / 'And your **9**
hair has become very white; / And yet you incessantly stand on
your head / – Do you think, at your age, it is right?'
Alice's Adventures in Wonderland ch5

'If everybody minded their own business, ... the world would **10**
go round a deal faster than it does.'
Alice's Adventures in Wonderland ch 6

'A cat may look at a king.' **11**
Alice's Adventures in Wonderland ch8

Soup of the evening, beautiful Soup! **12**
Alice's Adventures in Wonderland ch10

'Will you, won't you, will you, won't you, will you join the **13**
dance?'
Alice's Adventures in Wonderland ch 10

What I tell you three times is true. **14**
Hunting of the Snark Fit 1, 'The Landing'

But oh, beamish nephew, beware of the day, / If your Snark be **15**
a Boojum! For then / You will softly and suddenly vanish
away, / And never be met with again!
Hunting of the Snark Fit 3, 'The Baker's Tale'

Carter Jimmy (James Earl) 1924– . US politician 39th president of
the USA 1976–80.

We should live our lives as though Christ were coming this
afternoon.
Speech to Bible class in Plains, Georgia, March 1976

Casals Pablo 1876–1973. Catalan cellist, composer, and conductor.

To make divine things human, and human things divine; such is
Bach, the greatest and purest moment in music of all times.
Speech at Prades Bach Festival 1950

Casson Hugh 1910– . English architect.

The British love permanence more than they love beauty.
Observer 1964

Castro Fidel 1927–   . Cuban communist dictator.

History will absolve me.
After an unsuccessful assault on army barracks July 1953

Cather Willa (Sibert) 1873–1947. US novelist and short-story writer.

Religion and art spring from the same root and are close kin.
Economics and art are strangers.
Commonweal 17 Apr 1936

When kindness has left people, even for a few moments, we   *2*
become afraid of them as if their reason has left them.
My Mortal Enemy

I like trees because they seem more resigned to the way they   *3*
have to live than other things do.
O Pioneers!

Catherine II 1729–1796. Russian empress, known as 'the Great'.

I shall be an autocrat: that's my trade. And the good Lord will
forgive me: that's his.
Attributed remark

Catullus Gaius Valerius *c.* 84–54 BC. Roman lyric poet.

Let us live, my Lesbia, and let us love.
Carmina 5

I hate, I love.   *2*
Carmina 85

And so, my brother, forever, hail, and farewell!   *3*
Carmina 101

Cavell Edith Louisa 1865–1915. English hospital matron in World
War I.

I realize that patriotism is not enough. I must have no hatred or
bitterness towards any one.
Last words

Céline Louis–Ferdinand 1894–1961. French novelist.

If you aren't rich you should always look useful.
Journey to the End of the Night

Cellini Benvenuto 1500–1571. Italian sculptor and goldsmith.

The difference between a painting and a sculpture is the difference between a shadow and the thing that casts it.
letter to Benedetto Varchi 1547

Cervantes Saavedra 1547–1616. Spanish novelist and dramatist.

There are only two families in the world ... : the Haves and the Have-nots.

Don Quixote

Chamberlain Joseph 1836–1914. British Conservative politician.

The day of small nations has long passed away. The day of Empires has come.
Speech in Birmingham 12 May 1904

Chamberlain (Arthur) Neville 1869–1940. British Conservative politician.

Peace with honour. I believe it is peace for our time.
Speech from 10 Downing Street 30 Sept 1938

Chandler Raymond 1888–1959. US novelist.

If my books had been any worse, I should not have been invited to Hollywood, and if they had been any better, I should not have come.
Letter to Charles W. Morton 12 Dec 1945

When I split an infinitive, God damn it, I split it so it will stay split.   2
Letter to Edward Weeks 18 Jan 1947

Down these mean streets a man must go who is not himself mean, who is neither tarnished nor afraid.   3
'The Simple Art of Murder'

Chaplin Charlie (Charles Spencer) 1889–1977. English film actor and director.

All I need to make a comedy is a park, a policeman and a pretty girl.

My Autobiography

Charles II 1630–1685. King of Great Britain, 1644–85.

He had been, he said, an unconscionable time dying; but he hoped that they would excuse it.

T B Macaulay, *History of England*

Let not poor Nelly starve.   *2*

Quoted in Gilbert Burnet, *History of My Own Time*

That is very true: for my words are my own, and my actions are   *3*
my ministers'.

Reply to Lord Rochester's Epitaph on him

Charles 1948– . Prince of Wales.

A monstrous carbuncle on the face of a much-loved and elegant friend.

On a 1984 proposal for an extension
to the National Gallery, London

Chateaubriand 1768–1848. French writer and politician.

The original writer is not he who refrains from imitating others, but he who can be imitated by none.

Le Génie du Christianisme

Chaucer Geoffrey *c.* 1340–1400. English poet.

A Clerk ther was of Oxenford also.

Canterbury Tales, Prologue

He was a verray parfit gentil knight.   *2*

Canterbury Tales, Prologue

She was a worthy womman al hir lyve, / Housbondes at chirche-   *3*
dore she hadde fyve, / Withouten other companye in youthe.

Canterbury Tales, Prologue

Whanne that Aprille with his shoures sote / The droghte of
Marche hath perced to the rote.

Canterbury Tales, Prologue

4

So was hir joly whistle wel y-wet.

Canterbury Tales, The Reve's Tale

5

Go, litel book, go litel myn tragedie.

Troilus and Criseyde

6

Chekhov Anton (Pavlovich) 1860–1904. Russian dramatist and writer.

Medvedenko: Why do you wear black all the time?
Masha: I'm in mourning for my life, I'm unhappy.

The Seagull

Chesterfield Philip Dormer Stanhope, 4th Earl of Chesterfield
1694–1773. English politician and writer.

I recommend you to take care of minutes; for hours will take
care of themselves.

Letter to his Son 1747

Advice is seldom welcome; and those who want it the most
always like it the least.

Letter to his Son 1748

2

Religion is by no means a proper subject of conversation in a
mixed company.

Letter to his Godson No. 112

3

Tyrawley and I have been dead these two years; but we don't
choose to have it known.

Quoted in Boswell's *Life of Johnson*

4

Chesterton G(ilbert) K(eith) 1874–1936. English novelist, essayist,
and poet.

I tell you naught for your comfort, / Yea, naught for your desire,
/ Save that the sky grows darker yet / And the sea rises higher.

Ballad of the White Horse

The devil's walking parody / Of all four-footed things.

The Donkey

2

One bears great things from the valley, only small things from   *3*
the peak.
                                                    The Hammer of God

Don John of Austria is going to the war.   *4*
                                                            Lepanto

From all the easy speeches / That comfort cruel men.   *5*
                                          O God of Earth and Altar

Before the Roman came to Rye or out to Severn strode, / The   *6*
rolling English drunkard made the rolling English road.
                                          The Rolling English Road

That night we went to Birmingham by way of Beachy Head.   *7*
                                          The Rolling English Road

And a few men talked of freedom, while England talked of ale.   *8*
                                                  The Secret People

Smile at us, pay us, pass us; but do not quite forget. / For we   *9*
are the people of England, that never have spoken yet.
                                                  The Secret People

And Noah he often said to his wife when he sat down to dine, / 'I *10*
don't care where the water goes if it doesn't get into the wine.'
                                                      Wine and Water

Chiang Kai-shek 1887–1975. Chinese politician, head of state
1928–49

We shall not talk lightly about sacrifice until we are driven to
the last extremity which makes sacrifice inevitable.
                            Speech to Fifth Congress of the Guomindang

Chomsky Noam 1928–   . US professor of linguistics.

Colourless green ideas sleep furiously.
            Example of a meaningless sentence, in *Syntactic Structures*

Churchill Charles 1731–1764. English satirical poet.

Just to the windward of the law.

                                                    The Ghost bk 3

A joke's a very serious thing.

The Ghost bk 4   2

Keep up appearances; there lies the test; / The world will give thee credit for the rest.

Night   3

Churchill Randolph (Henry Spencer) 1849–1894. English Conservative politician.

Ulster will fight; Ulster will be right.

Letter, 1886

Churchill Winston (Leonard Spencer) 1874–1965. English Conservative politician.

It cannot be classified as slavery in the extreme acceptance of the word without some risk of terminological inexactitude.

Hansard 22 Feb 1906

The British people have taken for themselves this motto – 'Business carried on as usual during alterations on the map of Europe'.

Speech at the Guildhall 9 Nov 1914   2

The belief that security can be obtained by throwing a small state to the wolves is a fatal delusion.

On Czechoslovakia, 21 Sept 1938   3

I cannot forecast to you the action of Russia. It is a riddle wrapped in a mystery inside an enigma.

Radio broadcast 1 Oct 1939   4

We shall go on to the end. We shall fight in France, we shall fight on the seas and oceans, we shall fight with growing confidence and growing strength in the air, we shall defend our island, whatever the cost may be. We shall fight on the beaches, we shall fight on the landing grounds, we shall fight in the fields and in the streets, we shall fight in the hills; we shall never surrender.

Hansard 4 June 1940   5

'This was their finest hour.'

Hansard 18 June 1940   6

Never in the field of human conflict was so much owed by so   *7*
many to so few.
>   Of the British airmen at the battle
>   of Britain, *Hansard* 20 Aug 1940

We are waiting for the long-promised invasion. So are the fishes.   *8*
>   Radio broadcast to the French people 21 Oct 1940

Give us the tools and we will finish the job.   *9*
>   Speech on radio 9 Feb 1942

The people of London with one voice would say to Hitler: ...   *10*
You do your worst – and we will do our best.'
>   Speech at County Hall London 14 July 1942

I have not become the King's First Minister in order to preside   *11*
over the liquidation of the British Empire.
>   Speech in London 10 Nov 1942

Some chicken! Some neck!   *12*
>   Of the French assertion in World War II that 'In
>   three weeks England will have her neck wrung like a
>   chicken', speech to Canadian Parliament 30 Dec 1942

There is no finer investment for any community than putting   *13*
milk into babies. Healthy citizens are the greatest asset any
country can have.
>   Speech on radio 21 Mar 1943

From Stettin in the Baltic to Trieste in the Adriatic, an iron   *14*
curtain has descended across the Continent.
>   Speech at Westminster College, Fulton, Missouri, 5 Mar 1946

I am prepared to meet my Maker. Whether my Maker is   *15*
prepared for the great ordeal of meeting me is another matter.
>   news conference, Washington 1954

To jaw-jaw is always better than to war-war.   *16*
>   Speech at White House 26 June 1954

A modest man who has a good deal to be modest about.   *17*
>   Of Clement Attlee, *Chicago Sunday Tribune*
>   *Magazine of Books* 27 June 1954

In defeat unbeatable: in victory unbearable.   *18*
   Of Viscount Montgomery in Marsh *Ambrosia and Small Beer*

Don't talk to me about naval tradition. It's nothing but rum,   *19*
sodomy and the lash.
                           Quoted in Peter Gretton *Former Naval Person*

In war: resolution. In defeat: defiance. In victory: magnanimity.   *20*
In peace: goodwill.
                           Second World War, 'Moral of the Work'

It may almost be said, 'Before Alamein we never had a victory.   *21*
After Alamein we never had a defeat.'
                           Second World War vol4, ch3

Cicero Marcus Tullius 106–43 BC. Roman orator, writer, and politician.

The good of the people is the chief law.
                                          De Legibus

The highest good.   *2*
                                          De Officiis I. 2

Let wars yield to peace.   *3*
                                          De Officiis I. 22

What times, what customs!   *4*
                                          In Catilinam

To whose profit.   *5*
                                          Pro Milone

Cimino Michael 1943– . US film director.

A film lives, becomes alive, because of its shadows, its spaces.
                                          Variety July 1980

Clare John 1793–1864. English poet.

He could not die when trees were green, / For he loved the time
too well.
                                          'The Dying Child'

Clarke Arthur C(harles) 1917– . English science-fiction and
nonfiction writer.

Any sufficiently advanced technology is indistinguishable from
magic.
                                          The Lost Worlds of 2001

Clay Henry 1777–1852. US politician.

I had rather be right than be President.
To Senator Preston of South Carolina, 1839

Clemenceau Georges 1841–1929. French politician and journalist.

It is easier to make war than to make peace.
Speech at Verdun 20 July 1919

Clinton Bill (William Jefferson) 1946–   . 42nd president of the USA.

There is nothing wrong with America that cannot be cured
by what is right with America.
Inaugural speech as US president, 1993

Clive Robert, Baron Clive of Plassey 1725–1774. English soldier
and administrator.

By God, Mr. Chairman, at this moment I stand astonished at
my own moderation!
Reply during Parliamentary cross-examination, 1773

I feel that I am reserved for some end or other.   *2*
Comment after failed suicide attempt

Clough Arthur Hugh 1819–1861. English poet.

Grace is given of God, but knowledge is bought in the market.
The Bothie of Tober-na-Vuolich

Do not adultery commit; / Advantage rarely comes of it.   *2*
'The Latest Decalogue'

Thou shalt not kill; but need'st not strive / Officiously to keep   *3*
alive.
'The Latest Decalogue'

Say not, the struggle naught availeth, / The labour and the   *4*
wounds are vain. / 'Say not the struggle naught availeth' / If
hopes were dupes, fears may be liars. / 'Say not the struggle
naught availeth' / And not by eastern windows only, / When
daylight comes, comes in the light, / In front, the sun climbs
slow, how slowly, / But westward, look, the land is bright.
'Say Not, the Struggle Naught Availeth'

Cobbett William 1763–1835. English Radical politician and journalist.

From a very early age, I had imbibed the opinion, that it was every man's duty to do all that lay in his power to leave his country as good as he had found it.
Political Register 22 Dec 1832

Give me, Lord, neither poverty nor riches. 2
Political Register 22 Dec 1832

Coborn Charles 1852–1945. English actor.

Two lovely black eyes, / Oh! what a surprise! / Only for telling a man he was wrong, / Two lovely black eyes!
'Two Lovely Black Eyes'

Cochran C(harles) B(lake) 1872–1951. English impresario.

I am interested in everything so long as it is well done. I would rather see a good juggler than a bad Hamlet.
Secrets of a Showman

Cocteau Jean 1889–1963. French poet, dramatist, and film director.

Life is a horizontal fall.

Opium

If it has to choose who is to be crucified, the crowd will always 2 save Barabbas.
Recall to Order, 'The Cock and the Harlequin'

The worst tragedy for a poet is to be admired through being 3 misunderstood.
Recall to Order, 'The Cock and the Harlequin'

Coke Edward 1552–1634. Lord Chief Justice of England 1613–17.

For a man's house is his castle.
Institutes, Commentary upon Littleton, Third Institute, ch 73

Coleridge Hartley 1796–1849. English poet and essayist.

But what is Freedom? Rightly understood, A universal licence to be good.
'Liberty'

Coleridge Samuel Taylor 1772–1834. English Romantic poet.

Prose = words in their best order; poetry = the *best* words in the best order.

Table Talk 12 July 1827

'God save thee, ancient Mariner! / From the fiends that plague   **2**
thee thus! – / Why look'st thou so?' – With my cross-bow / I
shot the Albatross.

The Ancient Mariner pt 1

It is an ancient Mariner, / And he stoppeth one of three. / 'By   **3**
thy long grey beard and glittering eye, / Now wherefore
stopp'st thou me?'

The Ancient Mariner pt 1

As idle as a painted ship / Upon a painted ocean.   **4**
The Ancient Mariner pt 2

Water, water, everywhere. / Nor any drop to drink.   **5**
The Ancient Mariner pt 2

He prayeth well, who loveth well / Both man and bird and   **6**
beast. / He prayeth best, who loveth best / All things both
great and small.

The Ancient Mariner pt 7

A sadder and a wiser man, / He rose the morrow morn.   **7**
The Ancient Mariner pt 7

No man was ever yet a great poet, without being at the same   **8**
time a profound philosopher.

Biographia Literaria

That willing suspension of disbelief for the moment, which   **9**
constitutes poetic faith.

Biographia Literaria ch 14

Swans sing before they die – 'twere no bad thing / Did certain   **10**
persons die before they sing.

Epigram on a Volunteer Singer

The frost performs its secret ministry, / Unhelped by any wind.   **11**
Frost at Midnight

In Xanadu did Kubla Khan / A stately pleasure-dome decree. **12**

Kubla Khan

Colette Sidonie-Gabrielle 1873–1954. French novelist.

Don't ever wear artistic jewellery, it wrecks a woman's reputation.

Gigi

Collingwood Robin George 1889–1943. English philosopher.

Perfect freedom is reserved for the man who lives by his own work, and in that work does what he wants to do.

Speculum Mentis

Collins John Churton 1848–1908. English scholar and critic.

To ask advice is in nine cases out of ten to tout for flattery.

L C Collins *Life of John Churton Collins*

Collins Mortimer 1827–1876. English poet and novelist.

A man is as old as he's feeling, / A woman as old as she looks.

The Unknown Quantity

Collins William 1721–1759. English poet.

Too nicely Jonson knew the critic's part, / Nature in him was almost lost in Art.

Verses to Sir Thomas Hanmer

Colman George 1762–1836. English dramatist.

His heart runs away with his head.

Who Wants a Guinea? I. i

Colton Charles Caleb 1780–1832. English epigrammatic writer.

Imitation is the sincerest of flattery.

Lacon Vol. 1, No. 217

If you would be known, and not know, vegetate in a village; if you would know, and not be known, live in a city. **2**

Lacon Vol. 1, No. 334

Common Prayer Book of

Grant that the old Adam in this Child may be so buried, that the new man may be raised up in him.
Baptism Invocation of Blessing on the Child

Hear them, read, mark, learn, and inwardly digest them.   *2*
Collect for 2nd Sunday in Advent

The author of peace and lover of concord, in knowledge of   *3*
whom standeth our eternal life, whose service is perfect freedom.
Collect for Peace

That peace which the world cannot give.   *4*
Evening Prayer, Second Collect

Lighten our darkness, we beseech thee, O Lord.   *5*
Evening Prayer, Third Collect

We have left undone those things which we ought to have done;   *6*
/ And we have done those things which we ought not to have
done; / And there is no health in us.
General Confession

All the changes and chances of this mortal life.   *7*
Holy Communion, Collect after the Offertory

All sorts and conditions of men.   *8*
Prayer for All Conditions of Men

Out of the mouth of very babes and sucklings hast thou   *9*
ordained strength.
Psalm 8

What is man, that thou art mindful of him.   *10*
Psalm 8

The fool hath said in his heart: there is no God.   *11*
Psalm 14

Keep me as the apple of an eye: hide me under the shadow of   *12*
thy wings.
Psalm 17

The heavens declare the glory of God: and the firmament showeth his handiwork. **13**

Psalm 19

The Lord is my shepherd: therefore can I lack nothing. / He shall feed me in a green pasture: and lead me forth beside the waters of comfort. **14**

Psalm 23

For man walketh in a vain shadow, and disquieteth himself in vain: he heapeth up riches, and cannot tell who shall gather them. **15**

Psalm 39

God is our hope and strength: a very present help in trouble. **16**

Psalm 46

I had rather be a doorkeeper in the house of my God: than to dwell in the tents of ungodliness. **17**

Psalm 84

Mercy and truth are met together: righteousness and peace have kissed each other. **18**

Psalm 85

The days of our age are threescore years and ten. **19**

Psalm 90

Thou shalt not be afraid for any terror by night: nor for the arrow that flieth by day. For the pestilence that walketh in darkness: nor for the sickness that destroyeth in the noon-day. **20**

Psalm 91

Wine that maketh glad the heart of man: and oil to make him a cheerful countenance, and bread to strengthen man's heart. **21**

Psalm 104

They that go down to the sea in ships: and occupy their business in great waters; / These men see the works of the Lord: and his wonders in the deep. **22**

Psalm 107

The fear of the Lord is the beginning of wisdom. **23**

Psalm 111

I will lift up mine eyes unto the hills: from whence cometh my *24*
help.

Psalm 121

The Lord shall preserve thy going out, and thy coming in: from *25*
this time forth for evermore.

Psalm 121

O pray for the peace of Jerusalem: they shall prosper that love *26*
thee.

Psalm 122

Except the Lord build the house: their labour is but lost that *27*
build it. / Except the Lord keep the city: the watchman waketh
but in vain.

Psalm 127

Like as the arrows in the hand of the giant: even so are the young *28*
children. / Happy is the man that hath his quiver full of them.

Psalm 127

By the waters of Babylon we sat down and wept: when we *28*
remembered thee, O Sion.

Psalm 137

O put not your trust in princes, nor in any child of man: for *30*
there is no help in them.

Psalm 146

If any of you know cause, or just impediment, why these two *31*
persons should not be joined in holy Matrimony, ye are to
declare it.

Solemnization of Matrimony, Banns

Compton-Burnett Ivy 1892–1969. English novelist.

As regards plots I find real life no help at all. Real life seems
to have no plots

R Lehmann et al. *Orion I*

Comte Auguste 1798–1857. French philosopher.

Men are not allowed to think freely about chemistry and

biology, why should they be allowed to think freely about
political philosophy?

Positive Philosophy

Condillac Étienne Bonnot de 1715–1780. French philosopher.
We cannot recollect the ignorance in which we were born.

Traités des Sensations

Congreve William 1670–1729. English dramatist and poet.
She lays it on with a trowel.

The Double Dealer

Oh fie Miss, you must not kiss and tell.   2

Love for Love

Musick has charms to sooth a savage breast.   3

The Mourning Bride I. i

Heav'n has no rage, like love to hatred turn'd, / Nor Hell a   4
fury, like a woman scorn'd.

The Mourning Bride I. viii

Courtship to marriage, as a very witty prologue to a very dull   5
Play.

The Old Bachelor

I nauseate walking; 'tis a country diversion, I loathe the country.   6

The Way of the World

Connolly Billy 1942–   . Scottish comedian.
Marriage is a wonderful invention; but, then again, so is a
bicycle repair kit.

Quoted in D Campbell *Billy Connolly*

Connolly Cyril 1903–1974. English critic and author.
As repressed sadists are supposed to become policemen or
butchers so those with irrational fear of life become publishers.

Enemies of Promise ch 3

Whom the gods wish to destroy they first call promising.   2

Enemies of Promise ch 13

There is no more sombre enemy of good art than the pram in   3
the hall.
Enemies of Promise ch 14

Better to write for yourself and have no public, than to write for   4
the public and have no self.
New Statesman 25 Feb 1933

It is closing time in the gardens of the West and from now on   5
an artist will be judged only by the resonance of his solitude or
the quality of his despair.
Horizon Dec 1949

As bees their sting, so the promiscuous leave behind them in   6
each encounter something of themselves by which they are
made to suffer.
The Unquiet Grave

In the sex-war thoughtlessness is the weapon of the male,   7
vindictiveness of the female.
The Unquiet Grave

We are all serving a life-sentence in the dungeon of self.   8
The Unquiet Grave

Connolly James 1868–1916. Irish Labour leader

The worker is the slave of capitalist society, the female worker   9
is the slave of that slave.
Re-conquest of Ireland

Conrad Joseph. Pen name of Teodor Jozef Conrad Korzeniowski
1857–1924. English novelist, born in the Ukraine of Polish parents.

The conquest of the earth, which mostly means the taking it away
from those who have a different complexion or slightly flatter
noses than ourselves, is not a pretty thing when you look into it.
Heart of Darkness ch 1

He [Kurtz] cried in a whisper at some image, at some vision, –   2
he cried out twice, a cry that was no more than a breath – 'The
horror! The horror!'.
Heart of Darkness ch 3

Any work that aspires, however humbly, to the condition of art **3**
should carry its justification in every line.

The Nigger of the Narcissus author's note

The terrorist and the policeman both come from the same **4**
basket.

Secret Agent

All ambitions are lawful except those which climb upwards on **5**
the miseries or credulities of mankind.

Some Reminiscences

A belief in a supernatural source of evil is not necessary; men **6**
alone are quite capable of every wickedness.

Under Western Eyes

Conran Shirley 1932– . English author.

Life is too short to stuff a mushroom.

Superwoman

Coolidge (John) Calvin 1872–1933. 30th president of the USA
1923–29.

Civilization and profits go hand in hand.

Speech, 27 Nov 1920

The chief business of the American people is business. **2**

Speech, 17 Jan 1925

There is no right to strike against the public safety by anybody, **3**
anywhere, any time.

Telegram to Samuel Gompers

Cope Wendy 1945– . English poet.

There are so many kinds of awful men – / One can't avoid them
all. She often said / She'd never make the same mistake again:/
She always made a new mistake instead.

'Rondeau Redoublé'

Corday Charlotte 1768–1793. French Girondin.

I have done my task, let others do theirs.

On being interrogated for the murder of Marat July 1793

Corneille Pierre 1606–1684. French dramatist.

When there is no peril in the fight, there is no glory in the triumph.
Le Cid

Cornford Frances 1886–1960. English poet.

O fat white woman whom nobody loves, / Why do you walk through the fields in gloves, ... / Missing so much and so much?
To a Fat Lady Seen from a Train

Cornford Francis M 1874–1943. English philosopher.

Every public action, which is not customary, either is wrong, or, if it is right, is a dangerous precedent. It follows that nothing should ever be done for the first time.
Microcosmographia Academica

Cornforth John Warcup 1917–   . Australian chemist.

For him [the scientist], truth is so seldom the sudden light that shows new order and beauty; more often, truth is the uncharted rock that sinks his ship in the dark.
Nobel prize address 1975

Cornuel Madame 1605–1694. French wit and woman of letters.

No man is a hero to his valet.
Lettres de Mlle Aissé

Cortés Hernando 1485–1547. Spanish conqueror of Mexico

I and my companions suffer from a disease of the heart that can be cured only with gold.
Message sent to Montezuma 1519

Coubertin Piérre de 1863–1937. French scholar and educator.

The important thing in life is not the victory but the contest; the essential thing is not to have won but to have run the race.
Speech, 24 July 1908

Coué Émile 1857–1926. French chemist and psychotherapist.

Every day, in every way, I am getting better and better.

Slogan that Coué advised his patients to repeat, *De la suggestion
et de ses applications* (On Suggestion and its Applications)

Courbet Gustave 1819–1877. French artist.

I deny that art can be taught.

> Letter to prospective students 1861

Coward Noël 1899–1973. English dramatist and actor.

Dear 338171 (May I call you 338?)

> Letter to T E Lawrence, 25 Aug 1930

Don't let's be beastly to the Germans / When our Victory is
ultimately won.   *2*

> 'Don't Let's Be Beastly to the Germans'

I believe that since my life began / The most I've had is just /
A talent to amuse.   *3*

> 'If Love Were All'

Mad dogs and Englishmen / Go out in the midday sun.   *4*

> 'Mad Dogs and Englishmen'

Don't put your daughter on the stage, Mrs Worthington.   *5*

> 'Mrs Worthington'

Poor little rich girl / You're a bewitched girl, / better beware!   *6*

> 'Poor Little Rich Girl'

Extraordinary how potent cheap music is.   *7*

> *Private Lives*

The Stately Homes of England, / How beautiful they stand, / To   *8*
prove the upper classes / Have still the upper hand.

> 'The Stately Homes of England'

I never realized before that Albert married beneath him.   *9*

> On seeing a certain actress playing the part of
> Queen Victoria, in K Tynan 'A Tribute to Mr Coward'

Cowley Abraham 1618–1667. English poet.

God the first garden made, and the first city Cain.

> *The Garden*

Cowper William 1731–1800. English poet.

The poplars are fell'd, farewell to the shade / And the whispering sound of the cool colonnade.
The Poplar-Field

Talks of darkness at noon-day.   *2*
Progress of Error

God made the country, and man made the town.   *3*
The Task bk 1

Variety's the very spice of life, / That gives it all its flavour.   *4*
The Task bk 2

I am monarch of all I survey.   *5*
Verses Supposed to be Written by Alexander Selkirk

Crisp Quentin 1908– . English writer.

There was no need to do any housework at all. After the first four years the dirt doesn't get any worse.
Naked Civil Servant ch 15

An autobiography is an obituary in serial form with the last   *2*
instalment missing.
Naked Civil Servant ch 29

Critchley Julian 1930– . British Conservative politician.

The only safe pleasure for a parliamentarian is a bag of boiled sweets.
Listener 10 June 1982

Cromwell Oliver 1599–1658. English general and politician.

A few honest men are better than numbers.
Letter to W. Spring, Sept 1643

I beseech you, in the bowels of Christ, think it possible you   *2*
may be mistaken.
Letter to the General Assembly of the
Church of Scotland 3 Aug 1650

Take away these baubles. **3**
> Referring to the symbols of parliamentary
> power when he dismissed parliament 1653

cummings e(dward) e(stlin) 1894–1962. US poet.

Listen: there's a hell of a good universe next door: let's go.
> *Pity this busy monster, manunkind*

Cummings William Thomas 1903–1945. US priest.

There are no atheists in the foxholes.
> Quoted in C P Romulo *I Saw the Fall of the Philippines* ch 15

D

Dali Salvador 1904–1989. Spanish painter and designer.

There is only one difference between a madman and me. I am not mad.

The American July 1956

Surrealism is destructive, but it destroys only what it considers to be shackles limiting our vision.   2

Declaration

Dana Charles Anderson 1819–1897. US journalist.

When a dog bites a man that is not news, but when a man bites a dog that is news.

'What is News?' in *The New York Sun* 1882

Dante Alighieri 1265–1321. Italian poet.

In the middle of the road of our life.

Divine Comedy 'Inferno' I

All hope abandon, ye who enter here.   2

Divine Comedy 'Inferno' III

The love that moves the sun and the other stars.   3

Divine Comedy 'Paradiso' XXXIII

Davies John 1569–1626. English poet.

Skill comes so slow, and life so fast doth fly, / We learn so little and forget so much.

Nosce Teipsum introduction

Judge not the play before the play be done.   2

Respice Finem

Davies W(illiam) H(enry) 1871–1940. Welsh poet.

What is this life if, full of care, / We have no time to stand and stare?

'Leisure'

de Gaulle Charles André Joseph Marie 1890–1970. French general and president.

France has lost a battle. But France has not lost the war!
Proclamation 18 June 1940

If I am not France, what am I doing in your office?   *2*
  Making claim to Winston Churchill to lead the Free French 1940

No country without an atom bomb could properly consider   *3*
itself independent.
New York Times 1968

How can you govern a country which has 246 varieties of   *4*
cheese?
E Mignon Les Mots du Général

Since a politician never believes what he says, he is quite   *5*
surprised to be taken at his word
E Mignon Les Mots du Général

de la Mare Walter 1873–1956. English poet.

Look thy last on all things lovely, / Every hour.
Fare Well

'Is there anybody there?' said the traveller, / Knocking on the   *2*
moonlit door.
'The Listeners'

De Vries Peter 1910– . US novelist.

It is the final proof of God's omnipotence that he need not exist
in order to save us.
Mackerel Plaza ch 1

Debs Eugene V(ictor) 1855–1926. US labour leader and socialist.

I said then, I say now, that while there is a lower
class, I am in it; while there is a criminal element, I am of it;
while there is a soul in prison, I am not free.
Speech at his trial 14 Sept 1918

Decatur Stephen 1779–1820. US naval hero.

Our country, right or wrong.
Toast given at Norfolk, Virginia 1816

Dekker Thomas *c*. 1572–*c*. 1632. English dramatist and
pamphleteer.

> Art thou poor, yet hast thou golden slumbers: / Oh sweet
> content! / Honest labour bears a lovely face.
>
> *Patient Grissill* I

> Golden slumbers kiss your eyes, / Smiles awake you when you   *2*
> rise.
>
> *Patient Grissill* IV. ii

Dempsey Jack (William Harrison) 1895–1983. US heavyweight
boxer.

> Honey, I just forgot to duck.
>
> Comment to his wife after losing his
> World Heavyweight title 23 Sept 1926

Dennis John 1657–1734. English critic and dramatist.

> A man who could make so vile a pun would not scruple to pick
> a pocket.
>
> *The Gentleman's Magazine*, 1781

> Damn them! They will not let my play run, but they steal my   *2*
> thunder!
>
> W S Walsh *Handy-book of Literary Curiosities*

Depardieu Gérard 1948–   . French actor.

> At twenty you have many desires that hide the truth, but
> beyond 40 there are only real and fragile truths—your abilities
> and your failings.
>
> *Observer* March 1991

Descartes René 1596–1650. French philosopher and mathematician.

> I think, therefore I am.
>
> *Le Discours de la Méthode*

Dewey John 1859–1952. US philosopher.

> For one man who thanks God that he is not as other men there
> are a few thousand to offer thanks that they are as other men,
> sufficiently as others to escape attention.
>
> *Human Nature and Conflict*

Díaz Porfiro 1830–1915. President of Mexico 1877–80, 1884–1911.

Poor Mexico, so far from God, and so close to the United States!
Attributed remark

Dibdin Charles 1745–1814. English songwriter and dramatist.

In every mess I finds a friend, / In every port a wife.
'Jack in his Element'

Dibdin Thomas 1771–1841. English songwriter.

Oh! what a snug little Island, / A right little, tight little Island!
'The Snug Little Island'

Dickens Charles 1812–1870. English novelist.

This is a London particular. ... A fog, miss.
Bleak House ch 3

Discipline must be maintained.   **2**
Bleak House ch 27

It is a melancholy truth that even great men have their poor   **3**
relations.
Bleak House ch 28

'God bless us every one!' said Tiny Tim, the last of all.   **4**
A Christmas Carol

'I am a lone lorn creetur',' were Mrs. Gummidge's words, / ...   **5**
'and everythink goes contrairy with me.'
David Copperfield ch 3

Annual income twenty pounds, annual expenditure nineteen   **6**
nineteen six, result happiness. Annual income twenty pounds,
annual expenditure twenty pounds ought and six, result misery.
Mr Micawber in *David Copperfield* ch 12

We are so very 'umble.   **7**
Uriah Heep in *David Copperfield* ch 12

Accidents will occur in the best-regulated families.   **8**
Mr Micawber in *David Copperfield* ch 28

It's only my child-wife.   **9**
Of Dora in *David Copperfield* ch 44

Now, what I want is, Facts. ... Facts alone are wanted in life.   *10*
                                    Mr Gradgrind in *Hard Times*

All is gas and gaiters.   *11*
                                        Nicholas Nickleby ch 49

Oliver Twist has asked for more!   *12*
                                              Oliver Twist ch 2

Known by the *sobriquet* of 'The artful Dodger.'   *13*
                                              Oliver Twist ch 8

'If the law supposes that,' said Mr. Bumble ... 'the law is a ass *14*
– a idiot.'
                                             Oliver Twist ch 51

I wants to make your flesh creep.   *15*
                                         Pickwick Papers ch 8

Anythin' for a quiet life, as the man said wen he took the   *16*
sitivation at the lighthouse.
                              Sam Weller in *Pickwick Papers* ch 43

It is a far, far better thing that I do, than I have ever done; it is *17*
a far, far better rest that I go to, than I have ever known.
                               A Tale of Two Cities bk 3, ch 15

Dickinson Emily (Elizabeth) 1830–1886. US poet.

Parting is all we know of heaven, / And all we need of hell.
                                                       'Parting'

Dickinson John 1732–1808. US lawyer and statesman.

Our cause is just. Our union is perfect.
                             Declaration on Taking Up Arms 1775

Dillon Wentworth *c* 1633–1685. English poet and translator.

But words once spoke can never be recall'd.
                                                  Art of Poetry

Choose an author as you choose a friend.   *2*
                                        Essay on Translated Verse

Dimnet 1869–1954. French churchman and writer.

Architecture, of all the arts, is the one which acts the most
slowly, but the most surely, on the soul.
                                               What We Live By pt 2, ch 12

Diogenes *c*. 412–323 BC. Greek philosopher.

Stand out of my sun a little.
                                    Response to Alexander the Great
                           when he asked him if he wanted anything

Dior Christian 1905–1957. French couturier.

My dream is to save [women] from nature.
                                               Quoted in *Collier's* 1955

Disraeli Benjamin, Earl of Beaconsfield 1804–1881. British
Conservative politician and novelist.

The Continent will not suffer England to be the workshop of the
world.
                             Speech in House of Commons 15 March 1838

The right Hon. Gentleman caught the Whigs bathing, and   *2*
walked away with their clothes.
     Of Sir Robert Peel, speech in House of Commons 28 Feb 1845

Justice is truth in action.   *3*
                             Speech in House of Commons 11 Feb 1851

Finality is not the language of politics.   *4*
                             Speech in House of Commons 28 Feb 1859

Is man an ape or an angel? Now I am on the side of the angels. *5*
         Speech at meeting of Society for Increasing Endowments of
               Small Livings in the Diocese of Oxford *25 Nov 1864*

Increased means and increased leisure are the two civilizers of *6*
man.
                                     Speech in Manchester 3 April 1872

All those institutions and all those principles ... in due time will *7*
become great and 'burning' questions.
                                  Speech in Manchester 20 March 1873

Read no history: nothing but biography, for that is life without   **8**
theory.
                                                        Contarini Fleming

His Christianity was muscular.   **9**
                                                                Endymion

Damn your principles! Stick to your party.   **10**
                                                        Latham, *Famous Sayings*

When a man fell into his anecdotage it was a sign for him to   **11**
retire from the world.
                                                            Lothair ch 28

You know who the critics are? The men who have failed in   **12**
literature and art.
                                                            Lothair ch 35

Little things affect little minds.   **13**
                                                        Sybil bk 3, ch 2

To do nothing and get something, formed a boy's ideal of a   **14**
manly career.
                                                            Sybil ch 5

Experience is the child of Thought, and Thought is the child of   **15**
Action. We cannot learn men from books.
                                                        Vivian Grey bk 5, ch 1

There is moderation even in excess.   **16**
                                                        Vivian Grey bk 6, ch 1

Donne John 1571–1631. English metaphysical poet.

Twice or thrice had I loved thee, / Before I knew thy face or
name. / So in a voice, so in a shapeless flame, / Angels affect us
soft, and worshipped be.
                                                        'Air and Angels'

For God's sake hold your tongue, and let me love.   **2**
                                                        'The Canonization'

No Spring, nor Summer beauty hath such grace, / As I have   **3**
seen in one Autumnal face.
                                                        Elegies No. 9, 'The Autumnal'

O my America! my new-found-land.   *4*
               Elegies No. 19, 'To his Mistress Going to Bed'

Go, and catch a falling star, / Get with child a mandrake root, /   *5*
Tell me, where all past years are, / Or who cleft the Devil's foot
               'Song, Go and Catch a Falling Star'

And now good morrow to our waking souls, / Which watch   *6*
not one another out of fear.
               'The Good-Morrow'

I wonder by my troth, what thou, and I / Did, till we lov'd?   *7*
were we not wean'd till then?
               'The Good-Morrow'

Death be not proud, though some have called thee / Mighty and   *8*
dreadful, for, thou art not so.
               Holy Sonnets No. 10, 'Death be not Proud'

Sweetest love, I do not go, / For weariness of thee, / Nor in   *9*
hope the world can show / A fitter Love for me.
               'Song, sweetest love, I do not go'

Busy old fool, unruly Sun, / Why dost thou thus, / Through   *10*
windows, and through curtains call on us?
               'The Sun Rising'

Love, all alike, no season knows, nor clime, / Nor hours, days,   *11*
months, which are the rags of time.
               'The Sun Rising'

I am two fools, I know, / For loving, and for saying so / In   *12*
whining Poetry.
               'The Triple Fool'

Dorman-Smith Reginald 1899–1977. British politician.

Let 'Dig for Victory' be the motto of every one with a garden
and of every able-bodied man and woman capable of digging
an allotment in their spare time.
               Radio broadcast 3 Oct 1939

Douglas Norman 1868–1952. English diplomat and travel writer.

To find a friend one must close one eye. To keep him – two.
Almanac

You can tell the ideals of a nation by its advertisements. 2
South Wind ch 6

Dowson Ernest 1867–1900. English poet.

And I was desolate and sick of an old passion.
'Non Sum Qualis Eram'

I have been faithful to thee, Cynara! in my fashion. 2
'Non Sum Qualis Eram'

They are not long, the weeping and the laughter, / Love and 3
desire and hate; / I think they have no portion in us after / We
pass the gate.
'Vitae Summa Brevis'

Doyle Arthur Conan 1859–1930. English writer.

It has long been an axiom of mine that the little things are
infinitely the most important.
The Adventures of Sherlock Holmes, 'A Case of Identity'

The giant rat of Sumatra, a story for which the world is not yet 2
prepared.
The Case Book, 'Sussex Vampire'

All other men are specialists, but his specialism is omniscience 3
His Last Bow, 'Bruce-Partington Plans'

You know my methods, Watson. 4
The Memoirs of Sherlock Holmes, 'The Crooked Man'

A long shot, Watson; a very long shot! 5
The Memoirs of Sherlock Holmes, 'The Silver Blaze'

How often have I said to you that when you have eliminated 6
the impossible, whatever remains, however improbable, must
be the truth?
The Sign of Four

The Baker Street irregulars.   7

The Sign of Four

Mediocrity knows nothing higher than itself, but talent   8
instantly recognizes genius.

The Valley of Fear

Drayton Michael 1563–1631. English poet.

How many paltry, foolish, painted things, / That now in coaches
trouble ev'ry street, / Shall be forgotten, whom no poet sings, /
Ere they be well wrapped in their winding sheet?

Sonnets 'Idea', 6

Since there's no help, come let us kiss and part.   2

Sonnets 61

Fair stood the wind for France.   3

To the Cambro-Britans, 'Agincourt'

For that fine madness still he did retain / Which rightly should   4
possess a poet's brain.

To Henry Reynolds, of Poets and Poesy

Had in him those brave translunary things, / That the first poets   5
had.

Of Marlowe, in *To Henry Reynolds, of Poets and Poesy*

Drinkwater John 1882–1937. English poet and dramatist.

Those book-learned fools who miss the world.

From Generation to Generation

Dryden John 1631–1700. English poet and dramatist.

Better one suffer, than a nation grieve.

Absalom and Achitophel pt 1

Beware the fury of a patient man.   2

Absalom and Achitophel pt 1

Great wits are sure to madness near alli'd   3

Absalom and Achitophel pt 1

In pious times, ere priestcraft did begin, / Before polygamy was   **4**
made a sin.
                                                                      Absalom and Achitophel pt 1

Youth, beauty, graceful action seldom fail: / But common   **5**
interest always will prevail.
                                                                      Absalom and Achitophel pt 1

None but the brave deserve the fair.   **6**
                                                                      Alexander's Feast

Men are but children of a larger growth; / Our appetites as apt   **7**
to change as theirs.
                                                                      All For Love

A knock-down argument; 'tis but a word and a blow.   **8**
                                                                      Amphitryon

Learn to write well, or not to write at all.   **9**
                                                                      Essay on Satire

All human things are subject to decay, / And, when fate   **10**
summons, monarchs must obey.
                                                                      MacFlecknoe

From harmony, from heavenly harmony / This universal frame   **11**
began: / From harmony to harmony / Through all the compass
of the notes it ran, / The diapason closing full in Man.
                                                                      St. Cecilia's Day

Joy rul'd the day, and Love the night.   **12**
                                                                      Secular Masque

And, dying, bless the hand that gave the blow.   **13**
                                                                      The Spanish Friar

Here lies my wife: here let her lie! / Now she's at rest, and so am I. **14**
                                                                      Epitaph intended for Dryden's wife

Dürer Albrecht 1471–1528. German artist and engraver.

If a man devotes himself to art, much evil is avoided that happens
otherwise if one is idle.
                                                                      Outline of a General Treatise on Painting

Duhamel Georges 1884–1966. French novelist.

I have too much respect for the idea of God to make it responsible for such an absurd world.

Le désert de Bièvres'

Dyer Edward d. 1607. English poet.

'My Mind to Me a Kingdom Is'

'In Praise of a contented mind'

Dylan Bob. Adopted name of Robert Allen Zimmerman 1941–   . US singer and songwriter.

How many roads must a man walk down / Before you can call him a man? ... / The answer, my friend, is blowin' in the wind, / The answer is blowin' in the wind.

'Blowin' in the Wind'

Money doesn't talk, it swears.

2

'It's Alright, Ma'

E

Earhart Amelia 1898–1937. US aviation pioneer and author.

Failure must be but a challenge to others.

Last Flight

Eastman George 1854–1932. US entrepreneur and inventor.

My work is done. Why wait?

Suicide note

Eban Abba 1915– . Israeli diplomat and politician.

History teaches us that men and nations behave wisely once they have exhausted other alternatives.

Speech, 16 Dec 1970

Ebbinghaus Hermann 1850–1909. German psychologist.

Psychology has a long past, but only a short history.

Summary of Psychology

Edgeworth Maria 1767–1849. Irish novelist.

Some people talk of morality, and some of religion, but give me a little snug property.

The Absentee

Edison Thomas Alva 1847–1931. US scientist and inventor.

Genius is one per cent. inspiration and ninety-nine per cent. perspiration.

Interview in *Life*

Edward III 1312–1377. King of England, 1327–77.

Let the boy win his spurs.

Of the Black Prince at Crécy, 1345

Edward VIII 1894–1972. Duke of Windsor.

The thing that impresses me most about America is the way parents obey their children.

Look 5 Mar 1957

Edwards Oliver 1711–1791. English lawyer.

I have tried too in my time to be a philosopher; but, I don't know how, cheerfulness was always breaking in.

Boswell's *Life of Johnson* 17 Apr 1778

Einstein Albert 1879–1955. German-born US physicist.

God is subtle but he is not malicious.

Remark made at Princeton University in 1921, later carved above the fireplace of the Common Room of Fine Hall (the Mathematical Institute)

At any rate, I am convinced that He [God] does not lay dice.   **2**

Letter to Max Born 4 Dec 1926

If my theory of relativity is proven correct, Germany will   **3** claim me as a German and France will declare that I am a citizen of the world. Should my theory prove untrue, France will say that I am a German and Germany will declare that I am a Jew.

Address at the Sorbonne, Paris, Dec 1929

The unleashed power of the atom has changed everything save   **4** our modes of thinking and we thus drift toward unparalleled catastrophe.

Telegram sent to prominent Americans 24 May 1946

If A is a success in life, then A equals x plus y plus z. Work is   **5** x; y is play; and z is keeping your mouth shut.

Observer 15 Jan 1950

Nationalism is an infantile sickness. It is the measles of the   **6** human race.

Quoted in H Dukas and B Hoffman *Albert Einstein, the Human Side*

Eisenhower Dwight David (*Ike*) 1890–1969. 34th president of the USA 1953–61.

Every gun that is made, every warship launched, every rocket fired signifies, in the final sense, a theft from those who hunger and are not fed, those who are cold and are not clothed.
                                                              Speech 16 Apr 1953

Your business is to put me out of business.   *2*
                              Addressing a graduating class at a university

Eliot George. Pen name of Mary Ann Evans 1819–1880. English novelist.

It's them as take advantage that get advantage i' this world.
                                                              Adam Bede ch 32

I'm not denyin' the women are foolish: God Almighty made   *2*
'em to match the men.

                                                              Adam Bede ch 53

The happiest women, like the happiest nations, have no history.   *3*
                                          The Mill on the Floss Bk6 ch 3

In every parting there is an image of death.
                              Scenes of Clerical Life, 'Amos Barton'

Nothing is so good as it seems beforehand.   *4*
                                                              Silas Marner

Eliot T(homas) S(tearns) 1888–1965. US poet and playwright, based in London.

I grow old ... I grow old ... / I shall wear the bottoms of my trousers rolled.

                                                      Love Song of J. Alfred Prufrock

April is the cruellest month, breeding / Lilacs out of the dead   *2*
land, mixing / Memory and desire.

                                                              The Waste Land

I will show you fear in a handful of dust.   *3*
                                                              The Waste Land

When lovely woman stoops to folly and / Paces about her room   **4**
again, alone, / She smoothes her hair with automatic hand, /
And puts a record on the gramophone.

The Waste Land

Elizabeth I 1533–1603. Queen of Great Britain, 1558–1603.

I know I have the body of a weak and feeble woman, but I
have the heart and stomach of a king, and of a king of England
too.

Speech to the troops at Tilbury on the approach
of the Armada, 1588

Though God hath raised me high, yet this I count the glory of   **2**
my crown: that I have reigned with your loves.

The Golden Speech 1601, D'Ewes' *Journal*

Anger makes dull men witty, but it keeps them poor.   **3**

Atributed remark

Elizabeth the *Queen Mother* 1900–   . Wife of King George VI of
England.

I'm glad we've been bombed. It makes me feel I can look the
East End in the face.

Said to a policeman 13 Sept 1940

Emerson Ralph Waldo 1803–1882. US philosopher, essayist, and
poet.

The shot heard round the world.

'Concord Hymn'

There is properly no history; only biography.   **2**

Essays, 'History'

All mankind love a lover.   **3**

Essays, 'Love'

In skating over thin ice, our safety is in our speed   **4**

Essays, 'Prudence'

By necessity, by proclivity, and by delight, we all quote.   **5**

Letters and Social Aims, 'Quotation and Originality'

A foolish consistency is the hobgoblin of little minds, adored   6
by little statesmen and philosophers and divines.
Essays, 'Self-Reliance'

Every hero becomes a bore at last.   7
Representative Men, 'Uses of Great Men'

Art is a jealous mistress.   8
Conduct of Life, 'Wealth'

The louder he talked of his honour, the faster we counted our
spoons.   9
Conduct of Life, 'Worship'

If a man write a better book, preach a better sermon, or make a   10
better mouse-trap than his neighbour, tho' he build his house
in the woods, the world will make a beaten path to his door.
Attributed remark

Essex Robert Devereux, 2nd Earl of Essex 1566–1601. English soldier
and politician.

Reasons are not like garments, the worse for wearing.
To Lord Willoughby 1598 or 1599

Estienne Henri 1531–1598. French classical scholar.

If youth knew; if age could.

Les Prémices

Evans Abel 1679–1737. English poet.

Under this stone, Reader, survey / Dead Sir John Vanbrugh's
house of clay. / Lie heavy on him, Earth! for he / Laid many
heavy loads on thee!
Epitaph on John Vanbrugh, architect of Blenheim Palace

F

Fanon Frantz 1925–1961. French political writer.

For the black man there is only one destiny. And it is white.
Black Skin White Masks

Farouk 1920–1965. King of Egypt 1936–52.

The whole world is in revolt. Soon there will be only five Kings left—the King of England, the King of Spades, the King of Clubs, the King of Hearts and the King of Diamonds.
Remark at a conference in Cairo 1948

Farquhar George 1677–1707. Irish dramatist.

My Lady Bountiful.
The Beaux Stratagem I. i

No woman can be a beauty without a fortune.   *2*
The Beaux Stratagem II.ii

How a little love and good company improves a woman!   *3*
The Beaux Stratagem IV. i

Spare all I have, and take my life.   *4*
The Beaux Stratagem V. ii

Faulkner William (Harrison) 1897–1962. US novelist.

If a writer has to rob his mother, he will not hesitate; the Ode on a / Grecian Urn is worth any number of old ladies.
Paris Review Spring 1956

I believe man will not merely endure, he will prevail. He is   *2*
immortal, not because he, alone among creatures, has an inexhaustible voice but because he has a soul, a spirit capable of compassion and sacrifice and endurance.
Nobel Prize speech 1950

Ferber Edna 1887–1968. US novelist and dramatist.

Being an old maid is like death by drowning, a really delightful
sensation after you cease to struggle.

R E Drennan *Wit's End*

Fermi Enrico 1901–1954. Italian-born US physicist.

Whatever Nature has in store for mankind, unpleasant as it
may be, man must accept, for ignorance is never better than
knowledge.

Atoms in the Family

Feyerabend Paul K 1924–   . US philosopher of science.

Variety of opinion is necessary for objective knowledge.

Against Method

Feynman Richard P(hillips) 1918–1988. US physicist.

One does not, by knowing all the physical laws as we know
them today, immediately obtain an understanding of anything
much.

The Character of Physical Law

Fielding Henry 1707–1754. English novelist.

Public schools are the nurseries of all vice and immorality.

Joseph Andrews

His designs were strictly honourable, as the phrase is; that is,   *2*
to rob a lady of her fortune by way of marriage.

Tom Jones

Fields W C. Stage name of William Claude Dukenfield 1879–1946.
US actor and screenwriter.

I always keep a supply of stimulant handy in case I see a snake
–which / I also keep handy.

C Ford *Time of Laughter*

Never give a sucker an even break.   *2*

Catch-phrase

Here lies W. C. Fields. I would rather be living in Philadelphia.   **3**
                                           Suggested epitaph for himself

Fitzgerald Edward 1809–1883. English poet and translator.

Ah, take the Cash in hand and waive the Rest; / Oh, the brave
Music of a distant Drum!

Omar Khayyám

Alas, that Spring should vanish with the Rose!   **2**

Omar Khayyám

Awake! for Morning in the Bowl of Night / Has flung the Stone   **3**
that puts the Stars to Flight: / And Lo! the Hunter of the East has
caught / The Sultan's Turret in a Noose of Light.

Omar Khayyám

Come, fill the Cup, and in the Fire of Spring / The winter   **4**
Garment of Repentance fling.

Omar Khayyám

Here with a Loaf of Bread beneath the bough, / A Flask of   **5**
Wine, a Book of Verse – and Thou / Beside me singing in the
Wilderness – / And Wilderness is Paradise enow.

Omar Khayyám

I sometimes think that never blows so red / The rose as where   **6**
some buried Caesar bled.

Omar Khayyám

The Moving Finger writes; and, having writ / Moves on: nor all   **7**
thy Piety nor Wit / Shall lure it back to cancel half a Line, / Nor
all thy Tears wash out a Word of it.

Omar Khayyám

'Who is the Potter, pray, and who the Pot?'   **8**

Omar Khayyám

Fitzgerald F Scott 1896–1940. US novelist.

Let me tell you about the very rich. They are different from you
and me.

All the Sad Young Men 'Rich Boy'

A big man has no time really to do anything but just sit and be   *2*
big.
This Side of Paradise

In a real dark night of the soul it is always three o'clock in the   *3*
morning, day after day.
'Handle with Care'

Flecker James Elroy 1884–1915. English poet.

And some to Meccah turn to pray, and I toward thy bed,
Yasmin.
Hassan I. ii

We take the Golden Road to Samarkand.   *2*
Hassan V. ii

It was so old a ship––who knows, who knows? / And yet so   *3*
beautiful, I watched in vain / To see the mast burst open with
a rose, / And the whole deck put on its leaves again.
The Old Ships

Foch Ferdinand 1851–1929. French marshal.

My centre is giving way, my right is in retreat; situation
excellent. I am attacking.
Attributed remark quoted in Aston, *Biography of Foch*

Foot Isaac 1880–1960. English Liberal politician.

Men of power have no time to read; yet men who do not read are
unfit for power.
Debts of Honour

Ford Henry 1863–1947. US automobile manufacturer.

People can have the Model T in any colour – so long as it's
black.
A Nevins *Ford*

History is bunk.   *2*
Remark

Ford John 1586–*c*. 1640. English poet and dramatist.

'Tis Pity She's a Whore.

Play title

Ford Lena Gilbert 1870–1916. English poet.

Keep the home fires burning.

Poem title

Ford Ford Madox. Adopted name of Ford Hermann Hueffer 1873–1939. English author.

There is a lady sweet and kind, / Was never face so pleased my mind; / I did but see her passing by, / And yet I love her till I die.
Music of Sundry Kinds

Forman Milos 1932– . Czech film director.

The Czechs voted for the jungle, while the Slovaks voted for the zoo. It is clear that a compromise is impossible.
Remark on the division of Czechoslovkia

Forster E(dward) M(organ) 1879–1970. English novelist.

The historian must have some conception of how men who are not historians behave. Otherwise he will move in a world of the dead.
Abinger Harvest, 'Captain Edward Gibbon'

It is not that the Englishman can't feel—it is that he is afraid to feel. He has been taught at his public school that feeling is bad form.   2
Abinger Harvest 'Notes on English Character'

Personal relations are the important thing for ever and ever, and not this outer life of telegrams and anger.   3
Howards End ch 19

Only connect!   4
Howards End ch 22

The so-called white races are really pinko-grey.   5
A Passage to India ch 7

The huge city which the West had built and abandoned with a   **6**
gesture of despair.

> On Bombay in *A Passage to India*

She ... joined the vast armies of the benighted, who follow   **7**
neither the heart nor the brain, and march to their destiny by
catchwords.

> *A Room with a View*

I suggest that the only books that influence us are those for   **8**
which we are ready, and which have gone a little farther down
our particular path than we have yet got ourselves.

> *Two Cheers for Democracy*, 'Books That Influenced Me'

Faith, to my mind, is a stiffening process, a sort of mental   **9**
starch, which should be applied as sparingly as possible.

> *Two Cheers for Democracy*' What I Believe'

I hate the idea of causes, and if I had to choose between   *10*
betraying my country and betraying my friend, I hope I
should have the guts to betray my country.

> *Two Cheers for Democracy*, 'What I Believe'

Foucault Michel 1926–1984. French philosopher.

Man is neither the oldest nor the most constant problem that
has been posed for human knowledge.

> *The Order of Things*

Fox Henry Richard, 3rd Baron Holland 1773–1840. English Liberal
statesman.

If Mr. Selwyn calls again, shew him up; if I am alive I shall be
delighted to see him; and if I am dead he would like to see me.

> Last words

France Anatole. Pen name of Jacques Anatole Thibault 1844–1924.
French writer.

They [the poor] have to labour in the face of the majestic
equality of the law, which forbids the rich as well as the poor to

sleep under bridges, to beg in the streets, and to steal bread.
The Red Lily ch 7

The good critic is he who relates the adventures of his soul
among masterpieces.　　　　　　　　　　　　　　　　　　*2*
The Literary Life, dedicatory letter

Francis I 1494–1547. King of France, 1515–47.

Out of all I had, only honour remains, and my life, which is safe.
Letter to his mother after losing Battle of Pavia 1525

Franklin Benjamin 1706–1790. US author, scientist, and statesman.

We must indeed all hang together, or, most assuredly, we shall
all hang separately.
Remark to John Hancock, at Signing of the
Declaration of Independence 4 July 1776

There never was a good war, or a bad peace.　　　　　　　*2*
Letter to Quincey 11 Sept 1783

But in this world nothing can be said to be certain, except death　*3*
and taxes.
Letter to Jean Baptiste Le Roy 13 Nov 1789

Remember, that time is money.　　　　　　　　　　　　　*4*
'Advice to Young Tradesman'

No nation was ever ruined by trade.　　　　　　　　　　　*5*
'Thoughts on Commercial Subjects'

Freud Clement 1924–　. English journalist.

If you resolve to give up smoking, drinking and loving, you
don't actually live longer; it just seems longer.
Observer Dec 1964

Freud Sigmund 1856–1939. Austrian physician and pioneer of
psychoanalysis.

Anatomy is destiny.
Collected Writings

Analogies decide nothing, that is true, but they can make one   *2*
feel more at home.
> *New Introductory Lectures on Psychoanalysis*

The great question that has never been answered ... is 'What   *3*
does a woman want?'
> Letter to Marie Bonaparte

Frost Robert (Lee) 1874–1963. US poet.

Most of the change we think we see in life / Is due to truths
being in or out of favour.
> 'The Black Cottage'

'Home is the place where, when you have to go there, / They   *2*
have to take you in.'
> 'Death of the Hired Man'

I never dared be radical when young / For fear it would make   *3*
me conservative when old.
> *Further Range*, 'Precaution'

I've given offence by saying that I'd as soon write free verse as   *4*
play tennis with the net down.
> E Lathem *Interviews with Robert Frost*

I would have written of me on my stone: / I had a lover's   *5*
quarrel with the world.
> 'Lesson for Today'

Something there is that doesn't love a wall.   *6*
> 'Mending Wall'

Poetry is what is lost in translation. It is also what is lost in   *7*
interpretation.
> Quoted in L Untermeyer *Robert Frost: a Backward Look*

Poetry is a way of taking life by the throat.   *8*
> Quoted in E S Sergeant *Robert Frost:*
> *the Trial by Existence* ch 18

We dance round in a ring and suppose, / But the Secret sits in   **9**
the middle and knows.

'The Secret Sits'

Fry Christopher 1907– . English dramatist.

I travel light; as light, / That is, as a man can travel who will /
Still carry his body around because / Of its sentimental value.
The Lady's not for Burning

Try thinking of love, or something. / Amor vincit insomnia.   **2**
A Sleep of Prisoners

I tell you, / Miss, I knows an undesirable character / When I   **3**
see one; I've been one myself for years.
Venus Observed

Fry Roger (Eliot) 1866–1934. English artist and art critic.

Bach almost persuades me to be a Christian.
V Woolf *Roger Fry*

Fuller R Buckminster 1895–1983. US architect and engineer.

Now there is one outstandingly important fact regarding
Spaceship Earth, and that is that no instruction book came with it.
Operating Manual for Spaceship Earth

G

Gabor Dennis 1900–1979. Hungarian-born British physicist.

Till now man has been up against Nature, from now on he
will be up against his own nature.

Inventing the Future

Gabor Zsa Zsa 1919– . Hungarian-born US film actress.

I never hated a man enough to give him his diamonds back.

Observer 25 Aug 1957

Galbraith John Kenneth 1908– . Canadian-born US economist.

Politics is not the art of the possible. It consists in choosing
between the disastrous and the unpalatable.

Letter to President Kennedy 2 Mar 1962

In the affluent society no useful distinction can be made   *2*
between luxuries and necessaries.

The Affluent Society

Gandhi Mohandas Karamchand, called *Mahatma* (*Great Soul*)
1869–1948. Indian nationalist leader.

What difference does it make to the dead, the orphans and the
homeless, whether the mad destruction is wrought under the
name of totalitarianism or the holy name of liberty or democracy?

Non-Violence in Peace and War vol 1, ch 142

The moment the slave resolves that he will no longer be a slave,   *2*
his fetters fall. He frees himself and shows the way to others.
Freedom and slavery are mental states.

Non-Violence in Peace and War vol 2, ch 5

Garrick David 1717–1779. English actor and theatre manager.

Heart of oak are our ships.

'Heart of Oak'

Gay John 1685–1732. English poet and dramatist.

Do you think your mother and I should have liv'd comfortably so long together, if ever we had been married?

The Beggar's Opera I.viii

If with me you'd fondly stray / Over the hills and far away.   2

The Beggar's Opera air I. xiii

How happy could I be with either, / Were t'other dear charmer   3
away!

The Beggar's Opera I. xiii

Life is a jest; and all things show it. / I thought so once; but   4
now I know it.

'My Own Epitaph'

Geldof Bob 1954–   . Irish fundraiser and rock singer.

Most people get into bands for three very simple rock and roll reasons: to get laid, to get fame, and to get rich.

Melody Maker 27 Aug 1977

I don't think that the possible death of 120 million people is a   2
matter for charity. It is a matter of moral imperative.

To Prime Minister Thatcher on the threatened famine in Africa 1985

George I 1660–1727. King of Great Britain, 1714–27.

I hate all Boets and Bainters.

Quoted in Campbell *Lives of the Chief Justices* ch 30

George II 1683–1760. King of Great Britain, 1727–60

Oh! he is mad, is he? Then I wish he would bite some other of my generals.

Reply when someone complained that
General James Wolfe was a madman

Gershwin Ira 1896–1983. US lyricist.

You like potato and I like po-tah-to, / You like tomato and I like to-mah-to; / Potato, po-tah-to, tomato, to-mah-to-/ Let's call the whole thing off!

'Let's Call the Whole Thing Off'

Holding hands at midnight / 'Neath a starry sky, / Nice work if   *2*
you can get it, / And you can get it if you try.
'Nice Work If You Can Get It'

Gibbon Edward 1737–1794. English historian.

[Antoninus Pius'] reign is marked by the rare advantage of
furnishing very few materials for history; which is, indeed, little
more than the register of the crimes, follies, and misfortunes of
mankind.
Decline and Fall of the Roman Empire ch 3

All taxes must, at last, fall upon agriculture.   *2*
Decline and Fall of the Roman Empire ch 8

Corruption, the most infallible symptom of constitutional liberty.   *3*
Decline and Fall of the Roman Empire ch 21

Dr. – well remembered that he had a salary to receive, and only   *4*
forgot that he had a duty to perform.
Memoirs of My Life

I sighed as a lover, I obeyed as a son.   *5*
Memoirs of My Life

It was at Rome, on the 15th of October, 1764, as I sat musing   *6*
amidst the ruins of the Capitol, while the barefooted friars were
singing vespers in the Temple of Jupiter, that the idea of
writing the decline and fall of the city first started to my mind.
Memoirs of My Life

I was never less alone than when by myself.   *7*
Memoirs of My Life

My early and invincible love of reading, which I would not   *8*
exchange for the treasures of India.
Memoirs of My Life

Gibbons Stella (Dorothea) 1902–1989. English journalist.

The dark flame of his male pride was a little suspicious of
having its leg pulled.
Cold Comfort Farm ch 7

When you were very small ... you had seen something nasty **2**
in the woodshed.

Cold Comfort Farm ch 10

Gibran Kahlil 1883–1931. Syrian poet.

Work is love made visible. And if you cannot work with love
but only with distaste, it is better that you should leave your
work and sit at the gate of the temple and take alms of those who
work with joy.

The Prophet 'On Work'

Gide André 1869–1951. French novelist, born in Paris.

Sadness is almost never anything but a form of fatigue.

Journal

Gilbert Fred 1850–1903. English songwriter.

The Man Who Broke the Bank at Monte Carlo.

Song title

Gilbert Humphrey *c.* 1539–1583. English soldier and navigator.

We are as near to heaven by sea as by land!

Hakluyt's Voyages

Gilbert W(illiam) S(chwenk) 1836–1911. English humorist and
dramatist.

He led his regiment from behind / He found it less exciting.

The Gondoliers

Take a pair of sparkling eyes. **2**

The Gondoliers

Now I am the Ruler of the Queen's Navee! **3**

H.M.S. Pinafore

Awaiting the sensation of a short, sharp shock, / From a cheap **4**
and chippy chopper on a big black block.

The Mikado

The flowers that bloom in the spring, Tra la, / Have nothing to **5**
do with the case.

The Mikado

The idiot who praises, with enthusiastic tone, / All centuries
but this, and every country but his own.   **6**

The Mikado

I've got a little list—I've got a little list / Of social offenders   **7**
who might well be under ground / And who never would be
missed – who never would be missed!

The Mikado

Modified rapture!   **8**

The Mikado

My object all sublime / I shall achieve in time / To make the   **9**
punishment fit the crime – / The punishment fit the crime.

The Mikado

Three little maids who, all unwary, / Come from a ladies'   **10**
seminary.

The Mikado

A wandering minstrel I / A thing of shreds and patches.   **11**

The Mikado

The policeman's lot is not a happy one.   **12**

Pirates of Penzance

I was a pale young curate then.   **13**

The Sorcerer

And many a burglar I've restored / To his friends and his   **14**
relations.

Trial by Jury

She may very well pass for forty-three / In the dusk with a light **15**
behind her!

Trial by Jury

Gilman Charlotte Perkins 1860–1935. US feminist poet, novelist, and
historian.

There is no female mind. The brain is not an organ of sex. As
well speak of a female liver.

Woman and Economics

Ginsberg (Irwin) Allen 1926– . US poet and political activist.

What if someone gave a war & Nobody came?

'Graffiti'

Gipp George *d.* 1920. US footballer.

Win just one for the Gipper.

Quoted by Knut Rockne *'Gipp the Great'*

Gladstone William Ewart 1809–1898. English Liberal politician, repeatedly prime minister.

All the world over, I will back the masses against the classes.

Speech in Liverpool *28 June 1886*

Glass George 1910–1984. US film producer and publicist.

An actor is a kind of a guy who if you ain't talking about him ain't listening.

B Thomas *Brando* ch 8

Godard Jean-Luc 1930– . French film writer and director.

Photography is truth. The cinema is truth 24 times per second.

Le Petit Soldat

Goebbels Joseph 1897–1945. German Nazi leader.

We can manage without butter but not, for example, without guns. If we are attacked we can only defend ourselves with guns not with butter.

Speech in Berlin 17 Jan 1936

Goethe Johann Wolfgang von 1749–1832. German poet, novelist, and dramatist.

He who seizes the right moment, / Is the right man.

Faust

Gogol Nicolai Vasilyevich 1809–1852. Russian writer.

Gambling is the great leveller. All men are equal – at cards.

Gamblers

Goldsmith Oliver 1728–1774. Anglo-Irish writer, poet and dramatist.

As writers become more numerous, it is natural for readers to become more indolent.
The Bee

And still they gaz'd, and still the wonder grew, / That one small head could carry all he knew.   2
The Deserted Village

Ill fares the land, to hast'ning ills a prey, / Where wealth accumulates, and men decay.   3
The Deserted Village

The man recover'd of the bite, / The dog it was that died.   4
'Elegy on the Death of a Mad Dog'

There is no arguing with Johnson; for when his pistol misses fire, he knocks you down with the butt end of it.   5
Remark quoted in Boswell's *Life of Johnson*

This is Liberty-Hall, gentlemen.   6
She Stoops to Conquer

When lovely woman stoops to folly / And finds too late that men betray, / What charm can soothe her melancholy, / What art can wash her guilt away?   7
The Vicar of Wakefield

She Stoops to Conquer.   8
Play title

Goldwyn Samuel. Adopted name of Samuel Goldfish 1882–1974. US film producer.

Pictures are for entertainment, messages should be delivered by Western Union.
Quoted in A Marx *Goldwyn*

Gentlemen, include me out.   2
The Goldwyn Touch

A verbal contract isn't worth the paper it is written on.   3
Quoted in A Johnston *The Great Goldwyn*

Any man who goes to a psychiatrist should have his head **4**
examined.

Quoted in N Zierold Moguls

Gordon Adam Lindsay 1833–1870. Australian poet.

Life is mostly froth and bubble, / Two things stand like stone, /
Kindness in another's trouble, / Courage in your own.

Ye Wearie Wayfarer

Gould Stephen Jay 1941– . US palaeontologist and author.

Science is all those things which are confirmed to such a degree that
it would be unreasonable to withhold one's provisional consent.

Lecture on Evolution

Graham Harry 1874–1936. British writer.

'There's been an accident,' they said, / 'Your servant's cut in
half; he's dead!' / 'Indeed!' said Mr Jones, 'and please, / Send
me the half that's got my keys.'

'Mr Jones'

Billy, in one of his nice new sashes, / Fell in the fire and was **2**
burnt to ashes; / Now, although the room grows chilly, /
I haven't the heart to poke poor Billy.

'Tender-Heartedness'

Grahame Kenneth 1859–1932. Scottish author.

Believe me, my young friend, there is *nothing* – absolutely
nothing—half so much worth doing as simply messing about in
boats.

Wind in the Willows ch 2

The clever men at Oxford / Know all that there is to be knowed. **2**
/ But they none of them know one half as much / As intelligent
Mr Toad!

Wind in the Willows ch 10

Grant Ulysses S(impson) 1822–1885. 18th president of the USA
1869–77.

I know no method to secure the repeal of bad or obnoxious laws

so effective as their stringent execution.
Inaugural Address 4 March 1869

Graves Robert (Ranke) 1895–1985. English poet and author.

In love as in sport, the amateur status must be strictly maintained.
Occupation: Writer

Goodbye to All That.   *2*
Title of autobiography

Gray Thomas 1716–1771. English poet.

The curfew tolls the knell of parting day, / The lowing herd winds slowly o'er the lea, / The ploughman homeward plods his weary way, / And leaves the world to darkness and to me.
'Elegy Written in a Country Churchyard' 1

Full many a flower is born to blush unseen, / And waste its   *2*
sweetness on the desert air. / Some village-Hampden, that with dauntless breast / The little tyrant of his fields withstood; / Some mute inglorious Milton here may rest, / Some Cromwell guiltless of his country's blood.
'Elegy Written in a Country Churchyard' 14–15

Far from the madding crowd's ignoble strife, / Their sober   *3*
wishes never learn'd to stray; / Along the cool sequester'd vale of life / They kept the noiseless tenor of their way.
'Elegy Written in a Country Churchyard' 19

A youth to fortune and to fame unknown.   *4*
'Elegy Written in a Country Churchyard' 30

Greeley Horace 1811–1872. US editor, publisher, and politician.

Go West, young man, and grow up with the country.
Hints toward Reform

Greene (Henry) Graham 1904–1991. English novelist.

Against the beautiful and the clever and the successful, one can wage a pitiless war, but not against the unattractive.
Heart of the Matter bk 1, pt 1, ch 2

In human relations, kindness and lies are worth a thousand truths. **2**
The Heart of the Matter bk 1, pt 2, ch 2

He felt the loyalty we all feel to unhappiness—the sense that **3**
that is where we really belong.
Heart of the Matter bk 3, pt 2, ch 2

Greer Germaine 1939–   . Australian feminist.

Human beings have an inalienable right to invent themselves;
when that right is pre-empted it is called brain-washing.
The Times 1 Feb 1986

Grenfell Joyce 1910–1975. English entertainer.

George – don't do that.

Catch-phrase

Grey Edward 1862–1933. British politician.

The lamps are going out all over Europe; we shall not see them
lit again in our lifetime.
On the impending war 3 Aug 1914 *Twenty-Five Years*

Gropius Walter Adolf 1883–1969. German architect who lived in the
USA from 1937.

The human mind is like an umbrella – it functions best when
open.
Observer 1965

Grossmith George 1847–1912, and Weedon 1854–1919. English
writers.

What's the good of a home if you are never in it?
The Diary of a Nobody ch 1

I left the room with silent dignity, but caught my foot in the mat. **2**
The Diary of a Nobody ch 12

Grotius Hugo 1583–1645. Dutch jurist and politician.

Not to know something is a great part of wisdom.
Docta Ignorantia

Gudmundsdottir Björk Icelandic pop singer.

I think I was lucky – I was loved but not brought up.
Remark on her unconventional childhood

Guedalla Philip 1889–1944. English writer.

The work of Henry James has always seemed divisible by a
simple dynastic arrangement into three reigns; James I, James
II, and the Old Pretender.
Supers and Supermen, 'Some Critics'

History repeats itself. Historians repeat each other.   2
Supers and Supermen, 'Some Historians'

Gulbenkian Nubar 1896–1972. Turkish oil magnate.

The best number for a dinner party is two – myself and a dam'
good head waiter.
Daily Telegraph 14 Jan 1965

H

Hâfiz 1326–1390. Persian lyric poet.

There is an ambush everywhere from the army of accidents;
therefore the rider of life runs with loosened reins.

Diwan

Haig Douglas, 1st Earl Haig 1861–1928. Scottish army officer.

A very weak-minded fellow I am afraid, and, like the feather
pillow, bears the marks of the last person who has sat on him.
Of 17th Earl of Derby in letter to Lady Haig 14 Jan 1918

Haldeman 1926– . US politician.

Once the toothpaste is out of the tube, it is awfully hard to get it
back in.

Comment on the Watergate affair 1973

Hall Peter (Reginald Frederick) 1930– . English theatre, opera, and
film director.

We do not necessarily improve with age: for better or worse we
become more like ourselves.

Observer Jan 1988

Halsey Margaret 1910– . US writer.

Englishwomen's shoes look as if they had been made by someone
who had often heard shoes described but had never seen any.
With Malice Toward Some

Hammarskjöld Dag 1905–1961. Swedish statesman. UN Secretary-
General, 1953–61

The only kind of dignity which is genuine is that which is not
diminished by the indifference of others.

Markings

Hands Terry 1941–   . English stage director.

We may pretend that we're basically moral people who make mistakes, but the whole of history proves otherwise.

                                                                                          Remark

Harding Warren G(amaliel) 1865–1923. 29th president of the USA 1921–23.

America's present need is not heroics, but healing; not nostrums but normalcy; not revolution, but restoration.

                                                                          Speech at Boston 14 May 1920

Hardy Thomas 1840–1928. English novelist and poet.

When the Present has latched its postern behind my tremulous stay, / And the May month flaps its glad green leaves like wings, / Delicate-filmed as new-spun silk, will the neighbours say, / 'He was a man who used to notice such things'?

                                                                                          'Afterwards'

Ah! stirring times we live in – stirring times.   2
                                                                          Far From the Madding Crowd

The President of the Immortals (in Æschylean phrase) had   3
ended his sport with Tess.

                                                                          Tess of the D'Urbervilles

Silent? Ah, he is silent! He can keep silence well. That man's silence is wonderful to listen to.

                                                                          Under the Greenwood Tree

Harington John 1561–1612. English translator and author.

Treason doth never prosper: what's the reason? / For if it prosper, none dare call it treason.

                                                                                          'Of Treason'

Harris Joel Chandler 1848–1908. US author.

Tar-baby ain't sayin' nuthin', en Brer Fox, he lay low.
                                                          Uncle Remus. Legends of the Old Plantation ch 2

Bred en bawn in a brier-patch!   2
                                                          Uncle Remus. Legends of the Old Plantation ch 4

Hartley L(eslie) P(oles) 1895–1972. English novelist.

> The past is a foreign country: they do things differently there.
> *The Go-Between*, prologue

Harvey F W 1835–1901. US restauranteur.

> From troubles of the world / I turn to ducks / Beautiful comical things.
> 'Ducks'

Hawker R S 1803–1875. English poet.

> And have they fixed the where and when? / And shall Trelawny die? / Here's twenty thousand Cornish men / Will know the reason why!
> 'Song of the Western Men'

Hazlitt William 1778–1830. English essayist and critic.

> We can scarcely hate any one that we know.
> *Table Talk*, 'On Criticism'

Heath Edward (Richard George) 1916– . English politician and prime minister 1970–4.

> It is the unpleasant and unacceptable face of capitalism.
> On the Lonrho Scandal, *Hansard* 15 May 1973

Heisenberg Werner Carl 1901–1976. German physicist.

> An expert is someone who knows some of the worst mistakes that can be made in his subject and how to avoid them.
> *The Part and the Whole*

Heller Joseph 1923– . US novelist.

> I'd like to see the government get out of war altogether and leave the whole field to private industry.
> *Catch-22*

> Some men are born mediocre, some men achieve mediocrity, and some men have mediocrity thrust upon them. With Major Major it had been all three.
> *Catch-22*

2

There was only one catch and that was Catch-22, which specified   *3*
that a concern for one's own safety in the face of dangers that
were real and immediate was the process of a rational mind.
                                                          Catch-22

Hellman Lillian 1907–1984. US dramatist.

I cannot and will not cut my conscience to fit this year's fashions.
Letter to the House Un-American Activities Committee May 1952

Cynicism is an unpleasant way of saying the truth.   *2*
                                                       The Little Foxes

Hemans Felicia 1793–1835. English poet.

The boy stood on the burning deck / Whence all but he had fled.
                                                         Casabianca

The stately homes of England, / How beautiful they stand!   *2*
                                                    The Homes of England

Hemingway Ernest (Miller) 1899–1961. US novelist.

Grace under pressure.
                                    Defining 'guts' in interview with Dorothy
                                    Parker, *New Yorker* 30 Nov 1929

The most essential gift for a good writer is a built-in, shock-   *2*
proof shit detector. This is the writer's radar and all great
writers have had it.
                                                  Paris Review Spring 1958

Cowardice, as distinguished from panic, is almost always simply   *3*
a lack of ability to suspend the functioning of the imagination.
                                                         Men at War

If you are lucky enough to have lived in Paris as a young man,   *4*
then wherever you go for the rest of your life, it stays with you,
for Paris is a movable feast.
                                                    A Movable Feast

A man can be destroyed but not defeated.   *5*
                                                The Old Man and the Sea

Henley W E 1849–1903. English poet.

I am the master of my fate: / I am the captain of my soul.

'Invictus'

My head is bloody, but unbowed.   *2*

'Invictus'

Henry IV 1367–1413. King of France 1399–1413.

Paris is well worth a mass.

Attributed remark on his conversion to Catholicism

Henry O Pen name of William Sydney Porter.1862–1910. US short-story writer.

If men knew how women pass the time when they are alone, they'd never marry.

'Memoirs of a Yellow Dog'

It was beautiful and simple as all truly great swindles are.   *2*

'Octopus Marooned'

Turn up the lights; I don't want to go home in the dark.   *3*

Last words

Henry Patrick 1736–1799. US politician.

I know not what course others may take; but as for me, give me liberty, or give me death!

Speech in the Virginia Convention 23 Mar 1775

Henry William 1774–1836. English chemist.

Another damned, thick, square book! Always scribble, scribble, scribble! Eh! Mr. Gibbon?

Best's Literary Memorials

Heraclitus 544BC–483BC. Greek philosopher.

All is flux, nothing is stationary.

Quoted in Aristotle *De Caelo*

Herbert A P 1890–1971. English writer and politician.

The Farmer will never be happy again; / He carries his heart in

his boots; / For either the rain is destroying his grain / Or the drought is destroying his roots.
>   'The Farmer'

The critical period in matrimony is breakfast-time.   2
>   'Is Marriage Lawful?'

Let's find out what everyone is doing, / And then stop everyone   3
from doing it.
>   'Let's Stop Somebody from Doing Something'

Let's stop somebody from doing something!   4
>   _Let's Stop Somebody_

This high official, all allow, / Is grossly overpaid. / There   5
wasn't any Board; and now / There isn't any trade.
>   On the President of the Board of Trade

The Common Law of England has been laboriously built about   6
a mythical figure—the figure of 'The Reasonable Man'.
>   'The Reasonable Man'

Well, fancy giving money to the Government! / Might as well   7
have put it down the drain. / Fancy giving money to the
Government! / Nobody will see the stuff again.
>   'Too Much!'

Holy Deadlock.   8
>   Title of novel

Herbert George 1593–1633. English poet.

Be calm in arguing; for fierceness makes Error a fault and truth
discourtesy.
>   _The Church Porch_

Let all the world in ev'ry corner sing / My God and King.   2
>   'Antiphon'

Love bade me welcome; yet my soul drew back, / Guilty of dust   3
and sin.
>   'Love'

King of glory, King of peace, / I will love Thee.   **4**
'Praise'

Sweet spring, full of sweet days and roses, / A box where   **5**
sweets compacted lie.
'Virtue'

Herrick Robert 1591–1674. English poet and cleric.

Cherry ripe, ripe, ripe, I cry, / Full and fair ones; come and buy.
'Cherry Ripe'

Fair daffodils, we weep to see / You haste away so soon.   **2**
'Daffodils'

A sweet disorder in the dress / Kindles in clothes a wantonness. **3**
'Delight in Disorder'

Love is a circle that doth restless move / In the same sweet   **4**
eternity of love.
'Love What It Is'

Bid me to live, and I will live / Thy Protestant to be: / Or bid **5**
me love, and I will give / A loving heart to thee.
'To Anthea, Who May Command Him Anything'

Sweet, be not proud of those two eyes, / Which star-like   **6**
sparkle in their skies.
'To Dianeme'

Gather ye rosebuds while ye may, / Old Time is still a-flying: / **7**
And this same flower that smiles to-day, / To-morrow will be
dying.
'To the Virgins, to Make Much of Time'

When as in silks my Julia goes, / Then, then (methinks) how   **8**
sweetly flows / That liquefaction of her clothes.
'Upon Julia's Clothes'

Hewart Gordon 1870–1943. English lawyer and politician.

It is not merely of some importance, but is of fundamental
importance that justice should not only be done, but should

manifestly and undoubtedly be seen to be done.

> Rex v Sussex Justices 9 Nov 1923

Hickson William Edward 1803–1870. English educationalist.

If at first you don't succeed, / Try, try again.

> 'Try and Try Again'

Hill Rowland 1795–1879. English inventor of the postage stamp.

He did not see any reason why the devil should have all the good tunes.

> E W Broome, *Rev. Rowland Hill*

Hilton James 1900–1954. English novelist.

Nothing really wrong with him – only anno domini, but that's the most fatal complaint of all, in the end.

> *Goodbye, Mr Chips*

Hitchcock Alfred 1899–1980. English-born US film director.

Television has brought back murder into the home— where it belongs.

> *Observer* 19 Dec 1965

Hobbes Thomas 1588–1679. English political philosopher.

No arts; no letters; no society; and which is worst of all, continual fear and danger of violent death; and the life of man, solitary, poor, nasty, brutish, and short.

> *Leviathan* pt 1, ch 13

The Papacy is not other than the Ghost of the deceased Roman   *2*
Empire, sitting crowned upon the grave thereof.

> *Leviathan* pt 4, ch 47

I am about to take my last voyage, a great leap in the dark.   *3*

> Last words

Hodgson Ralph 1871–1962. English poet.

'Twould ring the bells of Heaven / The wildest peal for years, / If Parson lost his senses / And people came to theirs, / And he

and they together / Knelt down with angry prayers / For tamed and shabby tigers / And dancing dogs and bears, / And wretched, blind, pit ponies, / And little hunted hares.
'The Bells of Heaven'

But fidgety Phil, / He won't sit still; / He wriggles / And giggles, / And then, I declare, / Swings backwards and forwards, / And tilts up his chair. *2*
'Fidgety Philip'

Time, you old gypsy man, / Will you not stay, / Put up your caravan / Just for one day? *3*
'Time, You Old Gypsy Man'

Hoffa Jimmy (James Riddle) 1913–75. US labour leader.

An ego is just imagination. And if a man doesn't have imagination he'll be working for someone else for the rest of his life.
Esquire

Hoffman Heinrich 1809–1874. German writer.

Anything to me is sweeter / Than to see Shock-headed Peter.
'Shock-Headed Peter'

Hogg James 1770–1835. Scottish novelist and poet.

Will you no come back again?
'Will You No Come Back Again'

And Charlie he's my darling, / My darling, my darling. *2*
'The Young Chevalier'

Holmes Oliver Wendell 1809–1894. US writer and physician.

To be seventy years young is sometimes far more cheerful and hopeful than to be forty years old.
'On the Seventieth Birthday of Julia Ward Howe'

It is the province of knowledge to speak and it is the privilege of wisdom to listen. *2*
The Poet at the Breakfast Table

A moment's insight is sometimes worth a life's experience.   *3*
                                        The Poet at the Breakfast Table

And, when you stick on conversation's burrs, / Don't strew   *4*
your pathway with those dreadful urs.
                                                        'A Rhymed Lesson'

Honegger Arthur 1892–1955. French composer.

There is no doubt that the first requirement for a composer is to
be dead.
                                                        I am a composer

Hood Thomas 1799–1845. English poet and humorist.

There are three things which the public will always clamour for,
sooner or later: namely, Novelty, novelty, novelty.
                                    Announcement of Comic Annual for 1836

They went and told the sexton, and / The sexton toll'd the bell.   *2*
                                                        'Faithless Sally Brown'

I remember, I remember, / The house where I was born.   *3*
                                                        'I Remember'

It was the time of roses, / We plucked them as we passed!   *4*
                                                        'It Was Not in the Winter'

Hoover Herbert Clark 1874–1964. 31st president of the USA 1929–33.

The American system of rugged individualism.
                                                        Campaign speech 1928

Hope Anthony. Pen name of Anthony Hope Hawkins 1863–1933.
English novelist.

Economy is going without something you do want in case you
should, some day, want something you probably won't want.
                                                        Dolly Dialogues

He is very fond of making things which he doesn't want, and   *2*
then giving them to people who have no use for them.
                                                        Dolly Dialogues

'I wish you would read a little poetry sometimes. Your ignorance cramps my conversation.'   *3*

Dolly Dialogues

'You oughtn't to yield to temptation.' / 'Well, somebody must, or the thing becomes absurd.'   *4*

Dolly Dialogues

Hopkins Gerard Manley 1844–1889. English poet and Jesuit priest.

Not, I'll not, carrion comfort, Despair, not feast on thee.

'Carrion Comfort'

The world is charged with the grandeur of God.   *2*

'God's Grandeur'

I have desired to go / Where springs not fail, / To fields where flies no sharp and sided hail / And a few lilies blow. / And I have asked to be / Where no storms come, / Where the green swell is in the havens dumb, / And out of the swing of the sea.   *3*

'Heaven-Haven'

What would the world be, once bereft / Of wet and of wildness? Let them be left, / O let them be left, wildness and wet; / Long live the weeds and the wilderness yet.   *4*

'Inversnaid'

Glory be to God for dappled things.   *5*

'Pied Beauty'

Horace 65–8 BC. Roman lyric poet and satirist.

But if worthy Homer nods for a moment, I think it a disgrace.

Ars Poetica

Mountains will be in labour, the birth will be a ridiculous mouse.   *2*

Ars Poetica

Dare to be wise.   *3*

Epistles I, 2

Seize the day.   *4*

Odes I. 11

Life's short span forbids us to embark on far-reaching hopes.   5
                                                    Odes I. 4

It is a sweet and becoming thing to die for one's country.   6
                                                    Odes III. 2

I have raised a memorial more enduring than brass.   7
                                                    Odes III. 30

Housman A E 1859–1936. English scholar and poet.

This great College, of this ancient University, has seen some
strange sights. It has seen Wordsworth drunk and Porson sober.
And here am I, a better poet than Porson, and a better scholar
than Wordsworth, betwixt and between.
                        Speech at Trinity College, Cambridge

Loveliest of trees, the cherry now / Is hung with bloom along   2
the bough, / And stands about the woodland ride / Wearing
white for Eastertide.
                                            A Shropshire Lad 2

When I was one-and-twenty / I heard a wise man say, / 'Give   3
crowns and pounds and guineas / But not your heart away.'
                                            A Shropshire Lad 13

The lads that will die in their glory and never be old.   4
                                            A Shropshire Lad 23

That is the land of lost content, / I see it shining plain, / The   5
happy highways where I went / And cannot come again.
                                            A Shropshire Lad 40

Malt does more than Milton can, / To justify God's ways to man.   6
                                            A Shropshire Lad 62

Howe Julia Ward 1819–1910. US feminist and antislavery campaigner.

Mine eyes have seen the glory of the coming of the Lord: / He is
trampling out the vintage where the grapes of wrath are stored.
                        'Battle Hymn of the American Republic'

Howitt Mary 1799–1888. English writer.

'Will you walk into my parlour?' said a spider to a fly.
'The Spider and the Fly'

Hoyle Fred(erick) 1915–   . English astronomer and writer.

Space isn't remote at all. It's only an hour's drive away if your car could go straight upwards.
Observer Sept 1979

Hubbard Elbert 1856–1915. US writer.

Never explain – your friends do not need it and your enemies will not believe you anyway.
Motto Book

Life is just one damned thing after another.   *2*
A Thousand and One Epigrams

Little minds are interested in the extraordinary; great minds in   *3*
the commonplace.
Thousand and One Epigrams

One machine can do the work of fifty ordinary men. No   *4*
machine can do the work of one extraordinary man.
Thousand and One Epigrams

Hughes Thomas 1822–1896. English writer.

Life isn't all beer and skittles.
Tom Brown's Schooldays

Hume David 1711–1776. Scottish philosopher.

Avarice, the spur of industry.
'Of Civil Liberty'

The usual propensity of mankind towards the marvellous.   *2*
'On Miracles'

Hunt G W 1829–1904. English writer.

We don't want to fight, but, by jingo if we do, / We've got the ships, we've got the men, we've got the money too.
Music hall song

Huxley Aldous 1894–1963. English novelist.

There are few who would not rather be taken in adultery than in provincialism.

Antic Hay

If the world had any ends British Honduras would certainly   *2*
be one of them.

On *Belize* (formerly British Honduras) in
Beyond the Mexique Bay

Official dignity tends to increase in inverse ratio to the   *3*
importance of the country in which the office is held.

Beyond the Mexique Bay

That men do not learn very much from the lessons of history is   *4*
the most important of all the lessons that history has to teach.

Collected Essays, 'Case of Voluntary Ignorance'

So long as men worship the Caesars and Napoleons, Caesars   *5*
and Napoleons will duly arise and make them miserable.

Ends and Means

A bad book is as much of a labour to write as a good one; it   *6*
comes as sincerely from the author's soul.

Point Counter Point ch 13

There is no substitute for talent. Industry and all the virtues are   *7*
of no avail.

Point Counter Point ch 13

Brought up in an epoch when ladies apparently rolled along on   *8*
wheels, Mr Quarles was peculiarly susceptible to calves.

Point Counter Point ch 20

Facts do not cease to exist because they are ignored.   *9*

Proper Studies, 'Note on Dogma'

Huxley Julian 1887–1975. English biologist.

Operationally, God is beginning to resemble not a ruler but the
last fading smile of a cosmic Cheshire cat.

Religion without Revelation

Huxley Thomas Henry 1825–1895. English scientist and humanist.

Logical consequences are the scarecrows of fools and the beacons of wise men.

Science and Culture. 'On the Hypothesis
that Animals are Automatic'

Irrationally held truths may be more harmful than reasoned 2
errors.

Science and Culture, 'The Coming of Age
of the Origin of Species'

It is the customary fate of new truths to begin as heresies and 3
to end as superstitions.

Science and Culture,'The Coming of Age
of the Origin of Species'

I

Ibarruri Dolores, known as *La Pasionaria* ('the passion flower') 1895–1989. Spanish Basque politician, journalist, and orator.

Il vaut mieux mourir debout que de vivre à genoux! / It is better to die on your feet than to live on your knees.
Speech in Paris 3 Sept 1936

Ibsen Henrik (Johan) 1828–1906. Norwegian dramatist and poet.

The minority is always right.
An Enemy of the People IV

One should never put on one's best trousers to go out to battle   *2* for freedom and truth.
An Enemy of the People V

Castles in the air—they are so easy to take refuge in. And so   *3* easy to build, too.
The Master Builder

Illich Ivan 1926– . US radical philosopher and activist, born in Austria.

In a consumer society there are inevitably two kinds of slaves: the prisoners of addiction and the prisoners of envy.
Tools for Conviviality ch 3

Inge Wilham Ralph 1860–1954. English theologian.

The effect of boredom on a large scale in history is under-estimated. It is a main cause of revolutions, and would soon bring to an end all the static Utopias and the farmyard civilization of the Fabians.
End of an Age

To become a popular religion, it is only necessary for a   *2* superstition to enslave a philosophy.
Idea of Progress

Many people believe that they are attracted by God, or by   *3*
Nature, when they are only repelled by man.
                                        More Lay Thoughts of a Dean

It takes in reality only one to make a quarrel. It is useless for the   *4*
sheep to pass resolutions in favour of vegetarianism, while the
wolf remains of a different opinion.
                              Outspoken Essays: First Series, 'Patriotism'

A man may build himself a throne of bayonets, but he cannot   *5*
sit on it.
                              Quoted in Marchant, *Wit and Wisdom of Dean Inge*

Ingersoll Robert G 1833–1899. US lawyer and agnostic

In nature there are neither rewards nor punishments – there are
consequences.
                                        Lectures and Essays, 'Some Reasons Why'

Innocent III 1161–1216. Italian Pope from 1198.

Greediness closed Paradise; it beheaded John the Baptist.
                                                           De Contemptu Mundi

Irving Washington 1783–1859. US essayist and short-story writer.

I am always at a loss to know how much to believe of my own
stories.
                                                           Tales of a Traveller

The almighty dollar, that great object of universal devotion   *2*
throughout our land, seems to have no genuine devotees in
these peculiar villages.
                              Wolfert's Roost, 'The Creole Village'

Ivan IV (*the Terrible*) 1530–1584. Russian Emperor.

Did I ascend the throne by robbery or armed bloodshed? I was
born to rule by the grace of God ... I grew up upon the throne.
                                        Letter to Prince Kurbsky Sept 1577

J

Jackson Holbrook 1874–1948. English bibliophile and literary historian.

Pedantry is the dotage of knowledge.

Anatomy of Bibliomania

Jacobs Joe 1896–1940. US boxing manager

We was robbed!

After Max Schmeling was beaten in the
heavyweight title fight 21 June 1932

James Henry 1843–1916. US novelist, naturalized British 1915.

The deep well of unconscious cerebration.

The American preface

The historian, essentially, wants more documents than he can 2
really use; the dramatist only wants more liberties than he can
really take.

The Aspern Papers preface

It takes a great deal of history to produce a little literature. 3
Life of Nathaniel Hawthorne

Cats and monkeys – monkeys and cats – all human life is there! 4
The Madonna of the Future

The only reason for the existence of a novel is that it does 5
attempt to represent life.

Partial Portraits, 'Art of Fiction'

James William 1842–1910. US psychologist/philosopher, brother of
Henry.

Man, biologically considered, and whatever else he may be into
the bargain, is simply the most formidable of all the beasts of

prey, and, indeed, the only one that preys systematically on its own species.

Atlantic Monthly Dec 1904

The art of being wise is the art of knowing what to overlook.   *2*
Principles of Psychology

There is no more miserable human being than one in whom no   *3*
thing is habitual but indecision.

Principles of Psychology

An idea, to be suggestive, must come to the individual with the   *4*
force of a revelation.

Varieties of Religious Experience

There is no worse lie than a truth misunderstood by those who   *5*
hear it.

Varieties of Religious Experience

Jeans James Hopwood 1877–1946. English mathematician and scientist.

Life exists in the universe only because the carbon atom possesses certain exceptional properties.

Mysterious Universe

Jefferson Thomas 1743–1826. 3rd president of the USA 1801–09.

A little rebellion now and then is a good thing.
Letter to James Madison 30 Jan 1787

The tree of liberty must be refreshed from time to time   *2*
with the blood of patriots and tyrants. It is its natural manure.
Letter to W S Smith 13 Nov 1787

No government ought to be without censors, and where   *3*
the press is free, no one ever will.
Letter to George Washington 9 Sept 1792

Advertisements contain the only truths to be relied on   *4*
in a newspaper.

Letter 1819

When a man assumes a public trust, he should consider himself   5
as public property.

Remark

Jenkins David 1925–   . English theologian.

In institutions—including religious institutions—when people
talk about unity, they're talking about keeping quiet.

Remark

Jerome Jerome K(lapka) 1859–1927. English journalist and writer.

It is always the best policy to speak the truth – unless, of
course, you are an exceptionally good liar.

The Idler Feb 1892

It is impossible to enjoy idling thoroughly unless one   2
has plenty of work to do.

Idle Thoughts of an Idle Fellow, 'On Being Idle'

Love is like the measles; we all have to go through it   3

Idle Thoughts of an Idle Fellow, 'On Being in Love'

I want a house that has got over all its troubles; I don't want   4
to spend the rest of my life bringing up a young and
inexperienced house.

They and I

But there, everything has its drawbacks, as the man said   5
when his mother-in-law died, and they came down upon him
for the funeral expenses.

Three Men in a Boat ch 3

I like work: it fascinates me. I can sit and look at it for hours.   6
I love to keep it by me: the idea of getting rid of it nearly breaks
my heart.

Three Men in a Boat ch 15

Jerrold Douglas 1803–1857. English dramatist.

Earth is here so kind that just tickle her with a hoe and she
laughs with a harvest.

On Australia, in *A Man Made of Money*

Some people are so fond of ill-luck that they run half-way to   2
meet it.

'Meeting Troubles Half-way'

We love peace, as we abhor pusillanimity; but not peace   3
at any price.

'Peace'

Love's like the measles – all the worse when it comes late in   4
life.

'A Philanthropist'

In your time we have the opportunity to move not only toward
the rich society and the powerful society, but upward to the
Great Society.

Speech at University of Michigan 22 May 1964

Johnson Lyndon Baines 1908–1973. 36th president of the USA.

It's probably better to have him inside the tent pissing out, than
outside pissing in.

Of J Edgar Hoover, in D Halberstam *Best and Brightest*

We hope that the world will not narrow into a neighbourhood   2
before it has broadened into a brotherhood.

Speech at lighting of the Nation's Christmas Tree 22 Dec 1963

Johnson Philip (Cortelyou) 1906–   . US architect.

Architecture is the art of how to waste space.

New York Times 27 Dec 1964

Johnson Samuel, known as *Dr Johnson*, 1709–1784. English
lexicographer, author, critic, and conversationalist.

If you call a dog Hervey, I shall love him.

Boswell's *Life of Johnson* vol i

I had done all I could; and no man is well pleased to have his   2
all neglected, be it ever so little.

Letter to Lord Chesterfield in Boswell's
Life of Johnson vol i

Is not a Patron, my Lord, one who looks with unconcern on a   3 man struggling for life in the water, and, when he has reached ground, encumbers him with help?

> Letter to Lord Chesterfield in Boswell's
> *Life of Johnson* vol i

A man, Sir, should keep his friendship in constant repair. **4**

> Boswell's *Life of Johnson* vol i

Sir, let me tell you, the noblest prospect which a Scotchman **5** ever sees, is the high road that leads him to England!

> Boswell's *Life of Johnson* vol i

Sir, a woman's preaching is like a dog's walking on his hinder **6** legs. It is not done well; but you are surprised to find it done at all.

> Boswell's *Life of Johnson* vol i

They [Lord Chesterfield's Letters] teach the morals of a whore **7** and the manners of a dancing master.

> Boswell's *Life of Johnson* vol 1

Your levellers wish to level down as far as themselves; but **8** they cannot bear levelling up to themselves.

> Boswell's *Life of Johnson* vol i

I think the full tide of human existence is at Charing-Cross. **9**

> Boswell's *Life of Johnson* vol ii

It was the triumph of hope over experience. **10**

> Boswell's *Life of Johnson* vol ii, referring to the second
> marriage of a man whose first marriage had been unhappy

Patriotism is the last refuge of a scoundrel. **11**

> Boswell's *Life of Johnson* vol ii

Read over your compositions, and where ever you meet with a **12** passage which you think is particularly fine, strike it out.

> Boswell's *Life of Johnson* vol ii

Claret is the liquor for boys; port for men; but he who aspires to **13** be a hero must drink brandy.

> Boswell's *Life of Johnson* vol iii

Depend upon it, Sir, when a man knows he is to be **14** hanged in a fortnight, it concentrates his mind wonderfully.

> Boswell's *Life of Johnson* vol iii

If I had no duties, and no reference to futurity, I would spend   *15*
my life in driving briskly in a post-chaise with a pretty woman.
                        Boswell's *Life of Johnson* vol iii

No man but a blockhead ever wrote, except for money.   *16*
                        Boswell's *Life of Johnson* vol iii

When a man is tired of London, he is tired of life; for there is in   *17*
London all that life can afford.
                        Boswell's *Life of Johnson* vol iii

Sir, I look upon every day to be lost, in which I do not make a   *18*
new acquaintance.
                        Boswell's *Life of Johnson* vol iv

Sir, there is no settling the point of precedency between a louse   *19*
and a flea.
                        Boswell's *Life of Johnson* vol iv

We are not here to sell a parcel of boilers and vats, but the   *20*
potentiality of growing rich, beyond the dreams of avarice.
                        Boswell's *Life of Johnson* vol iv

The chief glory of every people arises from its authors.   *21*
                        Dictionary of the English Language

Dull. *To make dictionaries is dull work.*   *22*
                        Dictionary of the English Language

Every quotation contributes something to the stability or   *23*
enlargement of the language.
                        Dictionary of the English Language

Lexicographer. *A writer of dictionaries, a harmless drudge.*   *24*
                        Dictionary of the English Language.

Oats. *A grain, which in England is generally given to horses,*   *25*
but in Scotland supports the people.
                        Dictionary of the English Language

Patron. *Commonly a wretch who supports with insolence, and*   *26*
is paid with flattery.
                        Dictionary of the English Language

It is very strange, and very melancholy, that the paucity of human   *27*
pleasures should persuade us ever to call hunting one of them.
             G B Hill(ed.) *Johnsonian Miscellanies* vol i

I am disappointed by that stroke of death, which has eclipsed   *28*
the gaiety of nations and impoverished the public stock of
harmless pleasure.
Of Garrick's death, in *Lives of the English Poets* 'Edmund Smith'

Slow rises worth by poverty depress'd.   *29*
                                London

Notes are often necessary, but they are necessary evils.   *30*
             Plays of William Shakespeare, with Notes Preface

Human life is everywhere a state in which much is to be   *31*
endured, and little to be enjoyed.
                            Rasselas ch 11

Marriage has many pains, but celibacy has no pleasures.   *32*
                            Rasselas ch 26

How small, of all that human hearts endure, / That part which   *33*
laws or kings can cause or cure!
             Lines added to Goldsmith's *Traveller*

Let observation with extensive view, / Survey mankind, from   *34*
China to Peru.
                    Vanity of Human Wishes l. 1

He left the name, at which the world grew pale, / To point a   *35*
moral, or adorn a tale.
                 Vanity of Human Wishes l. 221

Fly fishing may be a very pleasant amusement; but angling or   *36*
float fishing I can only compare to a stick and a string, with a
worm at one end and a fool at the other.
                            Attributed remark

Jolson Al. Stage name of Asa Yoelson 1886–1950. Russian-born US
singer.

   'You ain't heard nuttin' yet!'
             Martin Abramson *Real Story of Al Jolson*

Jones John Paul 1747–1792. Scottish-born American naval officer.

> I have not yet begun to fight.
>> On being asked during a sea battle 1779, if he would
>> surrender, as his ship was sinking

Jonson Ben 1572–1637. English dramatist, poet, and critic.

> I remember the players have often mentioned it as an honour to
> Shakespeare that in his writing (whatsoever he penned) he never
> blotted out a line. My answer hath been 'Would he had blotted a
> thousand'.
>> *Discoveries*, 'De Shakespeare Nostrati'

> It is not growing like a tree / In bulk, doth make men better be;   **2**
>> 'A Pindaric Ode on the Death of Sir H. Morison'

> Drink to me only with thine eyes, / And I will pledge with mine;   **3**
> / Or leave a kiss but in the cup, / And I'll not look for wine.
>> 'To Celia'

> He was not of an age, but for all time!   **4**
>> *To the Memory of My Beloved, the Author,*
>> *Mr William Shakespeare*

> Small Latin, and less Greek.   **5**
>> *To the Memory of My Beloved, the Author,*
>> *Mr William Shakespeare*

> Sweet Swan of Avon!   **6**
>> *To the Memory of My Beloved, the Author,*
>> *Mr W illiam Shakespeare*

Joyce James (Augustine Aloysius) 1882–1941. Irish novelist.

> That ideal reader suffering from an ideal insomnia.
>> *Finnegans Wake* pt 1

> All moanday, tearsday, wailsday, thumpsday, frightday,   **2**
> shatterday till the fear of the Law.
>> *Finnegans Wake* pt 2

> Ireland is the old sow that eats her farrow.   **3**
>> *A Portrait of the Artist as a Young Man*

Jung Carl Gustav 1875–1961. Swiss psychiatrist, associate of Freud.

A man who has not passed through the inferno of his passions
has never overcome them.

Memories, Dreams, Reflections ch 9

As far as we can discern, the sole purpose of human existence   *2*
is to kindle a light in the darkness of mere being.

Memories, Dreams, Reflections ch 11

Every form of addiction is bad, no matter whether the narcotic   *3*
be alcohol or morphine or idealism.

Memories, Dreams, Reflections ch 12

Juvenal *c.* AD 60–   . Roman satirical poet.

But who will guard the guards themselves?

Satires 6

An inveterate itch of writing.

Satires 7

Your prayer must be that you may have a sound mind in a sound
body.

Satires 10

K

Kafka Franz 1883–1924. Czech novelist.

You may object that it is not a trial at all; you are quite right,
for it is only a trial if I recognize it as such.

The Trial ch 2

It's often better to be in chains than to be free. 2

The Trial ch 8

Kant Immanuel 1724–1804. German philosopher.

Two things fill the mind with ever-increasing wonder and awe,
… the starry heavens above me and the moral law within me.

Critique of Practical Reason conclusion

Karr Alphonse 1808–1890. French writer.

Plus ça change, plus c'est la même chose. / The more things
change, the more they remain the same.

Les Guêpes

Kaufman George S 1930–   . British Labour politician.

The longest suicide note in history.

Of the Labour Party's 1983 election manifesto,
D Healey *Time of My Life*

Kaunda Kenneth (David) 1924–   . Zambian politician, president
1964–91.

The inability of those in power to still the voices of their own
consciences is the great force leading to change.

Observer July 1965

Kearney Denis 1847–1907. US labour leader.

Horny-handed sons of toil.

Speech, San Francisco about 1878

Keats John 1795–1821. English Romantic poet.

Oh what can ail thee, Knight at arms / Alone and palely
loitering; / The sedge is wither'd from the lake, / And no birds
sing.

'La Belle Dame Sans Merci'

I am certain of nothing but of the holiness of the heart's   *2*
affections and the truth of imagination.

Letter to Benjamin Bailey 22 Nov 1817

Negative Capability, that is, when man is capable of being in   *3*
uncertainties, mysteries, doubts, without any irritable reaching
after fact and reason.

Letter to G and T Keats 21 Dec 1817

We hate poetry that has a palpable design upon us ... Poetry   *4*
should be great and unobtrusive, a thing which enters into
one's soul, and does not startle or amaze it with itself, but with
its subject.

Letter to J H Reynolds 3 Feb 1818

If poetry comes not as naturally as leaves to a tree it had better   *5*
not come at all.

Letter to John Taylor 27 Feb 1818

I think I shall be among the English Poets after my death.   *6*
Letter to Richard Woodhouse 14 Oct 1818

A thing of beauty is a joy for ever: / Its loveliness increases.   *7*
Endymion

St. Agnes' Eve – Ah, bitter chill it was! / The owl, for all his   *8*
feathers, was a-cold.

The Eve of S. Agnes

Do not all charms fly / At the mere touch of cold philosophy?   *9*
Lamia pt 2

'Beauty is truth, truth beauty,' – that is all / Ye know on earth,   *10*
and all ye need to know.

'Ode on a Grecian Urn'

Thou still unravish'd bride of quietness, / Thou foster-child of silence and slow time.   *11*

'Ode on a Grecian Urn'

A bright torch, and a casement ope at night, / To let the warm Love in!   *12*

'Ode to a Nightingale'

My heart aches, and a drowsy numbness pains / My sense.   *13*

'Ode to a Nightingale'

Now more than ever seems it rich to die, / To cease upon the midnight with no pain.   *14*

'Ode to a Nightingale'

O for a beaker full of the warm South, / Full of the true, the blushful Hippocrene, / With beaded bubbles winking at the brim, / And purple-stained mouth.   *15*

'Ode to a Nightingale'

Was it a vision, or a waking dream?   *16*

'Ode to a Nightingale'

Much have I travell'd in the realms of gold, / And many goodly states and kingdoms seen.   *17*

'On First Looking into Chapman's Homer'

Season of mists and mellow fruitfulness, / Close bosom-friend of the maturing sun.   *18*

'To Autumn'

O soft embalmer of the still midnight.   *19*

'To Sleep'

Here lies one whose name was writ in water.   *20*

His own epitaph

Keller Helen Adams 1880–1968. US deaf-blind author and campaigner.

Science may have found a cure for most evils; but it has found no remedy for the worst of them all—the apathy of human beings.

My Religion

Kempis Thomas à *c.* 1380–1471. German monk and writer.

Thus, the glory of the world passes away!

Imitatio Christi

Kennedy John F(itzgerald) *Jack* 1917–1963. 35th president of the USA 1961–63.

And so, my fellow Americans: ask not what your country can do for you—ask what you can do for your country.

Inaugural address 20 Jan 1962

Those who make peaceful revolution impossible will make   *2*
violent revolution inevitable.

Speech at White House 13 Mar 1962

Probably the greatest concentration of talent and genius in this   *3*
house except for perhaps those times when Thomas Jefferson
ate alone.

Of a White House dinner for Nobel Prizewinners,
in *New York Times* 30 Apr 1962

When we got into office, the thing that surprised me most was   *4*
to find that things were just as bad as we'd been saying they
were.

Speech at White House 27 May 1962

Ich bin ein Berliner.   *5*

Speech in West Berlin 26 June 1963

It was involuntary. They sank my boat.   *6*

Answer to question about how he became a war hero,
in A M Schlesinger Jr *A Thousand Days*

Kennedy Joseph P 1888–1969. US industrialist and diplomat.

When the going gets tough, the tough get going.

J H Cutler *Honey Fitz*

Kerouac Jack (Jean Louis) 1923–1969. US 'Beat Generation' novelist.

I had nothing to offer anybody except my own confusion.

On the Road

Key Francis Scott 1779–1843. US lawyer and poet.

'Tis the star-spangled banner; O long may it wave / O'er the land of the free, and the home of the brave!

'The Star-Spangled Banner'

Keynes John Maynard, 1st Baron Keynes 1883–1946. English economist.

The important thing for Government is not to do things which individuals are doing already, and to do them a little better or a little worse; but to do those things which at present are not done at all.

End of Laissez-Faire pt 4

I think that Capitalism, wisely managed, can probably be made   *2*
more efficient for attaining economic ends than any alternative system yet in sight, but that in itself it is in many ways extremely objectionable.

End of Laissez-Faire pt 5

It is better that a man should tyrannize over his bank balance   *3*
than over his fellow-citizens.

General Theory of Employment

But this *long run* is a misleading guide to current affairs. *In the*   *4*
long run we are all dead.

Tract on Monetary Reform

Khrushchev Nikita Sergeyevich 1894–1971. Soviet politician, premier 1958–64.

Comrades! We must abolish the cult of the individual decisively, once and for all.

Speech to the secret session of 20th Congress of the Communist Party 25 Feb 1956

Whether you like it or not, history is on our side. We will bury you.   *2*
Speech to Western diplomats at reception in Moscow 18 Nov 1956

Kilmer Joyce 1886–1918. US poet.

I think that I shall never see / A poem lovely as a tree.

'Trees'

King Henry 1592–1669. English bishop and poet.

> But hark! My pulse like a soft drum / Beats my approach, tells thee I come; / And slow howe'er my marches be, / I shall at last sit down by thee.
>
> *Exequy upon His Wife*

King Martin Luther Jr 1929–1968. US civil-rights campaigner, black leader, and Baptist minister.

> I want to be the white man's brother, not his brother-in-law.
> *New York Journal-American* 10 Sept 1962

> Injustice anywhere is a threat to justice everywhere.   *2*
> Letter from Birmingham jail, Alabama 16 Apr 1963

> I submit to you that if a man hasn't discovered something he   *3*
> will die for, he isn't fit to live.
> Speech in Detroit 23 June 1963

> I have a dream that my four little children will one day live in a   *4*
> nation where they will not be judged by the colour of their skin
> but by the content of their character.
> Speech at civil-rights march in Washington 28 Aug 1963

> Now, I say to you today my friends, even though we face the   *5*
> difficulties of today and tomorrow, I still have a dream. It is a
> dream deeply rooted in the American dream. I have a dream
> that one day this nation will rise up and live out the true
> meaning of its creed: – 'We hold these truths to be self-
> evident, that all men are creat ed equal.'
> Speech at civil-rights march in Washington 28 Aug 1963

> We must learn to live together as brothers or perish together as   *6*
> fools.
> Speech at St. Louis 22 Mar 1964

> Nothing in all the world is more dangerous than sincere   *7*
> ignorance and conscientious stupidity.
> *Strength to Love* ch 4

> The means by which we live have outdistanced the ends for   *8*

which we live. Our scientific power has outrun our spiritual power. We have guided missiles and misguided men.

Strength to Love ch 7

King Stoddard 1889–1933. English songwriter.

There's a long, long trail a-winding / Into the land of my dreams, / Where the nightingales are singing / And a white moon beams.

'The Long, Long Trail'

Kingsley Charles 1819–1875. English author and clergyman.

Be good, sweet maid, and let who will be clever.

'A Farewell'

For men must work, and women must weep, / And there's little   2
to earn, and many to keep.

'The Three Fishers'

As thorough an Englishman as ever coveted his neighbour's   3
goods.

The Water Babies

Kingsmill Hugh 1889–1949. English writer.

Friends ... are God's apology for relations.

M Holroyd *Best of Hugh Kingsmill*

Kinnock Neil 1942– . British Labour party leader 1983–92.

If Margaret Thatcher wins on Thursday, I warn you not to be ordinary, I warn you not to be young, I warn you not to fall ill, and I warn you not to grow old.

Speech at Bridgend 7 June 1983

Mr Shultz went off his pram.   2

Comment after meeting US Secretary of State

Kipling (Joseph) Rudyard 1865–1936. Indian-born English writer.

Oh, East is East, and West is West, and never the twain shall meet.

'The Ballad of East and West'

Land of our birth, we pledge to thee / Our love and toil in the   **2**
years to be.
'The Children's Song'

It's clever, but is it Art?   **3**
'The Conundrum of the Workshops'

When the Himalayan peasant meets the he-bear in his pride, /   **4**
He shouts to scare the monster, who will often turn aside. / But
the she-bear thus accosted rends the peasant tooth and nail / For
the female of the species is more deadly than the male.
'The Female of the Species'

And the Glory of the Garden it shall never pass away!   **5**
'The Glory of the Garden'

You're a better man than I am, Gunga Din!   **6**
'Gunga Din'

If you can dream – and not make dreams your master; / If you   **7**
can think – and not make thoughts your aim; / If you can meet
with Triumph and Disaster / And treat those two impostors just
the same.
'If'

If you can keep your head when all about you / Are losing   **8**
theirs and blaming it on you.
'If'

If you can talk with crowds and keep your virtue, / Or walk   **9**
with Kings – nor lose the common touch.
'If'

Then ye contended your souls / With the flannelled fools at the   **10**
wicket or the muddied oafs at the goals.
'The Islanders'

The Cat. He walked by himself, and all places were alike to him   **11**
Just-So Stories, 'The Cat That Walked By Himself'

An Elephant's Child – who was full of 'satiable curtiosity.   **12**
Just-So Stories, 'The Elephant's Child'

The great greygreen, greasy Limpopo River, all set about with　　**13**
fever trees.

Just So Stories 'The Elephant's Child'

A man of infinite-resource-and-sagacity.　　　　　　　　　　　　**14**

Just-So Stories, 'How the Whale Got His Throat'

There's a whisper down the field where the year has shot her　　**15**
yield, / And the ricks stand grey to the sun, / Singing: 'Over t
hen, come over, for the bee has quit the clover, / And your
English summer's done.'

'The Long Trail'

On the road to Mandalay, / Where the flyin'-fishes play, An'　**16**
 the dawn comes up like thunder outer China 'crost the / Bay!

Mandalay

But that is another story.　　　　　　　　　　　　　　　　　　**17**

Plain Tales from the Hills, 'Three and – an Extra'

Take my word for it, the silliest woman can manage a clever　　**18**
man; but it needs a very clever woman to manage a fool.

Plain Tales from the Hills, 'Three and – an Extra'

God our fathers, known of old, / Lord of our far-flung battle-　**19**
line, / Beneath whose awful Hand we hold / Dominion over
palm and pine – / Lord God of Hosts, be with us yet, / Lest we
forget – lest we forget!

'Recessional'

Them that asks no questions isn't told a lie. / Watch the wall,　**20**
my darling, while the Gentlemen go by!

'A Smuggler's Song'

I gloat! Hear me gloat!　　　　　　　　　　　　　　　　　　**21**

Stalky and Co.

Take up the White Man's burden　　　　　　　　　　　　　　　**22**

'The White Man's Burden'

Down to Gehenna or up to the Throne, / He travels the fastest　**23**
who travels alone.

'The Winners'

The Light that Failed.

24

Title of novel

Kissinger Henry 1923– . German-born US diplomat.

There cannot be a crisis next week. My schedule is already full.

New York Times Magazine 1 June 1969

Knox John *c*. 1505–1572 Founder of the Church of Scotland.

The First Blast of the Trumpet Against the Monstrous Regiment of Women.

Pamphlet title

Knox Ronald Arbuthnott 1888–1957. English Roman Catholic scholar.

There once was a man who said, 'God / Must think it exceedingly odd / If he finds that this tree / Continues to be / When there's no one about in the Quad.'

Langford Reed *Complete Limerick Book*

It is stupid of modern civilization to have given up believing in the devil, when he is the only explanation of it.

2

Let Dons Delight

Koestler Arthur 1905–1983. Hungarian writer.

The most persistent sound which reverberates through man's history is the beating of war drums.

Janus prologue

Koran The sacred book of Islam.

And do not say, regarding anything, 'I am going to do that tomorrow', but only, 'if God will'.

18:23–24

Kurosawa Akira 1929– . Japanese cinema director.

To be an artist means never to look away.

Guardian 1980

L

La Bruyère Jean de 1645–1696. French essayist.

Party loyalty lowers the greatest of men to the petty level of the masses.

The Characters

Laing R(onald) D(avid) 1927–1989. Scottish psychoanalyst.

We are effectively destroying ourselves by violence masquerading as love.

Politics of Experience

Lamb Charles 1775–1834. English essayist and critic.

I have been trying all my life to like Scotchmen, and am obliged to desist from the experiment in despair.

Essays of Elia, 'Imperfect Sympathies'

I love to lose myself in other men's minds. When I am not 2 walking, I am reading; I cannot sit and think. Books think for me.
Last Essays of Elia, 'Detached Thoughts on books and Reading'

The greatest pleasure I know, is to do a good action by stealth, 3 and to have it found out by accident.

'Table Talk by the late Elia'

Lambert Constant 1905–1951. English composer.

The whole trouble with a folk song is that once you have played it through there is nothing much you can do except play it over again and play it rather louder.

Music Ho!

Landor Walter Savage 1775–1864. English poet and essayist.

George the First was always reckoned / Vile, but viler George the

Second; / And what mortal ever heard / Any good of George the Third? / When from earth the Fourth descended / God be praised, the Georges ended!

'Epigram'

States, like men, have their growth, their manhood, their decrepitude, their decay. 2

Imaginary Conversations, 'Leonora di Este and Panigarola'

Lang Andrew 1844–1912. Scottish poet, historian, and folklorist.

The surge and thunder of the Odyssey.

'As One that for a Weary Space has Lain'

Langland William *c.* 1332–*c.* 1400. English poet.

A glotoun of wordes.

Piers Plowman Prologue

In a somer seson whan soft was the sonne. 2

Piers Plowman Prologue

Lao Zi or Lao Tzu *c.* 604–*c.* 531 BC. Chinese philosopher.

A journey of a thousand miles must begin with a single step.

Tao Tê Ching

Larkin Philip 1922–1985. English poet.

Far too many relied on the classic formula of a beginning, a muddle, and an end.

Of books entered for the 1977 Booker Prize in *New Fiction* Jan 1978

Deprivation is for me what daffodils were for Wordsworth. 2

Observer 1979

Sexual intercourse began / In nineteen sixty-three / (Which was rather late for me). 3

'Annus Mirabilis'

Lasch Christopher. US critic.

Nothing succeeds like the appearance of success.

The Culture of Narcissism

Lauder Harry. Stage name of Hugh MacLennan 1870–1950. Scottish music-hall comedian and singer.

Keep right on to the end of the road / Keep right on to the end.

'The End of the Road'

O! it's nice to get up in the mornin' / But it's nicer to lie in bed.   *2*

'It's Nice to Get Up In The Mornin'

I Love a Lassie.   *3*

Song title

Roamin' in the Gloamin'.   *4*

Song title

Lawrence D(avid) H(erbert) 1885–1930. English poet, essayist and novelist.

I like to write when I feel spiteful; it's like having a good sneeze.

Letter to Lady Cynthia Asquith 1913

The dead don't die. They look on and help.   *2*

Letter to J Middleton Murry 2 Feb 1923

To the Puritan all things are impure, as somebody says.   *3*

'Cerveteri'

How beastly the bourgeois is / Especially the male of the   *4*
species.

'How Beastly the Bourgeois Is'

Men! The only animal in the world to fear!   *5*

'Mountain Lion'

Pornography is the attempt to insult sex, to do dirt on it.   *6*

Phoenix, 'Pornography and Obscenity'

I never saw a wild thing / Sorry for itself.   *7*

'Self-Pity'

'Be a good animal, true to your instincts,' was his motto.   *8*

White Peacock

Don't you find it a beautiful clean thought, a world empty of   *9*

people, just uninterrupted grass, and a hare sitting up?
Women in Love

Le Carré John 1931–   . English novelist.

A committee is an animal with four back legs.
Tinker, Tailor, Soldier, Spy

Leacock Stephen Butler 1869–1944. Canadian political scientist, historian, and humorist.

Advertising may be described as the science of arresting human intelligence long enough to get money from it.
Garden of Folly 'The Perfect Salesman'

Leacock Stephen Butler 1869–1944. Canadian political scientist, historian, and humorist.

Lord Ronald ... flung himself from the room, flung himself upon his horse and rode madly off in all directions.
'Gertrude the Governess'

The North alone is silent and at peace. Give man time and he will spoil that too.
My Discovery of the West

Lear Edward 1812–1888. English artist and humorist.

Far and few, far and few, / Are the lands where the Jumblies live; / Their heads are green, and their hands are blue, / And they went to sea in a Sieve.
Nonsense Songs, 'The Jumblies'

The Owl and the Pussy-Cat went to sea / In a beautiful pea-green boat.   2
Nonsense Songs, 'The Owl and the Pussy-Cat'

They dined on mince, and slices of quince, / Which they ate   3
with a runcible spoon; / And hand in hand, on the edge of the sand, / They danced by the light of the moon.
Nonsense Songs, 'The Owl and the Pussy-Cat'

'How pleasant to know Mr. Lear!' / Who has written such   4 volumes of stuff! / Some think him ill-tempered and queer, / But a few think him pleasant enough.

Nonsense Songs preface

Leary Timothy 1920– . US psychologist who popularized "LSD".

Turn on, tune in and drop out.

The Politics of Ecstasy

Lease Mary 1853–1933. US writer and lecturer.

Kansas had better stop raising corn and begin raising hell.

Attributed remark

Lee Nathaniel 1653–1692. English dramatist.

See the conquering hero comes, / Sound the trumpets, beat the drums.

The Rival Queens

Lehmann Rosamond (Nina) 1901–1990. English novelist.

One can present people with opportunities. One cannot make them equal to them.

The Ballad and the Source

Lehrer Tom 1928– . US mathematician and satirical songwriter.

Life is like a sewer. What you get out of it depends on what you put into it.

Preamble to song 'We Will All Go Together When We Go'

Lenin Vladimir Ilyich. Adopted name of Vladimir Ilyich Ulyanov 1870–1924. Russian communist revolutionary leader.

Communism is Soviet power plus the electrification of the whole country.

Report to 8th Congress of the Communist Party 1920

It is true that liberty is precious – so precious that it must be rationed.

2

Quoted in S and B Webb *Soviet Communism*

Lennon John 1940–1980 and **McCartney** Paul 1942– . English
rock musicians.

All You Need Is Love.

Song title

For I don't care too much for money, / Money can't buy me
love.   2

'Can't Buy Me Love'

Give Peace a Chance.   3

Song title

It's been a hard day's night, / And I've been working like a dog.   4

'A Hard Day's Night'

Magical Mystery Tour.   5

Title of song and TV film

Will you still need me, will you still feed me, / When I'm sixty   6
four?

'When I'm Sixty Four'

Oh I get by with a little help from my friends.   7

'With a Little Help from My Friends'

Lennon John (Ono) 1940–1980. English rock musician.

Will the people in the cheaper seats clap your hands? All the
rest of you, if you'll just rattle your jewellery.

Royal Variety Performance 4 Nov 1963

We're more popular than Jesus now; I don't know which will   2
go first – rock 'n' roll or Christianity.

Of the Beatles *Evening Standard* 4 Mar 1966

Lenthall William 1591–1662. English lawyer.

I have neither eye to see, nor tongue to speak here, but as the
House is pleased to direct me.

Refusing to answer King Charles I's demand concerning the
five MPs whom the king wished to arrest 4 Jan 1642

Lerner Alan Jay 1918–1986. US lyricist.

Why can't a woman be more like a man?

'A Hymn to Him'

On a clear day (you can see forever).
> Song from musical *On a Clear Day* **2**

Lessing Gotthold Ephraim 1729–1781. German dramatist and critic.

A man who does not lose his reason over certain things has none to lose.
> *Emilia Galotti*

Levant Oscar 1906–1972. US pianist and actor.

Underneath this flabby exterior is an enormous lack of character.
> *Memoirs of an Amnesiac*

Leverhulme William Hesketh Lever, 1st Viscount 1851–1925. English industrialist.

Half the money I spend on advertising is wasted, and the trouble is I don't know which half.
> Quoted in D Ogilvy *Confessions of an Advertising Man.*

Lewis C S 1898–1963. English theologian and novelist.

She's the sort of woman who lives for others – you can always tell the others by their hunted expression.
> *Screwtape Letters*

Lewis (Harry) Sinclair 1885–1951. US novelist.

Our American professors like their literature clear and cold and pure and very dead.
> *The American Fear of Literature* (Nobel Prize Address, 12 Dec 1930)

Liddell Hart Basil 1895–1970. British military strategist.

Fifty years were spent in the process of making Europe explosive. Five days were enough to detonate it.
> *The Real War, 1914–1918*

Lincoln Abraham 1809–1865. 16th president of the USA 1861–5.

No man is good enough to govern another man without that other's consent.
> Speech 1854

The ballot is stronger than the bullet.   2
                          Speech 19 May 1856

You can fool all the people some of the time, and some of the   3
people all the time, but you can not fool all the people all of the
time.
                 Attributed words in a speech at Clinton 8 Sept 1858

I intend no modification of my oft-expressed personal wish   4
that all men everywhere could be free.
                          Letter to H Greeley 22 Aug 1862

In giving freedom to the slave, we assure freedom to the free, –   5
honourable alike in what we give and what we preserve.
                          Annual message to Congress I Dec 1862

With malice toward none; with charity for all; with firmness in   6
 the right, as God gives us to see the right.
                          Second Inaugural Address 4 Mar 1865

Fourscore and seven years ago our fathers brought forth upon   7
this continent a new nation, conceived in liberty, and dedicated
to the proposition that all men are created equal.
                          Gettysburg Address 19 Nov 1863

That we here highly resolve that the dead shall not have died in   8
vain, that this nation, under God, shall have a new birth of
freedom; and that government of the people, by the people,
and for the people, shall not perish from the earth.
                          Gettysburg Address 19 Nov 1863

People who like this sort of thing will find this the sort of thing 9
they like.
                                    Comment on a book

Linkletter Art 1912–   . US writer and broadcaster.

The four stages of man are infancy, childhood, adolescence and
obsolescence.
                     A Child's Garden of Misinformation

Linnaeus Carolus 1707–1778. Swedish naturalist and physician.
Nature does not make jumps.

Philosophia Botanica

Lippmann Walter 1889–1974. US liberal political commentator.
The final test of a leader is that he leaves behind him in other men the conviction and the will to carry on.

New York Herald Tribune 14 Apr 1945

Litvinov Maxim 1876–1951. Soviet politician.
Peace is indivisible.

Speech to League of Nations July 1936

Livingstone David 1813–1873. Scottish physician, missionary and explorer.
Men are immortal until their work is done.

Letter describing the death of Bishop Mackenzie, March 1862

Livy Titus Livius 59 BC–AD 17. Roman historian.
Woe to the vanquished.

History V. 48

Llewellyn Richard. Pen name of Richard Vivian Llewellyn Lloyd 1907–1983. Welsh writer.
How Green Was My Valley.

Book title

Lloyd George David 1863–1945. Welsh Liberal politician, prime minister of Britain 1916–22.
A fully-equipped duke costs as much to keep up as two Dreadnoughts; and dukes are just as great a terror and they last longer.

Speech at Newcastle 9 Oct 1909

What is our task? To make Britain a fit country for heroes to live in.   *2*

Speech at Wolverhampton 23 Nov 1918

The finest eloquence is that which gets things done; the worst is   *3*
that which delays them.
> Speech at Paris Peace Conference Jan 1919

He had sufficient conscience to bother him, but not sufficient to   *4*
keep him straight.
> Of Ramsay MacDonald, in A J Sylvester *Life with Lloyd George*

Locke John 1632–1704. English philosopher.

It is one thing to show a man that he is in error, and another to
put him in possession of the truth.
> *Essay Concerning Human Understanding*

Lodge David (John) 1935–   . English academic, writer and critic.

Literature is mostly about having sex and not much about having
children. Life is the other way round.
> *The British Museum is Falling Down*

Loesser Frank 1910–1969. US songwriter.

See what the boys in the back room will have / And tell them
I'm having the same.
> 'Boys in the Back Room'

I'd love to get you / On a slow boat to China.   *2*
> 'Slow Boat to China'

Longfellow Henry Wadsworth 1807–1882. US poet.

I shot an arrow into the air, / It fell to earth, I knew not where.
> 'The Arrow and the Song'

The men that women marry, / And why they marry them, will   *2*
always be / A marvel and a mystery to the world.
> *Michael Angelo*

Though the mills of God grind slowly, yet they grind   *3*
exceeding small.
> 'Retribution'

Ships that pass in the night, and speak each other in passing.   *4*
> *Tales of a Wayside Inn*, 'The Theologian's Tale'

It was the schooner Hesperus, / That sailed the wintry sea.   5
'The Wreck of the Hesperus'

Loos Anita 1893–1981. US humorous writer.

So this gentleman said a girl with brains ought to do something
with them besides think.

Gentlemen Prefer Blondes

Lorenz Konrad 1903–1989. Austrian zoologist.

It is a good morning exercise for a research scientist to discard a
pet hypothesis every day before breakfast. It keeps him young.
The So-Called Evil

Louis XIV 1638–1715. French monarch, known as "the Sun King".

I am the State.
Attributed remark before the Parlement of Paris 13 April 1655

Louis Joe. Assumed name of Joseph Louis Barrow 1914–1981. US
boxer.

He can run, but he can't hide.
Of his opponent Billy Conn, in *New York
Herald Tribune* 9 June 1946

Lovelace Richard 1618–1658. English poet.

Stone walls do not a prison make / Nor iron bars a cage.
'To Althea, From Prison'

I could not love thee (Dear) so much, / Lov'd I not honour more.   2
'To Lucasta, Going to the Wars'

Lowell James Russell 1819–1891. US poet and critic.

There is no good in arguing with the inevitable. The only
argument available with an east wind is to put on your overcoat.
Democracy and Addresses

Lowell Robert Traill Spence, Jr 1917–1977. US poet.

The Lord survives the rainbow of His will.
'The Quaker Graveyard in Nantucket'

If we see light at the end of the tunnel, / It's the light of the   *2*
oncoming train.

'Since 1939'

Lucas George 1944–   . US cinema director and producer.

May the force be with you.
Star Wars: from the Adventures of Luke Skywalker

Luce Clare Boothe 1903–1987. US journalist, playwright, and
politician.

But if God had wanted us to think just with our wombs, why
did He give us a brain?
Life 16 Oct 1970

Lucretius (Titus Lucretius Carus) *c*. 99–*c*. 55 BC. Roman poet and
Epicurean philosopher.

Nothing can be created out of nothing.
De Rerum Natura

Luther Martin 1483–1546. German Christian church reformer,
founder of Protestantism.

My conscience is taken captive by God's word, I cannot and
will not recant anything. ... Here I stand. I can do no other.
God help me. Amen.
Speech at the Diet of Worms 18 Apr 1521

Luxemburg Rosa 1870–1919. Polish-born German communist.

Freedom is always and exclusively freedom for the one who
thinks differently.
The Russian Revolution

Lyly John *c*. 1553–1606. English dramatist.

Night hath a thousand eyes.
Maides Metamorphose

Lyte Henry Francis 1793–1847. British cleric and hymn writer.

Abide with me; fast falls the eventide; / The darkness deepens;

Lord, with me abide.

'Abide with Me'

Where is death's sting? Where, Grave, thy victory?   *2*

'Abide with Me'

M

McCarthy Joseph 1908–1957. US rightwing politician.

McCarthyism is Americanism with its sleeves rolled.
Speech in Wisconsin 1952

McCarthy Mary 1912–1989. US novelist and critic.

If someone tells you he is going to make a 'realistic decision', you immediately understand that he has resolved to do something bad.
'American Realist Playwrights'

Macaulay Thomas Babington, Baron Macaulay 1800–1859. English historian.

The Puritan hated bear-baiting, not because it gave pain to the bear, but because it gave pleasure to the spectators.
History of England

Lars Porsena of Clusium / By the nine gods he swore / That the great house of Tarquin / Should suffer wrong no more. **2**
Lays of Ancient Rome, 'Horatius' 1

Now who will stand on either hand, / And keep the bridge with me? **3**
Lays of Ancient Rome, 'Horatius' 29

Was none who would be foremost / To lead such dire attack; / But those behind cried 'Forward!' / And those before cried 'Back!' **4**
Lays of Ancient Rome, 'Horatius' 50

And even the ranks of Tuscany / Could scarce forbear to cheer. **5**
Lays of Ancient Rome, 'Horatius' 60

As civilization advances, poetry almost necessarily declines. **6**
Literary Essays, 'Milton'

We know no spectacle so ridiculous as the British public in one 7
of its periodical fits of morality.
> *Literary Essays,* Moore's 'Life of Lord Byron'

McCoy Horace 1897–1955. US novelist and screenwriter.

They Shoot Horses Don't They.

> Title of novel

McCrae John 1872–1918. Canadian poet.

Take up our quarrel with the foe; / To you from falling hands
we throw / The torch; be yours to hold it high. / If ye break faith
with us who die / We shall not sleep, though poppies grow / In
Flanders fields.

> 'In Flanders Fields'

McCullers Carson 1917–1967. US novelist.

The Heart Is a Lonely Hunter.

> Title of novel

Macdonald George 1824–1905. Scottish novelist and children's
writer.

Here lie I, Martin Elginbrodde: / Hae mercy o' my soul, Lord
God; / As I wad do, were I Lord God, / And ye were Martin
Elginbrodde.

> *David Elginbrod*

Mackay Charles 1814–1849. English songwriter.

There's a good time coming, boys, / A good time coming.
> 'The Good Time Coming'

Mackenzie Compton 1883–1972. Scottish author.

Women do not find it difficult nowadays to behave like men, but
they often find it extremely difficult to behave like gentlemen.
> *Literature in My Time*

Mackintosh James 1765–1832. Scottish philosopher and historian.

Men are never so good or so bad as their opinions.
> *Ethical Philosophy*

The Commons, faithful to their system, remained in a wise and   **2**
masterly inactivity.
Vindiciæ Gallicæ

McLuhan Marshall 1911–1980. Canadian communications theorist.

The new electronic interdependence recreates the world in the
image of a global village.
Gutenberg Galaxy

For tribal man space was the uncontrollable mystery. For   **2**
technological man it is time that occupies the same role.
The Mechanical Bride

The medium is the message.   **3**
Understanding Media ch 1

The car has become the carapace, the protective and aggressive   **4**
shell, of urban and suburban man.
Understanding Media ch 22

Macmillan (Maurice) Harold, 1st Earl of Stockton 1894–1986. British
Conservative politician, prime minister 1957–63.

Most of our people have never had it so good.
Speech in Bedford 20 July 1957

The wind of change is blowing through this continent.   **2**
Speech in Cape Town 3 Feb 1960

As usual the Liberals offer a mixture of sound and original   **3**
ideas. Unfortunately none of the sound ideas is original and
none of the original ideas is sound.
Speech to London Conservatives 7 Mar 1962

MacNeice Louis 1907–1963. Irish-born British poet.

Better authentic mammon than a bogus god.
Autumn Journal

Time was away and somewhere else.   **2**
'Meeting Point'

The sunlight on the garden / Hardens and grows cold, / We   **3**
cannot cage the minute / Within its net of gold, / When all is told /

We cannot beg for pardon.

'Sunlight on the Garden'

Madonna stage name of Madonna Louise Ciccone 1958– . US pop singer and self-publicist.

Without you, I'm nothing ... without Elvis, you're nothing.

To her stage cast and crew

Maeterlinck Maurice, Count Maeterlinck 1862–1949. Belgian poet and dramatist.

We possess only the happiness we are able to understand.

Wisdom and Destiny

Maistre Josephe de 1753–1821. French monarchist.

Every country has the government it deserves.

Lettres et Opuscules Inédits

Malamud Bernard 1914–1986. US novelist and short-story writer.

The past exudes legend: one can't make pure clay of time's mud.

Dubin's Lives

Malcolm X adopted name of Malcolm Little 1926–1965. US black nationalist leader.

If someone puts his hand on you, send him to the cemetery.

Malcolm X Speaks

Mallory George Leigh 1886–1924. British mountaineer.

Because it's there.
Response to question 'Why do you want to climb Mount Everest?'

Mancroft Lord 1917–1987. British businessman and writer.

Cricket – a game which the English, not being a spiritual people, have invented in order to give themselves some conception of eternity.

Bees in Some Bonnets

Mao Zedong or *Mao Tse-tung* 1893–1976. Chinese Marxist leader and theoretician.

Letting a hundred flowers blossom and a hundred schools of thought contend is the policy for promoting progress in the arts and the sciences and a flourishing socialist culture in our land.

Speech in Peking 27 Feb 1957

Maradona Diego 1960–   . Argentine footballer.

The goal was scored a little bit by the hand of God, another bit by the head of Maradona.

After scoring a doubtful goal in the World Cup 1986

Marcus (Marcus Aurelius Antoninus) 121–180. Roman emperor and Stoic philosopher.

Men exist for the sake of one another. Either teach them or bear with them.

Meditations

Waste no more time arguing what a good man should be. Be one.   *2*

Meditations

Marie Antoinette 1755–1793. Queen of France 1774–93.

Let them eat cake.

Attributed remark, on being told that the poor had no bread

Marlowe Christopher 1564–1593. English poet and dramatist.

Why this is hell, nor am I out of it: / Thinkst thou that I who saw the face of God, / And tasted the eternal joys of heaven, / Am not tormented with ten thousand hells / In being deprived of everlasting bliss?

Doctor Faustus I. iii

Was this the face that launch'd a thousand ships, / And burnt   *2*
the topless towers of Ilium?

Doctor Faustus V. i

Stand still you ever-moving spheres of heaven, / That time   *3*
may cease, and midnight never come.

Doctor Faustus V. ii

Cut is the branch that might have grown full straight, / And   *4* burnèd is Apollo's laurel bough, / That sometime grew within this learned man.

Doctor Faustus epilogue

My men, like satyrs grazing on the lawns, / Shall with their goat feet dance an antic hay.   5

Edward II I. i

It lies not in our power to love, or hate, / For will in us is over-rul'd by fate.   6

Hero and Leander I.

Who ever loved that loved not at first sight?   7

Hero and Leander I.

I count religion but a childish toy, / And hold there is no sin but ignorance.   8

The Jew of Malta prologue

Infinite riches in a little room.   9

The Jew of Malta I. i

Come live with me and be my love; / And we will all the pleasures prove / That hills and valleys, dales and fields, / Woods or steepy mountain yields.   10

'The Passionate Shepherd to his Love'

Is it not passing brave to be a King, / And ride in triumph through Persepolis?   11

Tamburlaine I

Marquis Don(ald Robert Perry) 1878–1937. US author.

Honesty is a good thing but it is not profitable to its possessor unless it is kept under control.

'archygrams'

Now and then there is a person born who is so unlucky that he runs into accidents which started to happen to somebody else.   2

'archy says'

An optimist is a guy that has never had much experience.   3

'certain maxims of archy'

Writing a book of poetry is like dropping a rose petal down the   *4*
Grand Canyon and waiting for the echo.
                         Quoted in E Anthony *O Rare Don Marquis*

There's a dance in the old dame yet toujours gai toujours gai.   *5*
                                        'the song of mehitabel'

Marryat Frederick (Captain) 1792–1848. British naval officer and writer.

As savage as a bear with a sore head.
                                                  The King's Own

If you please, ma'am, it was a very little one.   *2*
        Midshipman Easy (servant's excuse for her illegitimate baby)

I think it much better that ... every man paddle his own canoe.   *3*
                                               Settlers in Canada

Martial (Marcus Valerius Martialis) AD 41–104. Latin poet and
epigrammatist.

The country in town.

                                                      Epigrammata

Marvell Andrew 1621–1678. English metaphysical poet and satirist.

Annihilating all that's made / To a green thought in a green shade.
                                                     'The Garden'

How vainly men themselves amaze / To win the palm, the oak,   *2*
or bays; / And their uncessant labours see / Crown'd from
some single herb or tree.
                                                     'The Garden'

He nothing common did or mean / Upon that memorable scene: *3*
But with his keener eye / The axe's edge did try.
                                                   'Horatian Ode'

But at my back I always hear / Time's wingèd chariot hurrying   *4*
near. / And yonder all before us lie / Deserts of vast eternity.
                                               'To His Coy Mistress'

The grave's a fine and private place, / But none I think do   *5*
there embrace.
                                               'To His Coy Mistress'

Had we but world enough, and time, / This coyness Lady were **6**
no crime. / We would sit down, and think which way / To
walk, and pass our long love's day.

'To His Coy Mistress'

Mary I 1516–1558. Queen of England, 1553–58.

When I am dead and opened, you shall find 'Calais' lying in
my heart.

Attributed remark in Holished's *Chronicles*

Masefield John 1878–1967. English poet and novelist.

Dirty British coaster with a salt-caked smoke stack, / Butting
through the Channel in the mad March days, / With a cargo of
Tyne coal, / Road-rail, pig-lead, / Firewood, iron-ware, and
cheap tin trays.

'Cargoes'

Quinquireme of Nineveh from distant Ophir / Rowing home to **2**
haven in sunny Palestine, / With a cargo of ivory, / And apes
and peacocks, / Sandalwood, cedarwood, and sweet white wine.

'Cargoes'

I must go down to the seas again, to the lonely sea and the sky, / **3**
And all I ask is a tall ship and a star to steer her by.

'Sea Fever'

Massinger Philip 1583–1640. English dramatist.

He that would govern others, first should be / The master of
himself.

The Bondman

A New Way to Pay Old Debts. **2**

Play title

Maugham W Somerset 1874–1965. English novelist.

A woman will always sacrifice herself if you give her the
opportunity. It is her favourite form of self-indulgence.

The Circle III

We have long passed the Victorian Era when asterisks were **2**

followed after a certain interval by a baby.

The Constant Wife

No married man's ever made up his mind till he's heard what   *3*
his wife has got to say about it.

Lady Frederick

It is not true that suffering ennobles the character; happiness   *4*
does that sometimes, but suffering, for the most part, makes
men petty and vindictive.

Moon and Sixpence ch 17

Like all weak men he laid an exaggerated stress on not   *5*
changing one's mind.

Of Human Bondage ch 39

Money is like a sixth sense without which you cannot make a   *6*
complete use of the other five.

Of Human Bondage ch 51

Mauriac François 1885–1970. French novelist.

Let us be wary of ready-made ideas about courage and
cowardice: the same burden weighs infinitely more heavily on
some shoulders than on others.

Second Thoughts

Maxton James 1885–1946. Scottish politician.

All I say is, if you cannot ride two horses you have no right in
the circus.

On being told that he could not be in two
political parties, in *Daily Herald* 12 Jan 1932

Mayo Charles H 1865–1939. US physician.

The definition of a specialist as one who 'knows more and
more about less and less' is good and true.

Modern Hospital Sept 1938

Mead Margaret 1901–1978. US anthropologist.

Human beings do not carry civilization in their genes.

New York Times Magazine April 1964

Medawar Peter (Brian) 1915–1987. Brazilian-born British immunologist.

If politics is the art of the possible, research is surely the art of the soluble.

The Art of the Soluble

Melbourne William Lamb, 2nd Viscount 1779–1848. British prime minister.

I wish I was as cocksure of anything as Tom Macaulay is of everything.

Remark

Things have come to a pretty pass when religion is allowed to invade the sphere of private life. 2

Remark after listening to an evangelical sermon

Melville Herman 1819–1891. US novelist and short-story writer.

Call me Ishmael.

Moby Dick

Mencken H(enry) L(ouis) 1880–1956. US essayist and critic.

If, after I depart this vale, you ever remember me and have thought to please my ghost, forgive some sinner and wink your eye at some homely girl.

Smart Set Dec 1922

No one in this world, so far as I know – has ever lost money by underestimating the intelligence of the great masses of the plain people. 2

Chicago Tribune 19 Sept 1926

The saddest life is that of a political aspirant under democracy. His failure is ignominious and his success is disgraceful. 3

Baltimore Evening Sun 9 Dec 1929

Nineteen suburbs in search of a metropolis. 4

On Los Angeles, *Americana*

Puritanism. The haunting fear that someone, somewhere, may be happy. 5

Chrestomathy

Democracy is the theory that the common people know what   **6**
they want, and deserve to get it good and hard.
Little Book in C major

Injustice is relatively easy to bear; what stings is justice.   **7**
Prejudices

Meredith George 1828–1909. English novelist and poet.

Kissing don't last: cookery do!
The Ordeal of Richard Feverel ch 28

Speech is the small change of silence.   **2**
The Ordeal of Richard Feverel ch 34

Meredith Owen 1831–1891. Pen name of Edward Robert Bulwer
Lytton, 1st Earl of Lytton. English statesman and poet.

Genius does what it must, and Talent does what it can.
'Last Words of a Sensitive Second-Rate Poet'

Merritt Dixon Lanier 1879–1954. US writer.

Oh, a wondrous bird is the pelican! / His beak holds more than
his belican. / He takes in his beak / Food enough for a week. /
But I'll be darned if I know how the helican.
Nashville Banner 22 Apr 1913

Mikes George 1912–1987. Hungarian-born US humorist and writer.

Continental people have sex life; the English have hot-water
bottles.
How to be an Alien

An Englishman, even if he is alone, forms an orderly queue of one. **2**
How to be an Alien

Mill John Stuart 1806–1873. English liberal philosopher and economist.

Ask yourself whether you are happy, and you cease to be so.
Autobiography ch 5

No great improvements in the lot of mankind are possible, until   **2**
a great change takes place in the fundamental constitution of
their modes of thought.
Autobiography ch 7

The liberty of the individual must be thus far limited; he must
not make himself a nuisance to other people.   *3*

On Liberty ch 3

The worth of a State, in the long run, is the worth of the   *4*
individuals composing it.

On Liberty ch 5

Millay Edna St Vincent 1892–1950. US poet.

My candle burns at both ends; / It will not last the night; / But
ah, my foes, and oh, my friends – / It gives a lovely light.

'First Fig'

I only know that summer sang in me / A little while, that in me   *2*
sings no more.

Harp-Weaver and Other Poems sonnet 19

Miller Arthur 1915–   . US dramatist.

A good newspaper, I suppose, is a nation talking to itself.
Observer 26 Nov 1962

A salesman is got to dream, boy. It comes with the territory.   *2*
Death of a Salesman 'Requiem'

Milligan Spike (Terence Alan Milligan) 1918–   . English comic and
humorist.

Money couldn't buy friends but you got a better class of enemy.
Puckoon

Milne A A 1882–1956. English children's writer.

King John was not a good man – / He had his little ways.
'King John's Christmas'

You must never go down to the end of the town if you don't go   *2*
down with me.
When We Were Very Young, 'Disobedience'

I do like a little bit of butter to my bread!   *3*
When We Were Very Young, 'The King's Breakfast'

Isn't it funny / How a bear likes honey? / Buzz! Buzz! Buzz! / I   *4*
wonder why he does?

Winnie-the-Pooh ch 2

I am a Bear of Very Little Brain, and long words Bother me.   5
Winnie-the-Pooh ch 4

Time for a little something.   6
Winnie-the-Pooh ch 6

Milton John 1608–1674. English poet.

As good almost kill a man as kill a good book; who kills a man
kills a reasonable creature, God's image; but he who destroys a
good book, kills reason itself, kills the image of God, as it were
in the eye.
Areopagitica

Books are not absolutely dead things, but do contain a potency   2
of life in them to be as active as that soul was whose progeny
they are.
Areopagitica

A good book is the precious life-blood of a master spirit,   3
embalmed and treasured up on purpose to a life beyond life.
Areopagitica

I cannot praise a fugitive and cloistered virtue, unexercised and   4
unbreathed, that never sallies out and sees her adversary, but
slinks out of the race, where that immortal garland is to be run
for, not without dust and heat.
Areopagitica

What hath night to do with sleep?   5
Comus l. 122

Come, knit hands, and beat the ground, / In a light fantastic round. 6
Comus l. 143

Till old experience do attain / To something like prophetic strain. 7
Il Penseroso

Fame is the spur that the clear spirit doth raise / (That last   8
infirmity of noble mind) / To scorn delights, and live laborious
days.
Lycidas l. 70

Fame is no plant that grows on mortal soil. **9**

Lycidas l. 78

The hungry sheep look up, and are not fed. **10**

Lycidas l. 123

Time will run back, and fetch the age of gold, / And speckled **11**
Vanity / Will sicken soon and die.

On the Morning of Christ's Nativity

And out of good still to find means of evil. **12**

Paradise Lost bk 1

Better to reign in hell, than serve in heav'n. **13**

Paradise Lost bk 1

But O how fall'n! how changed / From him who, in the happy **14**
realms of light, / Clothed with transcendent brightness didst
outshine / Myriads though bright.

Paradise Lost bk 1

Fall'n Cherub, to be weak is miserable / Doing or suffering: **15**
but of this be sure, / To do ought good never will be our task, /
But ever to do ill our sole delight.

Paradise Lost bk 1

His form had yet not lost / All her original brightness, nor **16**
appeared / Less than archangel ruined, and th' excess / Of
glory obscur'd.

Paradise Lost bk 1

I may assert eternal Providence, / And justify the ways of God **17**
to Men.

Paradise Lost bk 1

The mind is its own place, and in it self / Can make a Heav'n **18**
of Hell, a Hell of Heav'n.

Paradise Lost bk 1

Of Man's first disobedience, and the fruit / Of that forbidden tree, **19**
whose mortal taste / Brought death into the world, and all our
woe, / With loss of Eden.

Paradise Lost bk 1

What though the field be lost? / All is not lost.   *20*
Paradise Lost bk 1

Who overcomes / By force, hath overcome but half his foe.   *21*
Paradise Lost bk 1

And princely counsel in his face yet shone, / Majestic though in   *22*
ruin.
Paradise Lost bk 2

To compare / Great things with small.   *23*
Paradise Lost bk 2

To sit in darkness here / Hatching vain empires.   *24*
Paradise Lost bk 2

With ruin upon ruin, rout on rout, / Confusion worse   *25*
confounded.
Paradise Lost bk 2

Abash'd the Devil stood, / And felt how awful goodness is, and   *26*
saw / Virtue in her shape how lovely.
Paradise Lost bk 4

Evil be thou my Good.   *27*
Paradise Lost bk 4

Millions of spiritual creatures walk the earth / Unseen, both   *28*
when we wake, and when we sleep.
Paradise Lost bk 4

With thee conversing I forget all time.   *29*
Paradise Lost bk 4

The serpent subtlest beast of all the field.   *30*
Paradise Lost bk 9

The world was all before them, where to choose / Their place   *31*
of rest, and Providence their guide: / They hand in hand with
wandering steps and slow, / Through Eden took their solitary
way.
Paradise Lost bk 12

Deep versed in books and shallow in himself.   *32*
Paradise Regained bk 4

And calm of mind all passion spent.   **33**
                                       Samson Agonistes

Love-quarrels oft in pleasing concord end.   **34**
                                       Samson Agonistes

Nothing is here for tears, nothing to wail / Or knock the breast;   **35**
no weakness, no contempt, / Dispraise or blame; nothing but
well and fair, / And what may quiet us in a death so noble.
                                       Samson Agonistes

O dark, dark, dark, amid the blaze of noon, / Irrecoverably   **36**
dark, total eclipse / Without all hope of day!
                                       Samson Agonistes

None can love freedom heartily, but good men; the rest love   **37**
not freedom, but licence.
                              Tenure of Kings and Magistrates

They also serve who only stand and wait.   **38**
                     'When I consider how my light is spent.'

Mitchell Margaret 1900–1949. US novelist.

Death and taxes and childbirth! There's never any convenient
time for any of them.
                                       Gone with the Wind ch 38

My dear, I don't give a damn.   *2*
                                       Gone with the Wind ch 57

Mitford Nancy 1904–1973. English writer.

An aristocracy in a republic is like a chicken whose head has
been cut off: it may run about in a lively way, but in fact it is
dead.
                                       Noblesse Oblige

Monmouth James Scott, Duke of Monmouth 1649–1685. Claimant
to the English crown.

Do not hack me as you did my Lord Russell.
                                       To his executioner

Montaigne Michel Eyquem de 1533–1592. French creator of the essay form.

> If you press me to say why I loved him, I feel that it can only be expressed by replying 'Because it was him; because it was me'.
>
> Explaining his friendship with Etienne de La Boëtie, *Essays* I, 28

> Marriage is like a cage; one sees the birds outside desperate to get in, and those inside equally desperate to get out. *2*
>
> *Essays* III

Moore George (Augustus) 1852–1933. Irish novelist.

> A man travels the world in search of what he needs and returns home to find it.
>
> *Brook Kerith*

Moore Thomas 1779–1852. Irish poet.

> 'Tis the last rose of summer / Left blooming alone; / All her lovely companions / Are faded and gone.
>
> 'Tis the Last Rose'

Mordaunt Thomas Osbert 1730–1809. English poet.

> Sound, sound the clarion, fill the fife, / Throughout the sensual world proclaim, / One crowded hour of glorious life / Is worth an age without a name.
>
> 'Verses Written During the War'

More (St) Thomas 1478–1535. English politician and author.

> I pray you, master Lieutenant, see me safe up, and my coming down let me shift for my self.
>
> Ascending the scaffold. Roper *Life of Sir Thomas Moore*

Morgan Augustus de 1806–1871. English mathematician.

> Great fleas have little fleas upon their backs to bite em, / And little fleas have lesser fleas, and so AD infinitum.
>
> *A Budget of Paradoxes*

Morris William 1834–1896. English designer.

Dreamer of dreams, born out of my due time, / Why should I
strive to set the crooked straight?
The Earthly Paradise 'An Apology'

The idle singer of an empty day.   *2*
The Earthly Paradise 'An Apology'

Have nothing in your houses that you do not know to be useful,   *3*
or believe to be beautiful.
Hopes and Fears for Art

Morrissey Stage name of Steven Patrick Morrissey 1959– .
English rock singer and lyricist.

I was looking for a job, and then I found a job / And heaven
knows I'm miserable now.
'Heaven Knows I'm Miserable Now'

I don't think black people and white people will ever really get   *2*
on. The English will never like the French. That tunnel will
collapse.
Remark on the Channel Tunnel

Motley John Lothrop 1814–1877. US historian and diplomat.

As long as he lived, he was the guiding-star of a brave nation,
and when he died the little children cried in the streets.
Rise of the Dutch Republic, of William of Orange

Give us the luxuries of life, and we will dispense with its   *2*
necessities.
Attributed remark

Mountbatten Louis, 1st Earl Mountbatten of Burma 1900–1979.
English admiral and administrator.

I can't think of a more wonderful thanksgiving for the life I
have had than that everyone should be jolly at my funeral.
Quoted in R Hough *Mountbatten*

Muggeridge Malcolm 1903–1990. English journalist and author.

An orgy looks particularly alluring seen through the mists of righteous indignation.

'Dolce Vita in a Cold Climate'

As has truly been said in his days as an active politician, he was   *2*
not only a bore; he bored for England.

Tread Softly, of Anthony Eden.

Mumford Lewis 1895–1990. US urban planner and social critic.

Every generation revolts against its fathers and makes friends with its grandfathers.

The Brown Decade

Murasaki Shikibu *c.* 978–*c.* 1015. Japanese writer, a lady at court.

There are those who do not dislike wrong rumours if they are about the right men.

The Tale of Genji

Murdoch Iris 1919–   . English novelist.

Writing is like getting married. One should never commit oneself until one is amazed at one's luck.

The Black Prince

N

Nabokov Vladimir 1899–1977. Russian-born US writer.

I am sufficiently proud of my knowing something to be
modest about my not knowing all.

Lolita

Life is a great surprise. I do not see why death should not be an   *2*
even greater one.

Pale Fire

Naipaul V(idiadhar) S(urajprasad) 1932–   . Trinidadian-born British
writer.

I'm the kind of writer that people think other people are reading.
Radio Times 1979

Nairne Lady 1766–1845. Scottish songwriter.

Will ye no come back again?

'Bonnie Charlie's now awa

Napoléon I 1769–1821. Emperor of France 1804–15.

Soldiers! From the summit of these pyramids, forty centuries
look down upon you.
  Exhortation to his troops before the Battle of the Pyramids 1798

England is a nation of shopkeepers.   *2*

Attributed remark

There is only one step from the sublime to the ridiculous.   *3*
Remark to the Polish ambassador, after the
retreat from Moscow

Nash Ogden 1902–1971. US poet.

The bronx? No thonx.

New Yorker 1931

The turtle lives 'twixt plated decks / Which practically conceal   2
its sex. / I think it clever of the turtle / In such a fix to be so fertile.
'Autres Bêtes, Autres Moeurs'

Oh, what a tangled web do parents weave / When they think   3
that their children are naïve.
'Baby, What Makes the Sky Blue'

The camel has a single hump; / The dromedary, two; / Or else   4
the other way around, / I'm never sure. Are you?
'The Camel'

Candy / Is dandy / But liquor / Is quicker.   5
'Reflections on Ice-breaking'

I sit in an office at 244 Madison Avenue, / And say to myself   6
You have a responsible job, havenue?
Spring comes to Murray Hill

Nashe Thomas 1567–1601. English poet and satirist.

Brightness falls from the air; / Queens have died young and
fair; / Dust hath closed Helen's eye.
'In Time of Pestilence'

Nellist David 1952– . English Labour politician.

The quickest way to become a left-winger in the Labour Party
today is to stand still for six months.
Remark

Nelson Horatio, Viscount Nelson 1758–1805. English admiral.

Before this time to-morrow I shall have gained a peerage, or
Westminister Abbey.
At the Battle of the Nile 1798

I have only one eye, I have a right to be blind sometimes: ... I   2
really do not see the signal!
At the Battle of Copenhagen 1801

England expects every man will do his duty.   3
At the Battle of Trafalgar 1805

Kiss me, Hardy. 4

Last words

Newbolt Henry John 1862–1938. English poet and naval historian.

Capten, art tha sleepin' there below?

'Drake's Drum'

But cared greatly to serve God and the King, / And keep the 2
Nelson touch.

'Minora Sidera'

Play up! play up! and play the game! 3

'Vitaï Lampada'

There's a breathless hush in the Close to-night – / Ten to make 4
and the match to win.

'Vitaï Lampada'

Newman John Henry 1801–1890. English Roman Catholic theologian.

May He support us all the day long, till the shades lengthen,
and the evening comes, and the busy world is hushed, and the
fever of life is over, and our work is done!

Sermon, 1834. 'Wisdom and Innocence'

Newton Isaac 1642–1727. English physicist and mathematician.

I do not know what I may appear to the world, but to myself
I seem to have been only a boy playing on the sea-shore, and
diverting myself in now and then finding a smoother pebble or
a prettier shell than ordinary, whilst the great ocean of truth
lay all undiscovered before me.

Quoted in L T More *Isaac Newton*

Niebuhr Reinhold 1892–1971. US Protestant Christian theologian.

God, give us the serenity to accept what cannot be changed;
Give us the courage to change what should be changed; Give
us the wisdom to distinguish one from the other.

Quoted in Richard Wightman Fox *Reinhold Niebuhr*

Nietzsche Friedrich Wilhelm 1844–1900. German philosopher.

Morality is the herd instinct in the individual.

The Joyous Science

Nin Anaïs 1903–1977. French-born US novelist and diarist.

Life shrinks or expands in proportion to one's courage.

Diary June 1941

Nixon Richard (Milhous) 1913–   . 37th president of the USA 1968–74.

There can be no whitewash at the White House.

Television speech on Watergate 30 Apr 1973

Nye Bill (Edgar Wilson Nye) 1850–1896. US humorist.

I have been told that Wagner's music is better than it sounds.

Quoted in Mark Twain *Autobiography*

O'Casey Sean. Adopted name of John Casey 1884–1964. Irish dramatist.

The whole worl's in a state o' chassis!

Juno and the Paycock

There's no reason to bring religion into it. I think we ought to have as great a regard for religion as we can, so as to keep it out of as many things as possible.

The Plough and the Stars

O'Neill Eugene (Gladstone) 1888–1953. US dramatist.

For de little stealin' dey gits you in jail soon or late. For de big stealin' dey makes you Emperor and puts you in de Hall o' Fame when you croaks.

The Emperor Jones

The Iceman Cometh. 2

Play title

A long day's journey into night. 3

Play title

Our lives are merely strange dark interludes in the electric 4 display of God the Father.

Strange Interlude

O'Shaughnessy Arthur 1844–1881. English poet.

We are the music makers, / We are the dreamers of dreams, ... / We are the movers and shakers / Of the world for ever, it seems.

'We are the Music Makers'

Oates Captain Lawrence 1880–1912. British Antarctic explorer.

I am just going outside and may be some time.

Last words, quoted in R F Scott's *Diary* 16–17 Mar 1912

Odets Clifford 1906–1963. US dramatist.

Go out and fight so life shouldn't be printed on dollar bills.

Awake and Sing

Olivier Laurence (Kerr), Baron Olivier 1907–1989. English actor and director.

What is acting but lying and what is good acting but convincing lying?

Autobiography

Opie John 1761–1807. English artist.

I mix them with my brains, sir.

When asked with what he mixed his colours

Orbach Susie 1946– . US psychotherapist and writer.

Fat Is a Feminist Issue.

Book title

Orczy Baroness Emmusca 1865–1947. Hungarian-born English novelist.

We seek him here, we seek him there, / Those Frenchies seek him everywhere. / Is he in heaven? Is he in hell? / That demmed, elusive Pimpernel?

The Scarlet Pimpernel

Ortega y Gasset José 1883–1955. Spanish philosopher and critic.

The poet begins where the man ends. The man's lot is to live his human life, the poet's to invent what is nonexistent.

The Dehumanization of Art

Civilization is nothing more than the effort to reduce the use of force to the last resort.   2

The Revolt of the Masses

War is not an instinct but an invention.   3

The Revolt of the Masses epilogue

Orton Joe 1933–1967. English dramatist.

Every luxury was lavished on you – atheism, breast-feeding, circumcision.

Loot I

Reading isn't an occupation we encourage among police   **2**
officers. We try to keep the paper work down to a minimum.
                                                                    Loot II

Orwell George. Pen name of Eric Arthur Blair 1903–1950. English
novelist and essayist.

To see what is in front of one's nose needs a constant struggle.
                                                    Tribune 22 Mar 1946

Four legs good, two legs bad.   **2**
                                                        Animal Farm ch 3

All animals are equal but some animals are more equal than   **3**
others.
                                                       Animal Farm ch 10

BIG BROTHER IS WATCHING YOU.   **4**
                                            Nineteen Eighty-Four pt 1, ch 1

War is peace. Freedom is slavery. Ignorance is strength.   **5**
                                            Nineteen Eighty-Four pt 1, ch 1

Doublethink means the power of holding two contradictory   **6**
beliefs in one's mind simultaneously, and accepting both of
them.
                                           Nineteen Eighty-Four pt II, ch 9

If you want a picture of the future, imagine a boot stamping   **7**
on a human face – for ever.
                                            Nineteen Eighty-Four pt 3, ch 3

It is only because miners sweat their guts out that superior   **8**
persons can remain superior.
                                                   The Road to Wigan Pier

Keep the Aspidistra Flying.   **9**
                                                             Title of novel

Osborne John (James) 1929–   . English dramatist.
Don't clap too hard – it's a very old building.
                                                           The Entertainer

They spend their time mostly looking forward to the past.   *2*
Look Back in Anger II.i

Osler William 1849–1919. Canadian physian.

One finger in the throat and one in the rectum makes a good
diagnostician.
Aphorisms from his Bedside Teachings

One of the first duties of the physician is to educate the masses   *2*
not to take medicine.
Aphorisms from his Bedside Teachings

Ovid (Publius Ovidius Naso) 43 BC–AD 17. Roman poet.

Time the devourer of all things.
Metamorphoses

Oz Amos 1939–   . Israeli writer.

He formulated his remarks as if the very existence of two
distinct exes was a disorder which multiplied agony in the
world, a disorder whose results people must do everything in
their power to mitigate.
My Michael

P

Paine Thomas 1737–1809. English left-wing political writer.

The sublime and the ridiculous are often so nearly related, that it is difficult to class them separately.

Age of Reason

These are the times that try men's souls.   2

The American Crisis

The final event to himself has been, that as he rose like a rocket,   3
he fell like the stick.

Of Edmund Burke, *Letter to the Addressers on the late Proclamation*

My country is the world, and my religion is to do good.   4
The Rights of Man

Palmerston Henry John Temple, 3rd Viscount Palmerston 1784–1865 British politician.

'Die, my dear Doctor, that's the last thing I shall do!'

Last words, attributed

Pankhurst Emmeline 1858–1928. English suffragette.

Is not a woman's life, is not her health, are not her limbs more valuable than panes of glass? There is no doubt of that, but most important of all, does not the breaking of glass produce more effect upon the Government?

Speech 16 Feb 1912

Pareto Vilfredo 1848–1923. Italian economist and political philosopher.

Give me fruitful error any time, full of seeds, bursting with its own corrections. You can keep your sterile truth for yourself.

The Mind and Society

Parker Dorothy 1893–1967. US writer and wit.

The affair between Margot Asquith and Margot Asquith will
live as one of the prettiest love stories in all literature.
   Review of Margot Asquith's *Lay Sermons, New Yorker* 1927

There's a hell of a distance between wise-cracking and wit. Wit
has truth in it; wise-cracking is simply callisthenics with words.
   Paris Review Summer 1956

One more drink and I'd have been under the host.   *3*
   H Teichmann *George S. Kaufman*

Men seldom make passes / At girls who wear glasses.   *4*
   'News Item'

Why is it no one ever sent me yet / One perfect limousine, do   *5*
you suppose? / Ah no, it's always just my luck to get / One
perfect rose.
   'One perfect Rose'

Sorrow is tranquillity remembered in emotion.   *6*
   'Sentiment'

Parkinson C Northcote 1909– . English writer and historian.

Work expands so as to fill the time available for its completion.
   Parkinson's Law

Pascal Blaise 1623–1662. French philosopher and mathematician.

The eternal silence of these infinite spaces [the heavens]
terrifies me.
   Pensées

The heart has its reasons which reason knows nothing of.   *2*
   Pensées

Pater Walter (Horatio) 1839–1894. English scholar, essayist and
art critic.

To burn always with this hard, gemlike flame, to maintain this
ecstasy, is success in life.
   Studies in the History of the Renaissance

Payn James 1830–1898. English writer and editor.

I had never had a piece of toast / Particularly long and wide, / But fell upon the sanded floor, / And always on the buttered side.

Chambers's Journal

Payne J H 1791–1852. US actor and dramatist.

Mid pleasures and palaces though we may roam, / Be it ever so humble, there's no place like home; ... / Home, home, sweet, sweet home! / There's no place like home! there's no place like home!

'Home, Sweet Home'

Paz Octavio 1914– . Mexican poet and essayist.

We are condemned to kill time: Thus we die bit by bit.

Cuento de los Jardines

Peacock Thomas Love 1785–1866. English satirical novelist and poet.

Marriage may often be a stormy lake, but celibacy is almost always a muddy horsepond.

Melincourt

Sir, I have quarrelled with my wife; and a man who has quarrelled with his wife is absolved from all duty to his country.   2

Nightmare Abbey

The mountain sheep are sweeter, / But the valley sheep are fatter; / We therefore deemed it meeter / To carry off the latter.   3

'The War-Song of Dinas Vawr'

Peele George 1558–1597. English dramatist.

His golden locks time hath to silver turn'd; / O time too swift, O swiftness never ceasing!

'A Farewell to Arms'

Péguy Charles 1873–1914. French publisher and poet.

He who does not bellow the truth when he knows the truth makes himself the accomplice of liars and forgers.

Lettre du Provincial 21 Dec 1899

Penn William 1644–1718. English Quaker.

It is a reproach to religion and government to suffer so much
poverty and excess.

Reflexions and Maxims pt 1, no. 52

Men are generally more careful of the breed of their horses and   *2*
dogs than of their children.

Reflexions and Maxims pt 1 no. 85

Let the people think they govern and they will be governed.   *3*
Some Fruits of Solitude

Pepys Samuel 1633–1703. English diarist.

And so to bed.

Diary 20 Apr 1660

But Lord! to see the absurd nature of Englishmen, that cannot   *2*
forbear laughing and jeering at everything that looks
strange.

Diary 27 Nov 1662

My wife, who, poor wretch, is troubled with her lonely life.   *3*
Diary 19 Dec 1662

Strange to see how a good dinner and feasting reconciles   *4*
everybody.

Diary 9 Nov 1665

Strange to say what delight we married people have to see   *5*
these poor fools decoyed into our condition.

Diary 25 Dec 1665

But it is pretty to see what money will do.   *6*
Diary 21 March 1667

I do hate to be unquiet at home.   *7*
Diary 22 Jan 1669

Pétain Henri Philippe 1856–1951. French marshal and politician.

To make a union with Great Britain would be a fusion with a
corpse.

In response to Churchill's proposal of an
Anglo-French union 1940

They shall not get past.   *2*

On the German army at Verdun 1916

Peter Laurence J 1910–1990. Canadian writer and teacher.

The Peter Principle: In a Hierarchy Every Employee Tends to Rise to His Level of Incompetence.

The Peter Principle

Work is accomplished by those employees who have not yet reached their level of incompetence.

The Peter Principle

Petronius Gaius, known as *Petronius Arbiter*, died *c.* AD 66. Roman author.

Beware of the dog.

Satyricon

Phelps Edward John 1822–1900. US lawyer and diplomat.

The man who makes no mistakes does not usually make anything.

Speech 1899

Phillips Wendell 1811–1884. US reformer.

Every man meets his Waterloo at last.

Lecture at Brooklyn 1859

One, on God's side, is a majority.   *2*

Lecture at Brooklyn 1859

Picasso Pablo Ruiz Y 1881–1973. Spanish artist.

I paint objects as I think them, not as I see them.

J Golding *Cubism*

People who try to explain pictures are usually barking up the   *2*
wrong tree.

D Ashton *Picasso on Art*, 'Two statements by Picasso'

Pirsig Robert M 1928– . US writer.

Zen and the Art of Motorcycle Maintenance.

Book title

Pisan Christine de 1364–1430. French poet and historian.

Just as women's bodies are softer than men's, so their understanding is sharper.

The City of Ladies

Pitkin Walter 1878–1953. US writer.

Life Begins at Forty.

Book title (1932)

Pitt William, *the Younger*, 1759–1806. British politician.

Necessity is the plea for every infringement of human freedom. It is the argument of tyrants; it is the creed of slaves.

Speech in House of Commons 18 Nov 1783

Roll up that map; it will not be wanted these ten years. 2

Referring to map of Europe, hearing of Napoleon's victory at Austerlitz 1805, in Stanhope's *Life of the Rt Hon William Pitt*

Pitt William, *the Elder*, 1st Earl of Chatham 1708–1778. British Whig politician.

The atrocious crime of being a young man ... I shall neither attempt to palliate nor deny.

Speech in House of Commons 27 Jan 1741

Our watchword is security. 2

Attributed remark

The parks are the lungs of London. 3

Attributed remark

Plath Sylvia 1932–1963. US poet and novelist.

Dying, / Is an art, like everything else. / I do it exceptionally well.

'Lady Lazarus'

Pliny 23–79. Roman naturalist and writer.

There is always something new out of Africa.

Historia Naturalis II. 8

There's truth in wine.   **2**

Historia Naturalis, II. 14

Attic wit.   **3**

Historia Naturalis, II.31

Poe Edgar Allan 1809–1849. US writer and poet.

I was a child and she was a child, / In this kingdom by the sea; / But we loved with a love which was more than love / I and my Annabel Lee.

'Annabel Lee'

To vilify a great man is the readiest way in which a little man can himself attain greatness.   **2**

Marginalia

Quoth the Raven, 'Nevermore'   **3**

The Raven

Thy hyacinth hair, thy classic face, / Thy Naiad airs have brought me home / To the glory that was Greece / And the grandeur that was Rome.   **4**

'To Helen'

Polo Marco 1254–1324. Venetian traveller and writer.

I have not told half of what I saw.

Last words

Pompadour Madame de (Antoinette Poisson, Marquise de Pompadour) 1721–1764. Mistress of Louise XV of France.

Après nous le déluge / After us the deluge.

Quoted in de Hausset *Mémoires*

Pompidou Georges 1911–1974. French conservative politician, president 1969–74.

A statesman is a politician who places himself at the service of the nation. A politician is a statesman who places the nation at his service.

Observer Dec 1973

Ponsonby 1871–1946. British politician and author.

When war is declared, Truth is the first casualty.
Falsehood in Wartime epigraph

Pope Alexander 1688–1744. English poet and satirist.

'Blessed is the man who expects nothing, for he shall never be disappointed', was the ninth beatitude which a man of wit (who, like a man of wit, was a long time in gaol) added to the eighth.
Letter 23 Sept 1725

The Right Divine of Kings to govern wrong.   2
The Dunciad bk 4

Stretch'd on the rack of a too easy chair.   3
The Dunciad bk 4

Thy hand, great Anarch! lets the curtain fall, / And universal   4
darkness buries all.
The Dunciad bk 4

Is there no bright reversion in the sky, / For those who greatly   5
think, or bravely die?
Elegy to the Memory of an Unfortunate Lady

What beck'ning ghost, along the moon-light shade /Invites my   6
steps, and points to yonder glade?
Elegy to the Memory of an Unfortunate Lady

Damn with faint praise, assent with civil leer, / And, without   7
sneering, teach the rest to sneer; / Willing to wound, and yet
afraid to strike, / Just hint a fault, and hesitate dislike.
Epistle to Dr. Arbuthnot

Let Sporus tremble. — A. What? that thing of silk, / Sporus,   8
that mere white curd of ass's milk? / Satire or sense, alas! can
Sporus feel? / Who breaks a butterfly upon a wheel?
Epistle to Dr. Arbuthnot

This painted child of dirt, that stinks and stings.   9
Epistle to Dr. Arbuthnot

Wit that can creep, and pride that licks the dust. **10**
Epistle to Dr. Arbuthnot

Nature and Nature's laws lay hid in night: / God said, *Let* **11**
Newton be! and all was light.
Epitaph intended for Sir Isaac Newton [Compare Squire 1.]

For fools rush in where angels fear to tread. **12**
Essay on Criticism

Let such teach others who themselves excel, / And censure **13**
freely who have written well.
Essay on Criticism

A little learning is a dangerous thing; / Drink deep, or taste not **14**
the Pierian spring: / There shallow draughts intoxicate the brain,
/ And drinking largely sobers us again.
Essay on Criticism

To err is human, to forgive, divine. **15**
Essay on Criticism

True ease in writing comes from art, not chance, / As those **16**
move easiest who have learned to dance.
Essay on Criticism

True wit is nature to advantage dressed, / What oft was thought, **17**
but ne'er so well expressed.
Essay on Criticism

Hope springs eternal in the human breast; / Man never is, but **18**
always to be blessed.
Essay on Man 1

Know then thyself, presume not God to scan, / The proper study **19**
of mankind is man.
Essay on Man 2

An honest man's the noblest work of God. **20**
Essay on Man 3

Do good by stealth, and blush to find it fame. **21**
Imitations of Horace

Has she no faults then (Envy says), Sir? / Yes, she has one, I
must aver; / When all the world conspires to praise her, / The
woman's deaf, and does not hear. **22**
> 'On a Certain Lady at Court'

I am his Highness' dog at Kew; / Pray tell me, sir, whose dog
are you? **23**
> 'On the Collar of a Dog which I gave to his Royal Highness'

What dire offence from am'rous causes springs, / What mighty
contests rise from trivial things! **24**
> *The Rape of the Lock* 1

Here thou, great Anna! whom three realms obey, / Dost
sometimes counsel take— and sometimes tea. **25**
> *The Rape of the Lock* 3

When men grow virtuous in their old age, they only make a
sacrifice to God of the devil's leavings. **26**
> *Thoughts on Various Subjects*

Popper Karl (Raimund) 1902– . Austrian philosopher of science.

We may become the makers of our fate when we have ceased
to pose as its prophets.
> *The Open Society and its Enemies* introduction

Porritt Jonathon 1950– . British environmental campaigner.

Green consumerism is a target for exploitation. There's a lot of
green froth on top, but murkiness lurks underneath.
> Speech at a Friends of the Earth Conference 1989

Porter Cole (Albert) 1892–1964. US composer and lyricist.

In olden days a glimpse of stocking / Was looked on as
something shocking / Now, heaven knows, / Anything goes.
> 'Anything Goes'

I get no kick from champagne, / Mere alcohol doesn't thrill me
at all / So tell me why should it be true / That I get a kick out of
you? **2**
> 'I Get a Kick Out of You'

Birds do it, bees do it, / Even educated fleas do it. / Let's do it,   3
let's fall in love.

> 'Let's Do It' (1954 version)

Potter Beatrix 1866–1943. English writer and illustrator.

Once upon a time there were four little Rabbits, and their names
were – Flopsy, Mopsy, Cottontail, and Peter.

> *Tale of Peter Rabbit*

It is said that the effect of eating too much lettuce is 'soporific'.   2
> *Tale of the Flopsy Bunnies*

Potter Dennis (Christopher George) 1935–   . English playwright.

The trouble with words is that you never know whose mouths
they have been in.

> Remark

Potter Stephen 1900–1969. English writer.

A good general rule is to state that the bouquet is better than the
taste, and vice versa.

> *One-Upmanship* ch 14

The Theory and Practice of Gamesmanship or The Art of   2
Winning Games Without Actually Cheating.

> Book title

Pound Ezra 1885–1972. US poet.

One of the pleasures of middle age is to *find out* that one was right,
and that one was much righter than one knew at say 17 *or 23*.
> *ABC of Reading* ch 2

Real education must ultimately be limited to one who insists on   2
knowing, the rest is mere sheep-herding.
> *ABC of Reading* ch 8

And even I can remember / A day when the historians left   4
blanks in their writings, / I mean for things they didn't know.
> *Draft of* XXX *Cantos*

Great literature is simply language charged with meaning to   5
the utmost possible degree.

How to Read

Winter is icummen in, / Lhude sing Goddamm, / Raineth drop   6
and staineth slop, / And how the wind doth ramm! / Sing:
Goddamm.

'Ancient Music'

Powell Anthony (Dymoke) 1905–   . English novelist.

He fell in love with himself at first sight and it is a passion to
which he has always remained faithful.

Acceptance World

Books Do Furnish a Room.   2

Title of novel

A Dance to the Music of Time.   3

Title of novel sequence

Powell (John) Enoch 1912–   . British Conservative politician.

As I look ahead, I am filled with foreboding. Like the Roman, I
seem to see 'the River Tiber foaming with much blood'.

Speech at Conservative Political
Centre, Birmingham 20 Apr 1968

All political lives, unless they are cut off in midstream at a   2
happy juncture, end in failure, because that is the nature of
politics and of human affairs.

Joseph Chamberlain epilogue

Priestley J(ohn) B(oynton) 1894–1984. English novelist and
playwright.

It is hard to tell where the MCC ends and the Church of
England begins.

New Statesman 20 July 1962

God can stand being told by Professor Ayer and Marghanita   2
Laski that He doesn't exist.

Listener 1 July 1965

Already we Viewers, when not viewing, have begun to whisper   *3*
to one another that the more we elaborate our means of
communication, the less we communicate.
> 'The Writer in a Changing Society'

Prior Matthew 1664–1721. English poet and diplomat.

Be to her virtues very kind; / Be to her faults a little blind; / Let
all her ways be unconfin'd; / And clap your padlock on her mind.
> *An English Padlock*

Cur'd yesterday of my disease, / I died last night of my physician.   *2*
> 'The Remedy Worse than the Disease'

Protagoras b *c.* 485 BC. Greek sophist.

Man is the measure of all things.

> Quoted in Plato *Theaetetus*

Proudhon Pierre-Joseph 1809–1865. French anarchist.

Property is theft.

> *What is Property?*

Proust Marcel 1871–1922. French novelist and critic.

Happiness is salutary for the body but sorrow develops the
powers of the spirit.

> *Time Regained*

As soon as one is unhappy one becomes moral.   *2*
> *Within a Budding Grove*

Pushkin Aleksandr 1799–1837. Russian poet and writer.

Habit is Heaven's own redress: it takes the place of happiness.
> *Eugene Onegin*

Putnam Israel 1718–1790. US revolutionary soldier.

Men, you are all marksmen—don't one of you fire until you see
the whites of their eyes.

> Order at the Battle of Bunker Hill 1775

Puzo Mario 1920– . US novelist.

He's a businessman. ... I'll make him an offer he can't refuse.
                                                              The Godfather ch 1

Q

Quarles Francis 1592–1644. English writer and poet.

Physicians of all men are most happy; what good success soever they have, the world proclaimeth, and what faults they commit, the earth covereth.

Hieroglyphics of the Life of Man

Quasimodo Salvatore 1901–1968. Italian poet.

Poetry is the revelation of a feeling that the poet believes to be interior and personal [but] which the reader recognizes as his own.

Speech 1960

R

Rabelais 1495–1553. French satirist, monk and physician.

I go to seek a great perhaps.
> Attributed remark on his deathbed

Ring down the curtain, the farce is over.   *2*
> Attributed remark on his deathbed

Raleigh Walter Alexander 1861–1922. English scholar.

An anthology is like all the plums and orange peel picked
out of a cake.
> Letter to Mrs Robert Bridges 15 Jan 1915

In Examinations those who do not wish to know ask   *2*
questions of those who cannot tell.
> 'Some Thoughts on Examinations'

Raleigh or *Ralegh* Walter *c.* 1552–1618. English courtier,
navigator and author.

O eloquent, just, and mighty Death!
> *A History of the World* bk 5, ch 6

If all the world and love were young, / And truth in every   *2*
shepherd's tongue, / These pretty pleasures might me move /
To live with thee, and be thy love.
> 'The Nymph's Reply to the Shepherd' [Compare Marlowe 10]

So the heart be right, it is no matter which way the head lies.   *3*
> Remark to the question which way he preferred to lay his
> head on the block, quoted in W Stebbing *Sir Walter Raleigh*

Even such is time, which takes in trust / Our youth, our joys,   *4*
and all we have, / And pays us but with age and dust, / Who in

the dark and silent grave, / When we have wandered all our
ways, / Shuts up the story of our days.

> Lines written the night before his death

Fain would I climb, yet fear I to fall.　　　　　　　　　　　　5

> Line written on a window-pane. Queen Elizabeth I
> wrote under it 'If thy heart fails thee, climb not at all.'

Ransome Arthur 1884–1967. English journalist and writer.

BETTER DROWNED THAN DUFFERS IF NOT DUFFERS
WONT DROWN.

> *Swallows and Amazons*

Grab a chance and you won't be sorry for a might-have-been.　　2

> *We Didn't Mean to Go to Sea* ch 2

Rattigan Terence 1911–1977. English dramatist.

Do you know what 'le vice Anglais' – the English vice – really
is? Not flagellation, not pederasty – whatever the French
believe it to be. It's our refusal to admit our emotions. We think
they demean us, I suppose.

> *In Praise of Love* II

Reagan Ronald (Wilson) 1911– . 40th president of the USA
1981–9.

Politics is supposed to be the second oldest profession. I have
come to realize that it bears a very close resemblance to the
first.

> At a conference in Los Angeles 2 Mar 1977

You know, by the time you reach my age, you've made plenty　　2
of mistakes if you've lived your life properly.

> *Observer* 1987

Reger (Johann Baptist Joseph) Max(imilian) 1873–1916. German
composer and pianist.

I am sitting in the smallest room of my house. I have your

review before me. In a moment it will be behind me.
> Letter to critic in response to review in
> *Münchener Neueste Nachrichten* 7 Feb 1906

Remarque Erich Maria 1898–1970. German novelist and soldier.

All Quiet on the Western Front.

> Book title.

Reuben David 1953– . US psychiatrist and author.

Everything You Always Wanted to Know about Sex, but Were
Afraid to Ask.

> Book title

Reynolds Joshua 1723–1792. English portrait painter.

If you have great talents, industry will improve them: if you
have but moderate abilities, industry will supply their
deficiency.
> Discourse to Students of the Royal Academy 11 Dec 1769

A mere copier of nature can never produce anyt'ing great. *2*
> Discourse to Students of the Royal Acade.ny 14 Dec 1770

Rhodes Cecil (John) 1853–1902. English-born South African
statesman.

So little done, so much to do.

> On the day he died

Rhys Jean 1894–1979. Dominican-born British novelist.

A room is a place where you hide from the wolves outside and
that's all any room is.

> *Good Morning, Midnight*

Rice Grantland 1880–1954. US sports journalist.

For when the One Great Scorer comes to mark against your
name, / He writes – not that you won or lost – but how you
played the Game.

> 'Alumnus Football'

Richelieu Armand Jean du Plessis de 1585–1642. French cardinal and politician.

Nothing is as dangerous for the state as those who would govern kingdoms with maxims found in books.

Political Testament

Robin Leo 1899–1984. US songwriter.

Diamonds Are a Girl's Best Friend.

Song title

Rochefoucauld Duc de la 1613–1680. French writer.

The height of cleverness is to be able to conceal cleverness.

Maxims

Hypocrisy is homage paid by vice to virtue.   2

Maxims

In the misfortune of our best friends, we find something which   3
is not displeasing to us.

Maxims

Rochester John Wilmot, 2nd Earl of Rochester 1647–1680. English poet and courtier.

Here lies a great and mighty king / Whose promise none relies on; / He never said a foolish thing, / Nor ever did a wise one.
'The King's Epitaph' [Compare Charles II 2]

A merry monarch, scandalous and poor.   2

A satire on King Charles II

Roddenberry Gene 1921–1991. US film producer.

These are the voyages of the starship Enterprise. Its five-year mission: to explore strange new worlds, to seek out new life and new civilizations, to boldly go where no man has gone before.
Introduction to television series *Star Trek*

Rogers Will 1879–1935. US actor and humorist.

You know everybody is ignorant, only on different subjects.
New York Times 31 Aug 1924

You can't say civilization don't advance, however, for in every   *2*
war they kill you in a new way.
                                        New York Times 23 Dec 1929

I don't make jokes – I just watch the government and report the   *3*
facts.
                                        Saturday Review 25 Aug 1962

Everything is funny as long as it is happening to Somebody Else.   *4*
                                        Illiterate Digest, 'Warning to Jokers'

Roland Madame (Marie-Jeanne Philipon) 1754–1793. French
intellectual and political figure.

O liberty! O liberty! what crimes are committed in thy name!
                                        Remark on seeing a statue of Liberty as
                                        she was taken to the scaffold

Romains Jules. Pen name of Louis Farigoule 1885–1972. French
novelist, playwright, and poet.

Every man who feels well is a sick man neglecting himself.
                                        Knock, or the Triumph of Medicine

Roosevelt (Anna) Eleanor 1884–1962. US social worker, lecturer,
and First Lady.

No one can make you feel inferior without your consent.
                                        Catholic Digest

Roosevelt Franklin D(elano) 1882–1945. 32nd president of the
USA 1933–45.

I pledge you – I pledge myself – to a new deal for the
American people.
                                        Speech 1932

In the field of world policy I would dedicate this Nation to the   *2*
policy of the good neighbour.
                                        Inaugural address 4 Mar 1933

Let me assert my firm belief that the only thing we have to fear   *3*
is fear itself – nameless, unreasoning, unjustified terror which

paralyses needed efforts to convert retreat into advance.
Inaugural address 4 Mar 1933

We must be the great arsenal of democracy.   *4*
Speech 1940

Roosevelt Theodore 1858–1919. 26th president of the USA 1901–09.

There is a homely old adage which runs: 'Speak softly and carry a big stick; you will go far.'
Speech at Chicago 3 Apr 1903

A man who is good enough to shed his blood for the country is   *2*
good enough to be given a square deal afterwards. More than that no man is entitled to, and less than that no man shall have.
Speech at the Lincoln Monument, Springfield, Illinois, 4 June 1903

I wish to preach, not the doctrine of ignoble ease, but the   *3*
doctrine of the strenuous life.
Speech 1899

The men with the muck-rakes are often indispensable to the   *4*
well-being of society; but only if they know when to stop raking the muck.
Speech in Washington 14 Apr 1906

A hyphenated American is not an American at all. This is just   *5*
as true of the man who puts 'native' before the hyphen as of the man who puts German or Irish or English or French before the hyphen.
Speech in New York 12 Oct 1915

Rosa Salvator 1615–1673. Italian Baroque painter, poet, and musician.

Be silent, unless what you have to say is better than silence.
Motto on self-portrait about 1645

Rosebery Archibald Philip Primrose, 5th Earl of Rosebery 1847–1929. Scottish Liberal politician.

It is beginning to be hinted that we are a nation of amateurs.
                                                        Address 1900

I must plough my furrow alone.   *2*
                                                        Speech 1901

Rossetti Christina (Georgina) 1830–1894. English poet.

Better by far you should forget and smile / Than that you
should remember and be sad.
                                                        'Remember'

Does the road wind up-hill all the way? / Yes, to the very end.   *2*
                                                        'Up-Hill'

When I am dead, my dearest, / Sing no sad songs for me.   *3*
                                                        'When I am dead'

Rossetti Dante Gabriel 1828–1882. English poet and painter.

I have been here before, / But when or how I cannot tell: / I
know the grass beyond the door, / The sweet keen smell, / The
sighing sound, the lights around the shore.
                                                        'Sudden Light'

Rostand Jean 1894–1977. French biologist and writer.

My pessimism goes to the point of suspecting the sincerity of
the pessimists.
                                                        Journal of a Character

To be adult is to be alone.   *2*
                                                        Thoughts of a Biologist

Rousseau Jean-Jacques 1712–1778. French philosopher and writer.

Censorship may be useful for the preservation of morality, but
can never be so for its restoration.
                                                        The Social Contract

Man is born free, and everywhere he is in chains.   *2*
                                                        The Social Contract

Routh Martin Joseph 1755–1854. English scholar.

You will find it a very good practice always to verify your references, sir!

Quoted in Burgon, *Memoir of Dr. Routh*

Rowland Helen 1875–1950. US writer.

A husband is what is left of a lover, after the nerve has been extracted.

A Guide to Men

When you see what some girls marry, you realize how they must hate to work for a living.

Reflections of a Bachelor Girl 2

Runyon (Alfred) Damon 1884–1946. US journalist.

I always claim the mission workers came out too early to catch any sinners on this part of Broadway. At such an hour the sinners are still in bed resting up from their sinning of the night before, so they will be in good shape for more sinning a little later on.

'The Idyll of Miss Sarah Brown'

'My boy,' he says, 'always try to rub up against money, for if you rub up against money long enough, some of it may rub off on you.'

'A Very Honourable Guy' 2

Ruskin John 1819–1900. English art critic and social critic.

Never expected to hear a coxcomb ask two hundred guineas for flinging a pot of paint in the public's face.

Comment on Whistler's *Nocturne in Black and Gold*

I believe the right question to ask, respecting all ornament, is simply this: Was it done with enjoyment – was the carver happy while he was about it?

'The Lamp of Life' 2

When we build, let us think that we build for ever.

The Seven Lamps of Architecture 3

To make your children *capable of honesty* is the beginning of   **4**
education.

Time and Tide

Government and co-operation are in all things the laws of life;   **5**
anarchy and competition the laws of death.

Unto this Last

Russell Bertrand (Arthur William), 3rd Earl Russell 1872–1970.
English philosopher and mathematician.

Three passions, simple but overwhelmingly strong, have
governed my life: the longing for love, the search for
knowledge, and unbearable pity for the suffering of mankind.

Autobiography prologue

Boredom is therefore a vital problem for the moralist, since   **2**
half the sins of mankind are caused by the fear of it.

Conquest of Happiness ch 4

A sense of duty is useful in work, but offensive in personal   **3**
relations. People wish to be liked, not to be endured with
patient resignation.

Conquest of Happiness ch 10

To be able to fill leisure intelligently is the last product of   **4**
civilization, and at present very few people have reached this
level.

Conquest of Happiness ch 14

The infliction of cruelty with a good conscience is a delight to   **5**
moralists. That is why they invented Hell.

'On the Value of Scepticism'

Man is a credulous animal, and must believe something; in the   **6**
absence of good grounds for belief, he will be satisfied with
bad ones.

'Outline of Intellectual Rubbish'

Russell John 1795–1883. English 'sporting parson'.

If peace cannot be maintained with honour, it is no longer peace.

Speech 1853

Rutherford Ernest 1871–1937. New Zealand physicist.

All science is either physics or stamp collecting.
                                   J B Birks *Rutherford at Manchester*

Ryle Gilbert 1900–1976. English philosopher.

The dogma of the Ghost in the Machine.

                                                        Concept of Mind ch 1

S

Saarinen Eero 1910–1961. Finnish-born US architect..

Always design a thing by considering it in its larger context—a chair in a room, a room in a house, a house in an environment, an environment in a city plan.

Time July 1956

Saint-Exupéry Antoine de 1900–1944. French author.

Grown-ups never understand anything for themselves, and it is tiresome for children to be always and forever explaining things to them.

The Little Prince 1943

Saint-Jean Perse pen name of Marie-René-Auguste-Alexis Saint-Leger 1887–1975. French poet and diplomat.

It is enough for the poet to be the bad conscience of his time.
Letter Dec 1941

Saki pen name of H(ugh) H(ector) Munro 1870–1916. Burmese-born English writer.

But, good gracious, you've got to educate him first. You can't expect a boy to be depraved until he's been to a good school.

'The Baker's Dozen'

'The man is a common murderer.' 'A common murderer, possibly, but a very uncommon cook.' 2

'The Blind Spot'

A little inaccuracy sometimes saves tons of explanation. 3
'The Comments of Moung Ka'

Waldo is one of those people who would be enormously improved by death. 4

'The Feast of Nemesis'

Children with Hyacinth's temperament don't know better as 5
they grow older; they merely know more.

> 'Hyacinth'

The people of Crete unfortunately make more history than they 6
can consume locally.

> 'The Jesting of Arlington Stringham'

All decent people live beyond their incomes nowadays, and 7
those who aren't respectable live beyond other peoples'. A few
gifted individuals manage to do both.

> 'The Match-Maker'

He's simply got the instinct for being unhappy highly developed. 8
> 'The Match-Maker'

Every reformation must have its victims. You can't expect the 9
fatted calf to share the enthusiasm of the angels over the
prodigal's return.

> 'Reginald on the Academy'

The cook was a good cook, as cooks go; and as cooks go she 10
went.

> 'Reginald on Besetting Sins'

People may say what they like about the decay of Christianity; 11
the religious system that produced green Chartreuse can never
really die.

> 'Reginald on Christmas Presents'

Samuel Lord (1st Viscount Samuel) 1870–1983. English Liberal
statesman.

A library is thought in cold storage.

> *A Book of Quotations*

It takes two to make a marriage a success and only one a failure. 2
> *A Book of Quotations*

Samuelson Paul 1915– . US economist and journalist.

Man does not live by GNP alone.

> *Economics* 1948

Sand George. Pen name of Amandine Aurore Lucie Dupin 1804–1876. French author.

We cannot tear out a single page of our life, but we can throw the whole book in the fire.

Mauprat

Sandburg Carl August 1878–1967. US poet.

Slang is a language that rolls up its sleeves, spits on its hands and goes to work.

New York Times 13 Feb 1959

I am an idealist. I don't know where I'm going but I'm on the way.   *2*

Incidentals

Sometime they'll give a war and nobody will come.   *3*

The People

Poetry is the opening and closing of a door, leaving those who   *4*
look through to guess about what is seen during a moment.

'Poetry Considered'

Santayana George 1863–1952. Spanish-born US philosopher and critic.

Fanaticism consists in redoubling your effort when you have forgotten your aim.

Life of Reason

It takes patience to appreciate domestic bliss; volatile spirits   *2*
prefer unhappiness.

Life of Reason

Those who cannot remember the past are condemned to repeat it.   *3*

Life of Reason

Sargent John Singer 1856–1925. US portrait painter.

Every time I paint a portrait I lose a friend.

N Bentley and E Esar *Treasury of Humorous Quotations*

Sartre Jean-Paul 1905–1980. French philosopher, dramatist and novelist.

I am condemned to be free.

Being and Nothingness

Hell is other people. 2

In Camera

I confused things with their names: that is belief. 3

The Words

Sassoon Siegfried 1886–1967. English poet and novelist.

Soldiers are dreamers; when the guns begin / They think of
firelit homes, clean beds, and wives.

'Dreamers' 1918

Does it matter? – losing your sight? ... / There's such splendid 2
work for the blind; / And people will always be kind, / As you sit
on the terrace remembering / And turning your face to the light.

'Does it Matter'

Everyone suddenly burst out singing. 3

'Everyone Sang'

Sayers Dorothy L(eigh) 1893–1957. English writer.

I admit it is better fun to punt than to be punted, and that a desire
to have all the fun is nine-tenths of the law of chivalry.

Gaudy Night ch 14

As I grow older and older, / And totter towards the tomb, / I 2
find that I care less and less / Who goes to bed with whom.

'That's Why I Never Read Modern Novels'

Schiller Johann Christoph Friedrich von 1759–1805. German
dramatist, poet, and historian.

Against stupidity the gods themselves struggle in vain.

The Maid of Orleans

Schnabel Artur 1882–1951. Austrian pianist and composer.

The notes I handle no better than many pianists. But the pauses
between the notes – ah, that is where the art resides!

Chicago Daily News 11 June 1958

Schumacher E F 1911–1977. German economist.

Small Is Beautiful.

Book title

Schweitzer Albert 1875–1965. French missionary surgeon.

'Reverence for Life'.

My Life and Thought ch 13

Scott Robert Falcon (known as *Scott of the Antarctic*) 1868–1912. English explorer.

Great God! this is an awful place.

On the South Pole, in Diary 17 Jan 1912

Scott Walter 1771–1832. Scottish novelist and poet.

Come fill up my cup, come fill up my can, / Come saddle your horses, and call up your men; / Come open the West Port, and let me gang free, / And it's room for the bonnets of Bonny Dundee!

'Bonnie Dundee'

But answer came there none. 2

The Bridal of Triermain

Look not thou on beauty's charming, / Sit thou still when kings 3
are arming, / Taste not when the wine-cup glistens, / Speak not when the people listens, / Stop thine ear against the singer, / From the red gold keep thy finger; / Vacant heart and hand, and eye, / Easy live and quiet die.

The Bride of Lammermoor

The hour is come, but not the man. 4

The Heart of Midlothian

Yet seem'd that tone, and gesture bland, / Less used to sue than 5
to command.

The Lady of the Lake

Breathes there the man, with soul so dead, / Who never to 6
himself hath said, / This is my own, my native land!

The Lay of the Last Minstrel VI. 1

O Caledonia! stern and wild, / Meet nurse for a poetic child!   **7**
> *The Lay of the Last Minstrel* VI. 2

O, young Lochinvar is come out of the west, / Through all the   **8**
wide Border his steed was the best.
> *Marmion* V. 12

And dar'st thou then / To beard the lion in his den, / The   **9**
Douglas in his hall?
> *Marmion* VI. 14

O what a tangled web we weave, / When first we practise to   **10**
deceive!
> *Marmion* VI. 17

O Woman! in our hours of ease, / Uncertain, coy, and hard to   **11**
please, ... / When pain and anguish wring the brow, / A
ministering angel thou!
> *Marmion* VI. 30

My heart's in the Highlands, my heart is not here, / My heart's   **12**
in the Highlands a-chasing the deer; / A-chasing the wild deer,
and following the roe, / My heart's in the Highlands wherever
I go.
> *Waverley*

Sedley Charles 1639–1701. English courtier and poet.

Love still has something of the sea / From whence his mother
rose.
> 'Love still has Something'

Seeger 1888–1916. US poet.

I have a rendezvous with Death / At some disputed barricade.
> 'I Have a Rendezvous with Death'

Selden John 1584–1654. English jurist and historian.

Old friends are best. King James used to call for his old shoes;
they were easiest for his feet.
> *Table Talk*, 'Friends'

'Tis not the drinking that is to be blamed, but the excess.   **2**
> *Table Talk*, 'Humility'

Ignorance of the law excuses no man; not that all men know the   *3*
law, but because 'tis an excuse every man will plead, and no
man can tell how to confute him.
>   *Table Talk*, 'Law'

Philosophy is nothing but discretion.   *4*
>   *Table Talk*, 'Philosophy'

Pleasure is nothing else but the intermission of pain.   *5*
>   *Table Talk*, 'Pleasure'

Sellar W C 1898–1951 and **Yeatman** R J 1898–1968. English writers.

The Roman Conquest was, however, a *Good Thing*, since the
Britons were only natives at the time.
>   *1066 and All That* ch 1

The utterly memorable Struggle between the Cavaliers (Wrong   *2*
but Wromantic) and the Roundheads (Right but Repulsive).
>   *1066 and All That* ch 35

Gladstone ... spent his declining years trying to guess the   *3*
answer to the Irish Question; unfortunately whenever he was
getting warm, the Irish secretly changed the Question.
>   *1066 and All That* ch 57

Seward Thomas 1708–1790. English cleric.

Seven wealthy towns contend for Homer dead, / Through
which the living Homer begg'd his bread.
>   'On Homer'

Shadwell Thomas 1642–1692. English dramatist and poet.

'Tis the way of all flesh.
>   *The Sullen Lovers*

The haste of a fool is the slowest thing in the world.   *2*
>   *A True Widow* III. i

Every man loves what he is good at.   *3*
>   *A True Widow* V. i

Shakespeare William 1564–1616. English dramatist and poet.

My friends were poor but honest.
All's Well That Ends Well I. iii

Praising what is lost / Makes the remembrance dear. **2**
All's Well That Ends Well V. iii

Let Rome in Tiber melt, and the wide arch / Of the rang'd **3**
empire fall! Here is my space. / Kingdoms are clay.
Antony and Cleopatra I. i

In Nature's infinite book of secrecy / A little I can read. **4**
Antony and Cleopatra I. ii

Eternity was in our lips and eyes. **5**
Antony and Cleopatra I. iii

My salad days, / When I was green in judgment. **6**
Antony and Cleopatra I. v

Age cannot wither her, nor custom stale / Her infinite variety. **7**
Antony and Cleopatra II. ii

I do not much dislike the matter, but / The manner of his speech. **8**
Antony and Cleopatra II. ii

The barge she sat in, like a burnish'd throne, / Burn'd on the **9**
water; the poop was beaten gold, / Purple the sails, and so
perfumed, that / The winds were love-sick with them, the oars
were silver, / Which to the tune of flutes kept stroke, and made /
The water which they beat to follow faster, / As amorous of
their strokes.
Antony and Cleopatra II. ii

No worse a husband than the best of men. **10**
Antony and Cleopatra II. ii

I laugh'd him out of patience; and that night / I laugh'd him **11**
into patience.
Antony and Cleopatra II. v

We have kiss'd away / Kingdoms and provinces. **12**
Antony and Cleopatra III. viii

Let's have one other gaudy night. **13**
Antony and Cleopatra III. xi

O infinite virtue! com'st thou smiling from / The world's great **14**
snare uncaught?
Antony and Cleopatra IV. viii

I am dying, Egypt, dying. **15**
Antony and Cleopatra IV. xiii

O! see my women, / The crown o' the earth doth melt. My lord! **16**
/ O! wither'd is the garland of the war, / The soldier's pole is
fall'n; young boys and girls / Are level now with men; the
odds is gone, / And there is nothing left remarkable / Beneath
the visiting moon.
Antony and Cleopatra IV. xiii

What's brave, what's noble, / Let's do it after the high Roman **17**
fashion, / And make death proud to take us.
Antony and Cleopatra IV. xiii

His delights / Were dolphin-like, they show'd his back above / **18**
The element they liv'd in.
Antony and Cleopatra V. ii

I have / Immortal longings in me. **19**
Antony and Cleopatra V. ii

A lass unparallel'd. **20**
Antony and Cleopatra V. ii

Sweet are the uses of adversity, ... / And this our life, exempt **21**
from public haunt, / Finds tongues in trees, books in the
running brooks, / Sermons in stones, and good in everything.
As You Like It II. i

Under the greenwood tree / Who loves to lie with me. **22**
As You Like It II. v

All the world's a stage, / And all the men and women merely **23**
players: / They have their exits and their entrances; / And one
man in his time plays many parts, / His acts being seven ages.
As You Like It II. vii

Blow, blow, thou winter wind, / Thou art not so unkind / As **24**
man's ingratitude.
As You Like It II. vii

Last scene of all, / That ends this strange eventful history, / Is 25
second childishness, and mere oblivion, / Sans teeth, sans eyes,
sans taste, sans everything.

As You Like It II. vii

Most friendship is feigning, most loving mere folly. 26

As You Like It II. vii

A motley fool. 27

As You Like It II. vii

I do desire we may be better strangers. 28

As You Like It III. ii

Men have died from time to time, and worms have eaten them, 29
but not for love.

As You Like It IV. i

It was a lover and his lass. 30

As You Like It V. iii

Fear no more the heat o' the sun, / Nor the furious winter's rages; 31
/ Thou thy worldly task hast done, / Home art gone and ta'en thy
wages: / Golden lads and girls all must, / As chimney-sweepers,
come to dust.

Cymbeline IV. ii

But, look, the morn, in russet mantle clad, / Walks o'er the dew 32
of yon high eastward hill.

Hamlet I. i

For this relief much thanks; 'tis bitter cold, / And I am sick at 33
heart.

Hamlet I. i

A countenance more in sorrow than in anger. 34

Hamlet I. ii

He was a man, take him for all in all, / I shall not look upon his 35
like again.

Hamlet I. ii

A little more than kin, and less than kind. 36

Hamlet I. ii

O! that this too too solid flesh would melt, / Thaw, and resolve   *37*
itself into a dew.

Hamlet I. ii

Thrift, thrift, Horatio! the funeral bak'd meats / Did coldly   *38*
furnish forth the marriage tables.

Hamlet I. ii

Neither a borrower, nor a lender be; / For loan oft loses both   *39*
itself and friend, / And borrowing dulls the edge of husbandry.
Hamlet I. iii

Costly thy habit as thy purse can buy, / But not express'd in   *40*
fancy, rich, not gaudy; / For the apparel oft proclaims the man.
Hamlet I. iii

The friends thou hast, and their adoption tried, / Grapple them   *41*
to thy soul with hoops of steel.

Hamlet I. iii

Meet it is I set it down, / That one may smile, and smile, and   *42*
be a villain.

Hamlet I. iv

Something is rotten in the state of Denmark.   *43*
Hamlet I. iv

There are more things in heaven and earth, Horatio, / Than are   *44*
dreamt of in your philosophy.

Hamlet I. iv

Though I am native here, / And to the manner born, – it is a   *45*
custom / More honour'd in the breach than the observance.
Hamlet I. iv

The time is out of joint; O cursed spite, / That ever I was born   *46*
to set it right!

Hamlet I. iv

To put an antic disposition on.   *47*
Hamlet I. iv

Brevity is the soul of wit.   *48*
Hamlet II. i

More matter with less art. **49**

Hamlet II. i

I could be bounded in a nut-shell, and count myself a king of **50**
infinite space, were it not that I have bad dreams.

Hamlet II. ii

That he is mad, 'tis true; 'tis true 'tis pity; / And pity 'tis 'tis true. **51**

Hamlet II. ii

There is nothing either good or bad, but thinking makes it so. **52**

Hamlet II. ii

Though this be madness, yet there is method in it. **53**

Hamlet II. ii

Get thee to a nunnery. **54**

Hamlet III. i

Let the doors be shut upon him, that he may play the fool **55**
nowhere but in's own house.

Hamlet III. i

O! what a noble mind is here o'erthrown: / The courtier's, **56**
soldier's, scholar's, eye, tongue, sword.

Hamlet III. i

Thus conscience doth make cowards of us all. **57**

Hamlet III. i

'Tis a consummation / Devoutly to be wish'd. **58**

Hamlet III. i

To be, or not to be: that is the question: / Whether 'tis nobler in **59**
the mind to suffer / The slings and arrows of outrageous fortune,
/ Or to take arms against a sea of troubles, / And by opposing
end them?

Hamlet III. i

The undiscover'd country from whose bourn / No traveller **60**
returns.

Hamlet III. i

With this regard their currents turn awry, / And lose the name **61**
of action.

Hamlet III. i

The lady doth protest too much, methinks.   *62*
Hamlet III. ii

A man that fortune's buffets and rewards / Hast ta'en with   *63*
equal thanks.
Hamlet III. ii

Suit the action to the word, the word to the action.   *64*
Hamlet III. iii

I must be cruel, only to be kind.   *65*
Hamlet III. iv

'Tis now the very witching time of night.   *66*
Hamlet III. iv

How all occasions do inform against me, / And spur my dull   *67*
revenge!
Hamlet IV. iii

Alas! poor Yorick. I knew him, Horatio; a fellow of infinite jest,   *68*
of most excellent fancy.
Hamlet V. i

Imperious Caesar, dead, and turn'd to clay, / Might stop a hole   *69*
to keep the wind away.
Hamlet V. i

A hit, a very palpable hit.   *70*
Hamlet V. ii

If thou didst ever hold me in thy heart, / Absent thee from   *71*
felicity awhile.
Hamlet V. ii

Not a whit, we defy augury; there's a special providence in the   *72*
fall of a sparrow. If it be now, 'tis not to come; if it be not to
come, it will be now; if it be not now, yet it will come: the
readiness is all.
Hamlet V. ii

The rest is silence.   *73*
Hamlet V. ii

There's a divinity that shapes our ends, / Rough-hew them how we will. **74**

> *Hamlet* V. ii

If all the year were playing holidays, / To sport would be as tedious as to work; / But when they seldom come, they wish'd for come. **75**

> *1 Henry IV* I. ii

Instinct is a great matter, I was a coward on instinct. **76**

> *1 Henry IV* II. iv

There live not three good men unhanged in England, and one of them is fat and grows old. **77**

> *1 Henry IV* II. iv

I am as vigilant as a cat to steal cream. **78**

> *1 Henry IV* IV. ii

Rebellion lay in his way, and he found it. **79**

> *1 Henry IV* V. i

The better part of valour is discretion. **80**

> *1 Henry IV* V. iv

I could have better spar'd a better man. **81**

> *1 Henry IV* V. iv

It is the disease of not listening, the malady of not marking, that I am troubled withal. **82**

> *2 Henry IV* I. ii

Uneasy lies the head that wears a crown. **83**

> *2 Henry IV* III. i

A soldier is better accommodated than with a wife. **84**

> *2 Henry IV* III. ii

We have heard the chimes at midnight. **85**

> *2 Henry IV* III. ii

Follow your spirit; and, upon this charge / Cry 'God for Harry! England and Saint George!' **86**

> *Henry V* III. i

Once more unto the breach, dear friends, once more.   **87**
                                            Henry V III. i

O God of battles! steel my soldiers hearts; / Possess them not   **88**
with fear.
                                            Henry V IV. i

We few, we happy few, we band of brothers.   **89**
                                            Henry V IV. iii

We would not die in that man's company / That fears his   **90**
fellowship to die with us.
                                            Henry V IV. iii

A little touch of Harry in the night.   **91**
                                      Henry V IV. chorus

Men's evil manners live in brass; their virtues / We write in   **92**
water.
                                        Henry VIII IV. ii

Beware the Ides of March.   **93**
                                       Julius Caesar I. i

For mine own part, it was Greek to me.   **94**
                                      Julius Caesar I. ii

He reads much; / He is a great observer, and he looks / Quite   **95**
through the deeds of men.
                                      Julius Caesar I. ii

Let me have men about me that are fat; / Sleek-headed men and   **96**
such as sleep o' nights; / Yond' Cassius has a lean and hungry
look; / He thinks too much: such men are dangerous.
                                      Julius Caesar I. ii

Men at some time are masters of their fates: / The fault, dear   **97**
Brutus, is not in our stars, / But in ourselves, that we are
underlings.
                                      Julius Caesar I. ii

Ye gods, it doth amaze me, / A man of such a feeble temper   **98**
should / So get the start of the majestic world, / And bear the

palm alone.
> *Julius Caesar* I. ii

But men may construe things after their own fashion, / Clean   **99**
from the purpose of the things themselves.
> *Julius Caesar* I. iii

It is the bright day that brings forth the adder; / And that craves   **100**
wary walking.
> *Julius Cæsar* II. i

That lowliness is young ambition's ladder, / Whereto the   **101**
climber-upward turns his face.
> *Julius Caesar* II. i

Cowards die many times before their deaths / The valiant   **102**
never taste of death but once.
> *Julius Cæsar* II. ii

The choice and master spirits of this age.   **103**
> *Julius Cæsar* III. i

O mighty Cæsar! dost thou lie so low?   **104**
> *Julius Cæsar* III. i

Thou art the ruins of the noblest man / That ever lived in the tide   **105**
of times.
> *Julius Cæsar* III. i

For Brutus is an honourable man; / So are they all, all   **106**
honourable men.
> *Julius Cæsar* III. ii

Friends, Romans, countrymen, lend me your ears; / I come to   **107**
bury Cæsar, not to praise him.
> *Julius Caesar* III. ii

If you have tears, prepare to shed them now.   **108**
> *Julius Cæsar* III. ii

Not that I loved Cæsar less, but that I loved Rome more.   **109**
> *Julius Cæsar* III. ii

This was the most unkindest cut of all.   **110**
> *Julius Caesar* III. ii

When that the poor have cried, Cæsar hath wept; / Ambition   ***111***
should be made of sterner stuff.

Julius Cæsar III. ii

There is a tide in the affairs of men, / Which, taken at the flood,   ***112***
leads on to fortune.

Julius Caesar IV. iii

O! that a man might know / The end of this day's business, ere   ***113***
it come; / But it sufficeth that the day will end, / And then the
end is known.

Julius Caesar V. i

This was the noblest Roman of them all.   ***114***

Julius Caesar V. v

To gild refined gold, to paint the lily, / To throw a perfume on   ***115***
the violet, ... / Is wasteful and ridiculous excess.

King John IV. ii

We make guilty of our disasters the sun, the moon, and the   ***116***
stars; as if we were villains by necessity, fools by heavenly
compulsion.

King Lear I. ii

Have more than thou showest, / Speak less than thou knowest, /   ***117***
Lend less than thou owest.

King Lear I. iv

How sharper than a serpent's tooth it is / To have a thankless   ***118***
child!

King Lear I. iv

O! that way madness lies; let me shun that.   ***119***

King Lear III. iv

The prince of darkness is a gentleman.   ***120***

King Lear III. iv

As flies to wanton boys, are we to the gods; / They kill us for   ***121***
their sport.

King Lear IV. i

Ay, every inch a king. *122*

King Lear IV. vi

When we are born we cry that we are come / To this great stage *123*
of fools.

King Lear IV. vi

I am a very foolish, fond old man, / Fourscore and upward, not *124*
an hour more or less; / And, to deal plainly, / I fear I am not in
my perfect mind.

King Lear IV. vii

Men must endure / Their going hence, even as their coming *125*
hither: / Ripeness is all.

King Lear V. ii

The gods are just, and of our pleasant vices / Make instruments *126*
to plague us.

King Lear V. iii

Her voice was ever soft, / Gentle, and low, an excellent thing in *127*
woman.

King Lear V. iii

The wheel has come full circle. *128*

King Lear V. iii

They have been at a great feast of languages, and stolen the *129*
scraps.

Love's Labour's Lost V. i

Cuckoo, cuckoo; O, word of fear, / Unpleasing to a married ear! *130*
Love's Labour's Lost V. ii

In russet yeas and honest kersey noes. *131*
Love's Labour's Lost V. ii

A world-without-end bargain. *132*
Love's Labour's Lost V. ii

Fair is foul, and foul is fair: / Hover through the fog and filthy air. *133*
Macbeth I. i

When shall we three meet again / In thunder, lightning, or in rain? *134*
Macbeth I. i

Yet do I fear thy nature; / It is too full o' the milk of human   *135*
kindness / To catch the nearest way.
                                                Macbeth I. v

But screw your courage to the sticking-place, / And we'll not fail.   *136*
                                                Macbeth I. vii

If it were done when 'tis done, then 'twere well / It were done   *137*
quickly.
                                                Macbeth I. vii

Is this a dagger which I see before me, / The handle toward my   *138*
hand?
                                                Macbeth II. i

The primrose way to the everlasting bonfire.   *139*
                                                Macbeth II. iii

Stand not upon the order of your going. / But go at once.   *140*
                                                Macbeth III. iv

But yet I'll make assurance double sure.   *141*
                                                Macbeth IV. i

By the pricking of my thumbs, / Something wicked this way   *142*
comes.
                                                Macbeth IV. i

A deed without a name.   *143*
                                                Macbeth IV. i

Double, double toil and trouble; / Fire burn, and cauldron   *144*
bubble.
                                                Macbeth IV. i

Out, damned spot!   *145*
                                                Macbeth IV. v

All the perfumes of Arabia will not sweeten this little hand.   *146*
                                                Macbeth V. i

I have lived long enough: my way of life / Is fall'n into the sear,   *147*
the yellow leaf; / And that which should accompany old age, /
As honour, love, obedience, troops of friends, / I must not look
to have.
                                                Macbeth V. iii

Blow, wind! come, wrack! / At least we'll die with harness on **148**
our back.

> *Macbeth* V. v

To-morrow, and to-morrow, and to-morrow, / Creeps in this **149**
petty pace from day to day, / To the last syllable of recorded
time; / And all our yesterdays have lighted fools / The way to
dusty death. Out, out, brief candle! / Life's but a walking
shadow, a poor player, / That struts and frets his hour upon the
stage, / And then is heard no more; it is a tale / Told by an idiot,
full of sound and fury, / Signifying nothing.

> *Macbeth* V. v

Man, proud man, / Drest in a little brief authority, / Most **150**
ignorant of what he's most assur'd, / His glassy essence, like
an angry ape, / Plays such fantastic tricks before high heaven, /
As make the angels weep.

> *Measure for Measure* II. ii

Be absolute for death; either death or life / Shall thereby be the **151**
sweeter.

> *Measure for Measure* III. i

Take, O take those lips away, / That so sweetly were forsworn. **152**
> *Measure for Measure* III. i

I am a kind of burr; I shall stick. **153**
> *Measure for Measure* III. iii

My daughter! O my ducats! O my daughter! / Fled with a **154**
Christian! O my Christian ducats!

> *The Merchant of Venice* II. viii

A Daniel come to judgment! **155**
> *The Merchant of Venice* IV. i

A harmless necessary cat. **156**
> *The Merchant of Venice* IV. i

The quality of mercy is not strain'd, / It droppeth as the gentle **157**
rain from heaven / Upon the place beneath: it is twice bless'd; / It
blesseth him that gives and him that takes.

> *The Merchant of Venice* IV. i

I will make a Star-Chamber matter of it.   *158*
                                The Merry Wives of Windsor I. i

Marry, this is the short and the long of it.   *159*
                                The Merry Wives of Windsor II. ii

Why, then the world's mine oyster.   *160*
                                The Merry Wives of Windsor II. ii

The course of true love never did run smooth.   *161*
                                A Midsummer Night's Dream I. i

Love looks not with the eyes, but with the mind, / And   *162*
therefore is wing'd Cupid painted blind.
                                A Midsummer Night's Dream I. i

I'll put a girdle round about the earth / In forty minutes.   *163*
                                A Midsummer Night's Dream II. i

Bless thee, Bottom! bless thee! thou art translated.   *164*
                                A Midsummer Night's Dream III. i

Jack shall have Jill; / Nought shall go ill; / The man shall have   *165*
his mare again, / And all shall be well.
                                A Midsummer Night's Dream III. ii

Lord, what fools these mortals be!   *166*
                                A Midsummer Night's Dream III. ii

The eye of man hath not heard, the ear of man hath not seen,   *167*
man's hand is not able to taste, his tongue to conceive, nor his
heart to report, what my dream was.
                                A Midsummer Night's Dream IV. i

And, as imagination bodies forth / The forms of things   *168*
unknown, the poet's pen / Turns them to shapes, and gives to
airy nothing / A local habitation and a name. / Such tricks hath
strong imagination, / That, if it would but apprehend some joy,
/ It comprehends some bringer of that joy; / Or in the night,
imagining some fear, / How easy is a bush suppos'd a bear!
                                A Midsummer Night's Dream V. i

The best in this kind are but shadows, and the worst are no worse, if imagination amend them.   ***169***
A Midsummer Night's Dream V. i

The lunatic, the lover, and the poet, / Are of imagination all compact.   ***170***
A Midsummer Night's Dream V. i

He is a very valiant trencher-man.   ***171***
Much Ado About Nothing I. i

Would it not grieve a woman to be over-mastered with a piece of valiant dust?   ***172***
Much Ado About Nothing I. ii

Sigh no more, ladies, sigh no more, / Men were deceivers ever.   ***173***
Much Ado About Nothing I. iii

There was a star danced, and under that was I born.   ***174***
Much Ado About Nothing I. iii

For there was never yet philosopher / That could endure the toothache patiently.   ***175***
Much Ado About Nothing V. i

The beast with two backs.   ***176***
Othello I. i

She lov'd me for the dangers I had pass'd, / And I lov'd her that she did pity them.   ***177***
Othello I. iii

Good name in man or woman, dear my lord, / Is the immediate jewel of their souls; / Who steals my purse steals trash; 'tis something, / nothing; / 'Twas mine, 'tis his, and has been slave to thousands; / But he that filches from me my good name / Robs me of that which not enriches him, / And makes me poor indeed.   ***178***
Othello III. iii

O! beware, my lord, of jealousy; / It is the green-ey'd monster which doth mock / The meat it feeds on.   ***179***
Othello III. iii

Sing willow, willow, willow: / Sing all a green willow must be   ***180***
my garland.

Othello IV. iii

I have done the state some service, and they know 't; / No more   ***181***
of that. I pray you, in your letters, / When you shall these
unlucky deeds relate, / Speak of me as I am; nothing extenuate,
/ Nor set down aught in malice: then, must you speak / Of one
that lov'd not wisely but too well; / Of one not easily jealous,
but, being wrought, / Perplex'd in the extreme.

Othello V. iii

There is no virtue like necessity.   ***182***

Richard II I. iii

This royal throne of kings, this scepter'd isle, / This earth of   ***183***
majesty, this seat of Mars, / This other Eden, demi-Paradise,
/ This fortress built by Nature for herself / Against infection
and the hand of war, / This happy breed of men, this little world,
/ This precious stone set in the silver sea, ... / This blessed plot,
this earth, this realm, this England.

Richard II II. i

How sour sweet music is, / When time is broke, and no   ***184***
proportion kept!

Richard II V. i

Now is the winter of our discontent / Made glorious summer   ***185***
by this sun of York.

Richard III I. i

An honest tale speeds best being plainly told.   ***186***

Richard III IV. ii

I am not in the giving vein to-day.   ***187***

Richard III IV. ii

A horse! a horse! my kingdom for a horse!   ***188***

Richard III V. iv

O Romeo, Romeo! wherefore art thou Romeo?   ***189***

Romeo and Juliet II. ii

What's in a name? that which we call a rose / By any other   **190**
name would smell as sweet.

Romeo and Juliet II. ii

A plague o' both your houses!   **191**

Romeo and Juliet III. i

This is the way to kill a wife with kindness.   **192**

The Taming of the Shrew IV. i

Full fathom five thy father lies; / Of his bones are coral made: /   **193**
Those are pearls that were his eyes: / Nothing of him that doth
fade, / But doth suffer a sea-change / Into something rich and
strange.

The Tempest I. ii

My library / Was dukedom large enough.   **194**

The Tempest I. ii

What seest thou else / In the dark backward and abysm of time?   **195**

The Tempest I. ii

You taught me language; and my profit on't / Is, I know how to   **196**
curse.

The Tempest I. ii

The isle is full of noises, / Sounds and sweet airs, that give   **197**
delight, and hurt not.

The Tempest III. ii

We are such stuff / As dreams are made on, and our little life / Is   **198**
rounded with a sleep.

The Tempest IV. i

Deeper than did ever plummet sound, / I'll drown my book.   **199**

The Tempest V. i

O brave new world, / That has such people in 't.   **200**

The Tempest V. i

Nothing emboldens sin so much as mercy.   **201**

Timon of Athens III. v

To be wise, and love, / Exceeds man's might.   **202**

Troilus and Cressida III. ii

Time hath, my lord, a wallet at his back, / Wherein he puts   ***203***
alms for oblivion.

Troilus and Cressida III. iii

If music be the food of love, play on; / Give me excess of it,   ***204***
that, surfeiting, / The appetite may sicken, and so die. / That
strain again! it had a dying fall.

Twelfth Night I. i

Many a good hanging prevents a bad marriage.   ***205***

Twelfth Night I. v

O! you are sick of self-love, Malvolio.   ***206***

Twelfth Night I. v

Dost thou think, because thou art virtuous, there shall be no   ***207***
more cakes and ale?

Twelfth Night II. iii

O mistress mine! where are you roaming? / O! stay and hear;   ***208***
your true love's coming, / That can sing both high and low. /
Trip no further, pretty sweeting; / Journeys end in lovers
meeting, / Every wise man's son doth know. / What is love?
'tis not hereafter; / Present mirth hath present laughter; / What's
to come is still unsure: / In delay there lies no plenty; / Then
come kiss me, sweet and twenty, / Youth's a stuff will not
endure.

Twelfth Night II. iii

Come away, come away, death, / And in sad cypress let me be   ***209***
laid.

Twelfth Night II. iv

She sat like patience on a monument, / Smiling at grief.   ***210***

Twelfth Night II. iv

Some men are born great, some achieve greatness, and some   ***211***
have greatness thrust upon them.

Twelfth Night II. v

Why, this is very midsummer madness.   ***212***

Twelfth Night III. iv

And thus the whirligig of time brings in his revenges. *213*
Twelfth Night V. i

When that I was and a little tiny boy, / With hey, ho, the wind *214*
and the rain; / A foolish thing was but a toy, / For the rain it
raineth every day.
Twelfth Night V. i

Who is Silvia? what is she, / That all our swains commend her? *215*
The Two Gentlemen of Verona IV. ii

A snapper-up of unconsidered trifles. *216*
The Winter's Tale IV. ii

I love a ballad in print, ... for then we are sure they are true. *217*
The Winter's Tale IV. iii

Exit, pursued by a bear. *218*
The Winter's Tale, stage direction

A sad tale's best for winter. *219*
The Winter's Tale II. i

Shall I compare thee to a summer's day? / Thou art more lovely *220*
and more temperate: / Rough winds do shake the darling buds
of May, / And summer's lease hath all too short a date.
Sonnet 18

Full many a glorious morning have I seen / Flatter the *221*
mountain-tops with sovereign eye.
Sonnet 33

Not marble, nor the gilded monuments / Of princes, shall *222*
outlive this powerful rhyme.
Sonnet 55

Like as the waves make towards the pebbled shore, / So do our *223*
minutes hasten to their end.
Sonnet 60

No longer mourn for me when I am dead / Than you shall hear *224*
the surly sullen bell / Give warning to the world that I am fled.
Sonnet 71

That time of year thou mayst in me behold / When yellow   *225*
leaves, or none, or few, do hang / Upon those boughs which
shake against the cold, / Bare ruin'd choirs, where late the
sweet birds sang.

> Sonnet 73

Lilies that fester smell far worse than weeds.   *226*

> Sonnet 94

To me, fair friend, you never can be old.   *227*

> Sonnet 104

Let me not to the marriage of true minds / Admit impediments. *228*

> Sonnet 116

My mistress' eyes are nothing like the sun.   *229*

> Sonnet 130

Good friend, for Jesu's sake forbear / To dig the dust enclosed *230*
here. / Blest be the man that spares these stones, / And curst be
he that moves my bones.

> Epitaph on Shakespeare's grave in Stratford-upon-Avon church

Shamir Yitzhak 1915– . Polish-born Israeli right-wing politician.

Our image has undergone a change from David fighting
Goliath to being Goliath.

> On Israel in the *Observer* Jan 1989

Shaw George Bernard 1856–1950. Irish dramatist.

Anarchism is a game at which the Police can beat you.

> *Misalliance*

There is only one religion, though there are a hundred versions *2*
of it.

> *Arms and the Man* preface

When a stupid man is doing something he is ashamed of, he *3*
always declares that it is his duty.

> *Caesar and Cleopatra* III

Do you think that the things people make fools of themselves **4**
about are any less real and true than the things they behave
sensibly about?

Candida I

We have no more right to consume happiness without **5**
producing it than to consume wealth without producing it.

Candida I

A lifetime of happiness: No man alive could bear it: it would be **6**
hell on earth.

Man and Superman I

The more things a man is ashamed of, the more respectable he is. **7**

Man and Superman I

An Englishman thinks he is moral when he is only **8**
uncomfortable.

Man and Superman III

There are two tragedies in life. One is not to get your heart's **9**
desire. The other is to get it.

Man and Superman IV

Do not do unto others as you would they should do unto you. **10**
Their tastes may not be the same.

Maxims for Revolutionists

Home is the girl's prison and the woman's workhouse. **11**

Maxims for Revolutionists

The fickleness of the women I love is only equalled by the **12**
infernal constancy of the women who love me.

The Philanderer

How can what an Englishman believes be heresy? It is a **13**
contradiction in terms.

St. Joan IV

Must then a Christ perish in torment in every age to save those **14**
that have no imagination?

St Joan Epilogue

Shawn Ted 1891–1972. US dancer and choreographer.

Dance is the only art of which we ourselves are the stuff of which it is made.

Time July 1955

Shelley Percy Bysshe 1792–1822. English lyric poet.

He hath awakened from the dream of life.

Adonais 39

From the contagion of the world's slow stain / He is secure, and now can never mourn / A heart grown cold, a head grown grey in vain.   **2**

Adonais 40

Poets are the unacknowledged legislators of the world.   **3**
A Defence of Poetry

I never was attached to that great sect, / Whose doctrine is, that each one should select / Out of the crowd a mistress or a friend, / And all the rest, though fair and wise, commend / To cold oblivion.   **4**

Epipsychidion

Let there be light! said Liberty, / And like sunrise from the sea, / Athens arose!   **5**

Hellas

I met Murder in the way – / He had a mask like Castlereagh.   **6**
The Mask of Anarchy

O wild West Wind, thou breath of Autumn's being, / Thou, from whose unseen presence the leaves dead / Are driven, like ghosts from an enchanter fleeing.   **7**

Ode to the West Wind

My name is Ozymandias, king of kings: / Look on my works, ye Mighty, and despair!   **8**

'Ozymandias'

Hail to thee, blithe spirit! / Bird thou never wert, / That from Heaven, or near it, / Pourest thy full heart / In profuse strains of   **9** unpremeditated art.

'To a Skylark'

Shenstone William 1714–1763. English poet and essayist.

Laws are generally found to be nets of such a texture, as the
little creep through, the great break through, and the middle-
sized are alone entangled in.

Essays, 'On Politics'

Sheridan Richard Brinsley 1751–1816. Irish dramatist and politician.

When a heroine goes mad she always goes into white satin.
The Critic III

'Tis safest in matrimony to begin with a little aversion.
The Rivals I.

2

Our ancestors are very good kind of folks; but they are the last
people I should choose to have a visiting acquaintance with.
The Rivals IV.

3

Here's to the maiden of bashful fifteen; / Here's to the widow of
fifty; / Here's to the flaunting, extravagant quean; / And here's
to the housewife that's thrifty.

4

The School for Scandal III

Sherman William Tecumseh 1820–1891. US Union general in the
American Civil War.

There is many a boy here to-day who looks on war as all glory,
but, boys, it is all hell.

Speech 1880

Shirley James 1596–1666. English dramatist.

The glories of our blood and state / Are shadows, not substantial
things;

The Contention of Ajax and Ulysses I

Shostakovich Dmitry (Dmitriyevich) 1906–1975. Soviet composer.

A Soviet composer's reply to just criticism.

Epigraph to his fifth symphony

Sidney Philip 1554–1586. English poet and soldier.

Thy necessity is yet greater than mine.
> On giving his water-bottle to a critically wounded
> soldier at the Battle of Zutphen 1586

Who shoots at the mid-day sun, though he be sure he shall   2
never hit the mark; yet as sure he is he shall shoot higher than
who aims but at a bush.
> *Arcadia* II

My true love hath my heart and I have his, / By just exchange   3
one for the other giv'n.
> *Arcadia* III

'Fool!' said my Muse to me, 'look in thy heart, and write.'   4
> *Astrophel and Stella* Sonnet 1

With how sad steps, O Moon, thou climb'st the skies! / How   5
silently, and with how wan a face!
> *Astrophel and Stella* Sonnet 31

With a tale forsooth he cometh unto you, with a tale which   6
holdeth children from play, and old men from the chimney
corner.
> *The Defence of Poesy*

Sieyès Emmanuel Joseph 1748–1836. French statesman.

I survived.
> Answer on being asked what he had
> done during the French Revolution

Sillitoe Alan 1928– . English novelist.

The Loneliness of the Long-Distance Runner.
> *Title of novel*

Slim William Joseph, 1st Viscount 1891–1970. British field marshal
in World War II.

In a battle nothing is ever as good or as bad as the first reports
of excited men would have it.
> *Unofficial History*

Smart Elizabeth 1913–1986. US poet.

By Grand Central Station I Sat Down and Wept.

Book title

Smiles Samuel 1812–1904. Scottish writer.

The shortest way to do many things is to do only one thing at once.
Self Help

A place for everything, and everything in its place. *2*

Thrift

Smith Adam 1723–1790. Scottish economist, often regarded as the founder of political economy.

To found a great empire for the sole purpose of raising up a people of customers, may at first sight appear a project fit only for a nation of shopkeepers. It is, however, a project altogether unfit for a nation of shopkeepers; but extremely fit for a nation that is governed by shopkeepers.

Wealth of Nations

Smith F E (1st Earl of Birkenhead) 1872–1930. English politician and lawyer.

The world continues to offer glittering prizes to those who have stout hearts and sharp swords.
Rectorial Address, Glasgow University 1923

We have the highest authority for believing that the meek shall *2* inherit the Earth; though I have never found any particular corroboration of this aphorism in the records of Somerset House.

'Marquess Curzon'

Smith Logan Pearsall 1865–1946. US-born English writer.

People say that life is the thing, but I prefer reading.
Afterthoughts

There are few sorrows, however poignant, in which a good *2* income is of no avail.

Afterthoughts

There are two things to aim at in life: first, to get what you *3*
want; and, after that, to enjoy it. Only the wisest of mankind
achieve the second.

Afterthoughts

Smith Stevie (Florence Margaret) 1902–1971. British poet and novelist.

I was much too far out all my life / And not waving but drowning.
'Not Waving but Drowning'

Smith Sydney 1771–1845. English journalist, clergyman and wit.

I have no relish for the country; it is a kind of healthy grave.
Letter to Miss G Harcourt 1838

Show me a man who cares no more for one place than another, *2*
and I will show you in that same person one who loves nothing
but himself. Beware of those who are homeless by choice.

The Doctor

What bishops like best in their clergy is a dropping-down- *3*
deadness of manner.

First Letter to Archdeacon Singleton

Poverty is no disgrace to a man, but it is confoundedly *4*
inconvenient.

His Wit and Wisdom

As the French say, there are three sexes – men, women, and *5*
clergymen.

Lady Holland, *Memoirs*

He has occasional flashes of silence, that make his conversation *6*
perfectly delightful.

Of J B Macaulay, in Lady Holland, *Memoirs*

It requires a surgical operation to get a joke well into a Scotch *7*
understanding. Their only idea of wit ... is laughing
immoderately at stated intervals.

Lady Holland, *Memoirs*

Not body enough to cover his mind decently with; his intellect *8*
is improperly exposed.

Lady Holland, *Memoirs*

I am just going to pray for you at St. Paul's, but with no very lively hope of success.   **9**

H Pearson, *The Smith of Smiths*

I never read a book before reviewing it; it prejudices a man so.   **10**
H Pearson, *The Smith of Smiths*

My idea of heaven is, eating *pâté de foie gras* to the sound of trumpets.   **11**

H Pearson, *The Smith of Smiths*

What a pity it is that we have no amusements in England but vice and religion!   **12**

H Pearson, *The Smith of Smiths*

Solzhenitsyn Alexander (Isayevich) 1918– . Soviet novelist, US citizen from 1974.

The salvation of mankind lies only in making everything the concern of all.

Nobel lecture 1970

You only have power over people as long as you don't take   **2**
everything away from them. But when you've robbed a man of *everything* he's no longer in your power – he's free again.

The First Circle

Sontag Susan 1933– . US critic, novelist, and screenwriter.

Interpretation is the revenge of the intellect upon art.

Against Interpretation

Sophocles *c*. 496–405 BC. Athenian dramatist.

None love the messenger who brings bad news.

Antigone

Wonders are many, and none is more wonderful than man.   **2**

Antigone

Southey Robert 1774–1843. English poet and author.

'And everybody praised the Duke, / Who this great fight did

win.' / 'But what good came of it at last?' / Quoth little
Peterkin. / 'Why that I cannot tell,' said he, / 'But 'twas a
famous victory.'

'The Battle of Blenheim'

Spark Muriel 1918– . Scottish novelist.

'I am putting old heads on your young shoulders ... and all my
pupils are the crème de la crème.'

The Prime of Miss Jean Brodie

Spencer Herbert 1820–1903. English philosopher.

Science is organized knowledge.

Education

The Republican form of Government is the highest form of   2
government; but because of this it requires the highest type
of human nature—a type nowhere, at present existing.

Essays, 'The Americans'

This survival of the fittest.   3

Principles of Biology

Education has for its object the formation of character.   4

Social Statics 2, ch 17

No one can be perfectly free till all are free; no one can be   5
perfectly moral till all are moral; no one can be perfectly happy
till all are happy.

Social Statics 4, ch 30

Spengler Oswald 1880–1936. German philosopher.

Christian theology is the grandmother of Bolshevism.

The Hour of Decision

Spenser Edmund *c.* 1552– . English poet.

Most glorious Lord of life, that on this day / Didst make thy
triumph over death and sin: / And, having harrow'd hell, didst
bring / Captivity thence captive, us to win.

Amoretti sonnet 68

A gentle knight was pricking on the plain.

The Faerie Queene I. 1

2

Sleep after toil, port after stormy seas, / Ease after war, death after life does greatly please.

The Faerie Queene I. 9

3

O goodly usage of those antique times, / In which the sword was servant unto right.

The Faerie Queene III. 1

4

O sacred hunger of ambitious minds.

The Faerie Queene V. 12

5

Sweet Thames, run softly, till I end my song.

Prothalamion

6

Spielberg Steven 1947– . US film director, writer, and producer.

I wanted the water to mean shark. The horizon to mean shark. I wanted the shark's presence to be felt everywhere.

On his film *Jaws*

Close Encounters of the Third Kind.

Film title

2

Spinoza Benedict or Baruch 1632–1677. Dutch philosopher.

We feel and know that we are eternal.

Ethics

Spooner William Archibald 1844–1930. Warden of New College, Oxford

Kinquering Congs their titles take.

Announcing the hymn in New College Chapel 1879

Squire J C 1884–1958. English journalist.

It did not last: the Devil howling 'Ho! / Let Einstein be!' restored the status quo.

Poems [Compare Pope 8]

Stanley Henry Morton. Adopted name of John Rowlands 1841–1904. Welsh-born US explorer and journalist.

Dr Livingstone, I presume?
> On meeting David Livingstone at Lake Tanganyika
> Nov 1871, in *How I Found Livingstone*

Stark Freya 1893–1993. English traveller, mountaineer, and writer.

The great and almost only comfort about being a woman is that one can always pretend to be more stupid than one is, and no one is surprised.
> *The Valley of the Assassins*

Steele Richard 1672–1729. Irish essayist and dramatist.

The insupportable labour of doing nothing.
> *Tatler*

To love her is a liberal education.   2
> *Tatler*

Steffens Lincoln 1866–1936. US journalist.

I have seen the future; and it works.
> Of the newly-formed Soviet Union,
> in letter to Marie Howe 3 Apr 1919

Stein Gertrude 1874–1946. US writer.

Anyone who marries three girls from St Louis hasn't learned much.
> Of Ernest Hemingway, in J R Mellow
> *Charmed Circle: Gertrude Stein and Company*

A rose is a rose is a rose, is a rose.   2
> *Sacred Emily*

You are all a lost generation.   3
> Ernest Hemingway *The Sun Also Rises* epigraph

Steinbeck John (Ernst) 1902–1968. US novelist.

I know this – a man got to do what he got to do.
> *Grapes of Wrath*

Steinem Gloria 1934–   . US journalist and liberal feminist.

A woman without a man is like a fish without a bicycle.
Attributed remark

Stendhal pen name of Marie Henri Beyle1783–1842. French novelist.

One can acquire everything in solitude except character.
On Love

Sterne Laurence 1713–1768. Irish writer.

I saw the iron enter into his soul!
A Sentimental Journey, 'The Captive'

There are worse occupations in this world than feeling a   2
woman's pulse.
A Sentimental Journey 'The Pulse'

They order, said I, this matter better in France.   3
A Sentimental Journey Opening words

A man should know something of his own country, too, before   4
he goes abroad.
Tristram Shandy

Said my mother, 'what is all this story about?' – 'A Cock and a   5
Bull,' said Yorick.
Tristram Shandy

'Tis known by the name of perseverance in a good cause, – and   6
of obstinacy in a bad one.
Tristram Shandy

Stevenson Adlai 1900–1965. US Democrat politician.

I suppose flattery hurts no one, that is, if he doesn't inhale.
TV broadcast 30 Mar 1952

There is no evil in the atom; only in men's souls.   2
Speech at Hartford Connecticut 18 Sept 1952

In America any boy may become President and I suppose it's   3
just one of the risks he takes!
Speech in Indianapolis 26 Sept 1952

My definition of a free society is a society where it is safe to be   **4**
unpopular.
                                        Speech in Detroit 7 Oct 1952

I have been thinking that I would make a proposition to my   **5**
Republican friends ... that if they will stop telling lies about the
Democrats, we will stop telling the truth about them.
                              Speech during 1952 presidential campaign

An editor is one who separates the wheat from the chaff and   **6**
prints the chaff.
                                              The Stevenson Wit

Stevenson Robert Louis 1850–1894. Scottish novelist.

Here lies one who meant well, tried a little, failed much: surely
that may be his epitaph, of which he need not be ashamed.
                          Across the Plains, 'A Christmas Sermon'

To make our idea of morality centre on forbidden acts is to   **2**
defile the imagination and to introduce into our judgments of
our fellow-men a secret element of gusto.
                          Across the Plains, 'A Christmas Sermon'

A child should always say what's true, / And speak when he is   **3**
spoken to, / And behave mannerly at table: / At least as far as
he is able.
              A Child's Garden of Verses, 'Whole Duty of Children'

I've a grand memory for forgetting.   **4**
                                                    Kidnapped

For my part, I travel not to go anywhere, but to go. I travel for   **5**
travel's sake. The great affair is to move.
                                        Travels with a Donkey

Fifteen men on the dead man's chest / Yo-ho-ho, and a bottle   **6**
of rum!
                                              Treasure Island

Go, little book, and wish to all / Flowers in the garden, meat in   **7**
the hall, / A bin of wine, a spice of wit, / A house with lawns

enclosing it, / A living river by the door, / A nightingale in the sycamore!

Underwoods, 'Envoy'

Under the wide and starry sky / Dig the grave and let me lie. /   8
Glad did I live and gladly die, / And I laid me down with a
will. / This be the verse you grave for me: / 'Here he lies where
he longed to be; / Home is the sailor, home from sea, / And the
hunter home from the hill.'

Underwoods, 'Requiem'

Stoppard Tom 1937–   . Czechoslovak-born English dramatist.

The bad end unhappily, the good unluckily. That is what
tragedy means.

Rosencrantz and Guildenstern Are Dead II

Eternity's a terrible thought. I mean, where's it all going to end?   2
Rosencrantz and Guildenstern Are Dead II

Life is a gamble, at terrible odds – if it was a bet, you wouldn't   3
take it.

Rosencrantz and Guildenstern Are Dead III

Stowe Harriet Beecher 1811–1896. US suffragist, abolitionist, and
author.

'Do you know who made you?' 'Nobody, as I knows on,' said
the child, with a short laugh. ... 'I 'spect I grow'd.'

Uncle Tom's Cabin

Stravinsky Igor 1882–1971. Russian-born composer.

Work brings inspiration, if inspiration is not discernible at the
beginning.

Chronicles of My Life

Suckling John 1609–1642. English poet and dramatist.

Why so pale and wan, fond lover? / Prithee, why so pale? / Will,
when looking well can't move her, / Looking ill prevail?

Aglaura, 'Song'

Suetonius (Gaius Suetonius Tranquillus) *c.* AD 69–   . Roman historian.

He so improved the city that he justly boasted that he found it brick and left it marble.
> *Lives of the Caesars*, 'Augustus'

Make haste slowly.   *2*
> *Lives of the Caesars*, 'Augustus'

Hail, Emperor, those who are about to die salute thee.   *3*
> *Lives of the Caesars*, 'Claudius'

So many men, so many opinions.   *4*
> *Phormio*

Surtees R S 1805–1864. English novelist

More people are flattered into virtue than bullied out of vice.
> *The Analysis of the Hunting Field*

'Unting is all that's worth living for ... it's the sport of kings,   *2*
the image of war without its guilt, and only five-and-twenty
per cent of its danger.
> *Handley Cross* ch 7

It ar'n't that I loves the fox less, but that I loves the 'ound   *3*
more.
> *Handley Cross* ch 16

He was a gentleman who was generally spoken of as having   *4*
nothing a-year, paid quarterly.
> *Mr Sponge's Sporting Tour*

Swaffer Hannen 1879–1962. British journalist.

Freedom of the press in Britain means freedom to print such of
the proprietor's prejudices as the advertisers don't object to.
> Tom Driberg *Swaff*

Swift Jonathan 1667–1745. Irish satirist and Anglican cleric.

Proper words in proper places, make the true definition of a style.
> *Letter to a Young Clergyman* 1720

Satire is a sort of glass, wherein beholders do generally   2
discover everybody's face but their own.

> *The Battle of the Books*

Whoever could make two ears of corn or two blades of grass to   3
grow upon a spot of ground where only one grew before, would
deserve better of mankind, and do more essential service to his
country than the whole race of politicians put together.

> *Gulliver's Travels*, 'Voyage to Brobdingnag'

I shall be like that tree, I shall die at the top.   4

> Walter Scott, *Memoirs of Swift*

Yet malice never was his aim; / He lash'd the vice, but spared   5
the name.

> *On the Death of Dr. Swift*

Few are qualified to shine in company; but it is in most   6
men's power to be agreeable.

> *Thoughts on Various Subjects*

We have just enough religion to make us hate, but not enough   7
to make us love one another.

> *Thoughts on Various Subjects*

Swinburne Algernon Charles 1837–1909. English poet.

From too much love of living, / From hope and fear set free, /
We thank with brief thanksgiving / Whatever gods may be /
That no man lives forever, / That dead men rise up never; /
That even the weariest river / Winds somewhere safe to sea.

> *The Garden of Proserpine*

Szasz Thomas 1920–   . Hungarian-born US psychiatrist

A child becomes an adult when he realizes that he has a right
not only to be right but also to be wrong.

> 'Childhood'

The stupid neither forgive nor forget; the naïve forgive and   2
forget; the wise forgive but do not forget.

> 'Personal Conduct'

Formerly, when religion was strong and science weak, men   *3*
mistook magic for medicine; now, when science is strong and
religion weak, men mistake medicine for magic.

'Science and Scientism'

T

Tagore Rabindranath 1861–1941. Bengali Indian writer.

The butterfly counts not months but moments, and has time enough.

Fireflies

Tarkington Booth 1869–1946. US novelist.

Arguments only confirm people in their own opinions.
Looking Forward to the Great Adventure

Tennyson Alfred, 1st Baron Tennyson 1809–1892. English poet.

Bare-footed came the beggar maid / Before the king Cophetua.
'The Beggar Maid'

Break, break, break, / On thy cold gray stones, O Sea! 2
'Break, Break, Break'

For men may come and men may go, / But I go on for ever. 3
'The Brook'

Half a league, half a league, / Half a league onward. 4
'The Charge of the Light Brigade'

Some one had blunder'd. 5
'The Charge of the Light Brigade'

Their's not to make reply, / Their's not to reason why, / Their's 6
but to do and die: / Into the valley of Death / Rode the six hundred.
'The Charge of the Light Brigade'

If thou shouldst never see my face again, / Pray for my soul. 7
More things are wrought by prayer / Than this world dreams of.
The Idylls of the king, 'The Passing of Arthur'

'The old order changeth, yielding place to new, / And God 8
fulfils himself in many ways.'
The Idylls of the King, 'The Passing of Arthur'

The whole round earth is every way / Bound by gold chains   **9**
about the feet of God.

The Idylls of the King, 'The Passing of Arthur'

Nature, red in tooth and claw.   **10**

In Memoriam 56

So many worlds, so much to do, / So little done, such things to be.   **11**
In Memoriam 73

Ring out, wild bells, to the wild sky. / Ring out the old, ring in   **12**
the new.

In Memoriam 106

Kind hearts are more than coronets, / And simple faith than   **13**
Norman blood.

'Lady Clara Vere de Vere'

The fairy tales of science, and the long result of Time.   **14**
'Locksley Hall'

He will hold thee, when his passion shall have spent its novel   **15**
force. / Something better than his dog, a little dearer than his
horse.

'Locksley Hall'

In the Spring a young man's fancy lightly turns to thoughts of   **16**
love.

'Locksley Hall'

A land / In which it seemed always afternoon.   **17**
'The Lotos-Eaters'

Come into the garden, Maud, / For the black bat, night, has flown.   **18**
Maud

Tears, idle tears, I know not what they mean, / Tears from the   **19**
depth of some divine despair.

The Princess 4

Now sleeps the crimson petal, now the white; / Nor waves the   **20**
cypress in the palace walk; / Nor winks the gold fin in the
porphyry font:/ The fire-fly wakens: waken thou with me.

The Princess 7

The woods decay, the woods decay and fall, / The vapours
weep their burthen to the ground, / Man comes and tills the field
and lies beneath, / And after many a summer dies the swan.

21

Tithonus

I will drink / Life to the lees: all times I have enjoy'd / Greatly,
have suffer'd greatly, both with those / That loved me, and alone.

22

Ulysses I. 6

Tho' much is taken, much abides; and tho' / We are not now
that strength which in old days / Moved earth and heaven; that
which we are, we are; / One equal temper of heroic hearts, /
Made weak by time and fate, but strong in will / To strive, to
seek, to find, and not to yield.

23

Ulysses I. 44

It little profits that an idle king, / By this still hearth, among
these barren crags, / Match'd with an aged wife, I mete and
dole / Unequal laws unto a savage race.

24

'Ulysses'

Terence (Publius Terentius Afer) 190–159 BC. Roman dramatist.

Fortune assists the brave.

Phormio

Thackeray William Makepeace 1811–1863. English novelist and
essayist.

He who meanly admires mean things is a Snob.

The Book of Snobs

'Tis not the dying for a faith that's so hard ... every man of
every nation has done that ... 'tis the living up to it that is
difficult.

6

3

The History of Henry Esmond bk 1, ch

'Tis strange what a man may do, and a woman yet think him an
angel.

74

The History of Henry Esmond bk 1, ch

We love being in love, that's the truth on't.

Vanity Fair bk 2, ch 15

Thatcher Margaret Hilda (born Roberts), Baroness Thatcher of
Kesteven 1925–   . British Conservative politician, prime minister
1979–90.

To those waiting with bated breath for that favourite media
catch-phrase, the U-turn, I have only one thing to say. You
turn if you want to. The lady's not for turning.
                              Speech to the Conservative Party Conference 1980

No one would remember the Good Samaritan if he'd only had   2
good intentions. He had money as well.
                              Television interview 6 Jan 1986

There is no such thing as Society. There are individual men and   3
women, and there are families.
                              Woman's Own 31 Oct 1987

I am extraordinarily patient, provided I get my own way in the   4
end.
                              Observer 4 Apr 1989

Theroux Paul (Edward) 1941–   . US novelist and travel writer.

Extensive travelling induces a feeling of encapsulation, and
travel, so broadening at first, contracts the mind.
                              The Great American Railway

Thomas Dylan (Marlais) 1914–1953. Welsh poet.

Do not go gentle into that good night, / Rage, rage against the
dying of the light.
                              'Do Not Go Gentle into That Good Night'

Now as I was young and easy under the apple boughs / About   2
the lilting house and happy as the grass was green.
                              'Fern Hill'

And before you let the sun in, mind it wipes its shoes.   3
                              Under Milk Wood

You're thinking, you're no better than you should be, / Polly,   4
and that's good enough for me. Oh, isn't life a terrible thing,
thank God?
                              Under Milk Wood

Thompson Francis 1859–1907. English poet.

The angels keep their ancient places; / Turn but a stone, and start a wing! / 'Tis ye, 'tis your estrangèd faces, / That miss the many-splendoured thing.

'The Kingdom of God'

Thompson Hunter S 1939– . US writer and journalist.

Fear and Loathing in Las Vegas.

Title of two articles in *Rolling Stone* Nov 1972

Thomson James 1700–1748. Scottish poet.

When Britain first, at heaven's command, / Arose from out the azure main, / This was the charter of the land, / And guardian angels sung this strain: / 'Rule, Britannia, rule the waves; / Britons never will be slaves.'

Alfred: a Masque

Thoreau Henry David 1817–1862. US author and naturalist.

The mass of men lead lives of quiet desperation.

Walden, 'Economy'

Some circumstantial evidence is very strong, as when you find a trout in the milk.   2

Miscellanies

It takes two to speak the truth, – one to speak, and another to hear.   3
A Week on the Concord and Merrimack Rivers

Simplify, simplify.   4
Walden, 'Where I Lived, and What I Lived For'

Thurber James (Grover) 1894–1961. US humorist.

It's a naïve domestic Burgundy without any breeding, but I think you'll be amused by its presumption.
Cartoon caption in *New Yorker* 27 Mar 1937

Well, if I called the wrong number, why did you answer the phone?   2

Cartoon caption in *New Yorker* 5 June 1937

Her own mother lived the latter years of her life in the horrible
suspicion that electricity was dripping invisibly all over the
house.   **3**
My Life and Hard Times

Thurlow Edward, 1st Baron Thurlow 1731–1806. English lawyer.

Corporations have neither bodies to be punished, nor souls to be
condemned, they therefore do as they like.
Poynder *Literary Extracts*

Tocqueville Alexis de 1805–1859. French politician and political
scientist.

Americans are so enamored of equality that they would rather
be equal in slavery than unequal in freedom.
Democracy in America

Democratic institutions generally give men a lofty notion of
country and themselves.   **2**
Democracy in America

When I refuse to obey an unjust law, I do not contest the right   **3**
of the majority to command, but I simply appeal from the
sovereignty of the people to the sovereignty of mankind.
Democracy in America

Tolstoy Leo Nikolaievich 1828–1910. Russian novelist.

All happy families resemble each other, but each unhappy
family is unhappy in its own way.
Anna Karenina

Townsend Sue 1946–   . English humorous novelist.
The Secret Diary of Adrian Mole Aged 13 ³/4.
Book title

Tree Herbert Beerbohm 1853–1917. English actor and theatre manager.
He is an old bore. Even the grave yawns for him.
Of Israel Zangwill, in Max Beerbohm *Herbert Beerbohm Tree*

Trinder Tommy 1909–1989. English entertainer.

Overpaid, overfed, oversexed, and over here.
Of US troops in Britain during World War II,
in *Sunday Times* 4 Jan 1976

Trollope Anthony 1815–1882. English novelist.

Three hours a day will produce as much as a man ought to write.
Autobiography

It's dogged as does it. It ain't thinking about it.   *2*
Last Chronicles of Barset

Trollope Frances 1780–1863. English novelist

Of course I draw from life—but I always pulp my acquaintance before serving them up. You would never recognize a pig in a sausage.

Remark

Trotsky Leon. Adopted name of Lev Davidovitch Bronstein 1879–1940. Russian revolutionary.

Old age is the most unexpected of all things that happen to a man.
Diary in Exile

Go where you belong from now on—into the dustbin of history!   *2*
Addressing the Mensheviks in *History of the Russian Revolution*

Truman Harry S 1884–1972. 33rd president of the USA 1945–53.

It's a recession when your neighbour loses his job; it's a depression when you lose yours.
Observer 13 Apr 1958

The buck stops here.   *2*

Sign on his presidential desk

Tucker Sophie 1884–1966. Russian-born US singer and entertainer.

From birth to 18 a girl needs good parents. From 18 to 35, she needs good looks. From 35 to 55, good personality. From 55 on, she needs good cash. I'm saving my money.
M Freedland *Sophie*

Twain Mark. Pen name of Samuel Langhorne Clemens 1835–1910. US writer.

There was things which he stretched, but mainly he told the truth.
The Adventures of Huckleberry Finn ch 1

The statements was interesting, but tough.   2
The Adventures of Huckleberry Finn ch 17

There are three kinds of lies: lies, damned lies, and statistics.   3
Autobiography

Are you going to hang him *anyhow* – and try him afterward?   4
Innocents at Home

Tynan Kenneth (Peacock) 1927–1980. English theatre critic and author.

A good drama critic is one who perceives what is happening in the theatre of his time. A great drama critic also perceives what is *not* happening.

Tynan Right and Left

U

Unamuno Miguel de 1864–1936. Spanish writer of Basque origin.

The chiefest sanctity of a temple is that it is a place to which men go to weep in common.

The Tragic Sense of Life 'The Man of Flesh and Bone'

Updike John (Hoyer) 1932– . US writer.

A healthy male adult bore consumes each year one and a half times his own weight in other people's patience.

'Confessions of a Wild Bore'

Neutrinos, they are very small. / They have no charge and have no mass / And do not interact at all.

2

'Cosmic Gall'

Ustinov Peter 1921– . English stage and film actor, writer, and director.

Laughter would be bereaved if snobbery died.

Observer 13 Mar 1955

Contrary to general belief, I do not believe that friends are necessarily the people you like best, they are merely the people who got there first.

2

Dear Me

A diplomat these days is nothing but a head-waiter who's allowed to sit down occasionally.

3

Romanoff and Juliet

V

Valéry 1871–1945. French poet and mathematician.

A poem is never finished; it's always an accident that puts a stop to it—i.e. gives it to the public.

Littérature

God made everything out of the void, but ⠀⠀void shows through.   2

Mauvaises pensées et autres

Politics is the art of preventing people from taking part in affairs which properly concern them.   3

Tel Quel 2, 'Rhumbs'

Van der Post Laurens (Jan) 1906– . South African writer.

Organized religion is making Christianity political, rather than making politics Christian.

Observer 9 Nov 1986

Vanderbilt William Henry 1821–1885. US financier and railway promoter.

The public be damned!
    Reply when asked if the public should be consulted about luxury trains. A W Cole's letter, in *New York Times* 25 August 1918

Vaughan Henry 1622–1695. Welsh poet and physician.

They are all gone into the world of light, / And I alone sit lingering here.

Silex Scintillans, 'They Are All Gone'

I saw Eternity the other night, / Like a great ring of pure and endless light.   2

Silex Scintillans, 'The World'

Veblen Thorstein (Bunde) 1857–1929. US social critic.

Conspicuous consumption of valuable goods is a means of reputability to the gentleman of leisure.

Theory of the Leisure Class

Vegetius 4th century– . Roman military writer

Let him who desires peace, prepare for war.

De Re Militare

Victoria 1819–1901. Queen of the UK 1837–1901.
We are not amused.

Notebooks of a Spinster Lady 2 Jan 1900

He speaks to Me as if I was a public meeting.   *2*
Remark about her Prime Minister Gladstone

Vidal Gore 1925– . US writer and critic.

A triumph of the embalmer's art.
Describing Ronald Reagan, *Observer* 26 Apr 1981

There is something about a bureaucrat that does not like a poem.   *2*
Sex, Death and Money Preface

Villiers George, 2nd Duke of Buckingham 1627–1687. English courtier and author.

What the devil does the plot signify, except to bring in fine things?
The Rehearsal III. i

Ay, now the plot thickens very much upon us.   *2*
The Rehearsal III ii

Villon François 1431–1465. French poet.

But where are the snows of yesteryear?
'Ballade des Dames du Temps Jadis'

Virgil (Publius Vergilius Maro) 70–19 BC. Roman poet.

Arms and the man I sing.

Aeneid I

Tears in the nature of thing.   2

Aeneid I

Roman, this is your task—these your arts—to hold sway over   3
the nations and to impose the law of peace, to spare the
humbled and to quell the proud!

Aeneid VI

Meanwhile, Time is flying—flying, never to return.   4

Georgics

Voltaire Pen name of François-Marie Arouet 1694–1778. French writer.

In this country [England] it is thought well to kill an admiral from
time to time to encourage the others.

Candide ch 23

'That is well said,' replied Candide, 'but we must cultivate our   2
garden.'

Candide ch 30

If God did not exist, it would be necessary to invent him.   3

Épîtres

W

Wagner Richard 1813–1883. German opera composer.

Where the speech of men stops short, then the art of music begins.
A Happy Evening

Wallace Edgar 1875–1932. English writer of thrillers.

What is a highbrow? He is a man who has found something more interesting than women.
New York Times 24 Jan 1932

Wallace George Corley 1919– . US politician.

Segregation now, segregation tomorrow and segregation forever!
Inaugural speech as Governor of Alabama Jan 1963

Wallace Henry Agard 1888–1965. US editor and public official.

The century on which we are entering—the century which will come out of this war—can be and must be the century of the common man.
Speech 8 May 1942

Waller Edmund 1606–1687. English poet.

Go, lovely Rose! / Tell her, that wastes her time and me, / That now she knows, / When I resemble her to thee, / How sweet and fair she seems to be.
'Go, Lovely Rose!'

Walpole Horace, 4th Earl of Orford 1717–1797. English novelist, letter writer and politician.

The balance of power.
Speech in House of Commons 1741

Our supreme governors, the mob.
Letter to Horace Mann 1743

2

This world is a comedy to those that think, a tragedy to those   *3*
that feel.
> Letter to the Countess of Upper Ossory 1776

Walpole Robert, 1st Earl of Orford 1676–1745. English statesman.

They now *ring* the bells, but they will soon *wring* their hands.
> Remark when war against Spain was declared 1739.

Walton Izaak 1593–1683. English author.

I love such mirth as does not make friends ashamed to look
upon one another next morning.
> *Compleat Angler* ch 5

Look to your health; and if you have it, praise God, and value it   *2*
next to a good conscience.
> *Compleat Angler* ch 21

Ward Artemus. Pen name of Charles Farrar Browne 1834–1867. US
humorist and writer.

My pollertics, like my religion, bein of a exceedin
accommodatin character.
> *Artemus Ward His Book*, 'The Crisis'

The ground flew up and hit me in the hed.   *2*
> *Artemus Ward His Book*, 'Thrilling Scenes in Dixie'

Warhol Andy. Adopted name of Andrew Warhola 1928–1987. US
Pop artist and filmmaker.

In the future everyone will be famous for 15 minutes.
> *Exposures*

Washington George 1732–1799. First president of the USA 1789–97.

Father, I cannot tell a lie.
> Attributed remark

Watts Isaac 1674–1748. English Nonconformist writer of hymns.

How doth the little busy bee / Improve each shining hour.
> *Divine Songs for Children*, 'Against Idleness and Mischief'

In works of labour, or of skill, / I would be busy too; / For Satan   2
finds some mischief still / For idle hands to do.
> *Divine Songs for Children*, 'Against Idleness and Mischief'

Let dogs delight to bark and bite, / For God hath made them so.   3
> *Divine Songs for Children*, 'Against Quarrelling'

'Tis the voice of the sluggard; I heard him complain, / 'You   4
have wak'd me too soon, I must slumber again'.
> *Moral Songs*, 'The Sluggard'

Waugh Evelyn (Arthur St John) 1903–1966. English novelist.

Manners are especially the need of the plain. The pretty can
get away with anything.
> *Observer* 15 Apr 1962

Any who have heard that sound will shrink at the recollection   2
of it; it is the sound of English county families baying for
broken glass.
> *Decline and Fall* 'Prelude'

I expect you'll be becoming a schoolmaster, sir. That's what   3
most of the gentlemen does, sir, that gets sent down for indecent
behaviour.
> *Decline and Fall* 'Prelude'

Any one who has been to an English public school will always   4
feel comparatively at home in prison.
> *Decline and Fall* pt 3, ch 4

Mr Salter's side of the conversation was limited to expressions   5
of assent. When Lord Copper was right, he said, 'Definitely,
Lord Copper'; when he was wrong, 'Up to a point'.
> *Scoop*

Brideshead Revisited.   6
> *Title of novel*

Webb Beatrice 1858–1943. English socialist and writer.

If I ever felt inclined to be timid as I was going into a room full
of people, I would say to myself, 'You're the cleverest member

of one of the cleverest families in the cleverest class of the
cleverest nation in the world, why should you be frightened?'
Bertrand Russell *Autobiography*

Weber Max 1864–1920. German sociologist.

The idea of duty in one's calling prowls about in our life like
the ghost of dead religious beliefs.
The Protestant Ethic

Weil Simone 1909–1943. French writer.

All sins are attempts to fill voids.
Gravity and Grace

Weissmuller Johnny 1904–1984. US actor.

Me Tarzan, you Jane.
Photoplay Magazine June 1932 (the words did not
occur in the film script of Tarzan, the Ape Man)

Welles (George) Orson 1915–1985. US actor and film and theatre director.

This is the biggest electric train set any boy ever had!
Of the RKO studio, in P Noble *The Fabulous Orson Welles*

Wells H(erbert) G(eorge) 1866–1946. English writer.

Human history becomes more and more a race between education
and catastrophe.
The Outline of History

If Max gets to Heaven he won't last long. He will be chucked   2
out for trying to pull off a merger between Heaven and Hell ...
after having secured a controlling interest in key subsidiary
companies in both places, of course.
Of Max Beaverbrook in A J P Taylor *Beaverbrook*

In England we have come to rely upon a comfortable time-lag   3
of fifty years or a century intervening between the
perception that something ought to be done and a serious
attempt to do it.
The Work, Wealth and Happiness of Mankind

The Shape of Things to Come.   4
Book title

The War that Will End War. 5

Book title

West Mae 1892–1980. US vaudeville, stage, and film actress.

Is that a gun in your pocket, or are you just glad to see me?

J Weintraub *Peel Me a Grape*

West Rebecca. Pen name of Cicely Isabel Fairfield 1892–1983.
English journalist, novelist, and feminist.

Journalism – an ability to meet the challenge of filling the space.

New York Herald Tribune 22 Apr 1956

The peculiar mathematics ... apply to many cases of desertion. 2
woman who loses her husband or her lover seems to lose more
by his absence than she ever gained by his presence.

Times Literary Supplement 26 July 1974

Wharton Edith 1862–1937. US novelist.

An unalterable and unquestioned law of the musical world
required that the German text of French operas sung by
Swedish artists should be translated into Italian for the clearer
understanding of English-speaking audiences.

Age of Innocence

Mrs. Ballinger is one of the ladies who pursue Culture in bands, 2
as though it were dangerous to meet it alone.

Xingu

Whately Richard 1787–1863. English churchman.

Happiness is no laughing matter.

Apophthegms

White E(lwyn) B(rooks) 1899–1985. US writer.

Democracy is the recurrent suspicion that more than half of the
people are right more than half of the time.

New Yorker 3 July 1944

White Patrick (Victor Martindale) 1912–1990. Australian writer.

Inspiration descends only in flashes, to clothe circumstances;

it is not stored up in a barrel, like salt herrings, to be doled out.
Voss

White T(erence) H(anbury) 1906–1964. English writer.

The Once and Future King.

Title of novel

Whitehead Alfred North 1861–1947. English philosopher and mathematician.

Intelligence is quickness to apprehend as distinct from ability, which is capacity to act wisely on the thing apprehended.
Dialogues 15 Dec 1939

Civilization advances by extending the number of important   2
operations which we can perform without thinking about them.
Introduction to Mathematics

Whitman Walt(er) 1819–1892. US poet.

Do I contradict myself? Very well then I contradict myself
(I am large, I contain multitudes).

'Song of Myself'

I celebrate myself, and sing myself.   2

'Song of Myself'

Whitton Charlotte 1896–1975. Canadian writer and politician.

Whatever women do they must do twice as well as men to be thought half as good. Luckily, this is not difficult.
Canada Month June 1963

Wilde Oscar (Fingal O'Flahertie Wills) 1854–1900. Irish writer.

Yet each man kills the thing he loves, ... / The coward does it with a kiss, / The brave man with a sword!
The Ballad of Reading Gaol

All women become like their mothers. That is their tragedy.   2
No man does. That's his.

Importance of Being Earnest I

In married life three is company and two none.

Importance of Being Earnest I

3

To lose one parent, Mr. Worthing, may be regarded as a misfortune; to lose both looks like carelessness.

Importance of Being Earnest I

4

On an occasion of this kind it becomes more than a moral duty to speak one's mind. It becomes a pleasure.

Importance of Being Earnest II

5

Experience is the name every one gives to their mistakes.

Lady Windermere's Fan

6

A man who knows the price of everything and the value of nothing.

Lady Windermere's Fan, definition of a cynic

7

A man cannot be too careful in the choice of his enemies.

Picture of Dorian Gray

8

The only way to get rid of a temptation is to yield to it.

Picture of Dorian Gray

9

There is no such thing as a moral or an immoral book. Books are well written, or badly written.

Picture of Dorian Gray

10

There is only one thing in the world worse than being talked about, and that is not being talked about.

Picture of Dorian Gray

11

A thing is not necessarily true because a man dies for it.

Sebastian Melmoth

12

One should never trust a woman who tells one her real age. A woman who would tell one that, would tell one anything.

A Woman of No Importance

13

I have nothing to declare except my genius.

Remark at the New York Customs House

14

Wilder Thornton 1897–1975. US dramatist and novelist.

Marriage is a bribe to make a housekeeper think she's a householder.

Merchant of Yonkers

Wilkes John 1727–1797. British Radical politician.

The chapter of accidents is the longest chapter in the book.

Attributed remark

Willans Geoffrey 1911–1958 and **Searl** Ronald 1920– . English writer and cartoonist.

The only good things about skool are the boys wizz who are noble brave fearless etc. although you hav various swots, bulies, cissies, milksops, greedy guts and oiks with whom I am forced to mingle hem-hem.

Down With Skool

Williams Tennessee (Thomas Lanier) 1911–1983. US dramatist.

We're all of us guinea pigs in the laboratory of God. Humanity is just a work in progress.

Camino Real

Wilson Sandy 1924– . English songwriter.

It's never too late to have a fling, / For Autumn is just as nice as Spring, / And it's never too late to fall in love.

'It's Never too Late to Fall in Love'

Wilson Woodrow 1856–1924. 28th president of the USA 1913–21.

The world must be made safe for democracy.

Address to Congress 2 Apr 1917

Wister Owen 1860–1938. US novelist.

When you call me that, smile!

The Virginian

Wither George 1588–1667. English poet and pamphleteer.

Shall I, wasting in despair, / Die because a woman's fair? ..

'Sonnet'

Wittgenstein Ludwig 1889–1951. Austrian philosopher.

Philosophy ... is a fight against the fascination which forms of expression exert upon us.

The Blue Book

The limits of my language mean the limits of my world.   2
Tractatus Logico-Philosophicus

The world is everything that is the case.   3
Tractatus Logico-Philosophicus

Wodehouse P(elham) G(renville) 1881–1975. English novelist.

What good are brains to a man? They only unsettle him.
The Adventures of Sally

He spoke with a certain what-is-it in his voice, and I could see   2
that, if not actually disgruntled, he was far from being gruntled.
The Code of the Woosters

It is no use telling me that there are bad aunts and good aunts.   3
At the core, they are all alike. Sooner or later, out pops the
cloven hoof.

The Code of the Woosters

Slice him where you like, a hellhound is always a hellhound.   4
The Code of the Woosters

The Right Hon. was a tubby little chap who looked as if he   5
had been poured into his clothes and had forgotten to say
'When!'.

'Jeeves and the Impending Doom'

Wolfe Charles 1791–1823. Irish curate.

Not a drum was heard, not a funeral note, / As his corse to the
rampart we hurried.
'The Burial of Sir John Moore at Corunna'

We carved not a line, and we raised not a stone – / But we left   2
him alone with his glory.
'The Burial of Sir John Moore at Corunna'

Wolfe Humbert 1886–1940. Italian-born English poet.

You cannot hope to bribe or twist, thank God! the British journalist. / But, seeing what the man will do unbrided, there's no occasion to.

'Over the Fire'

Wolsey Thomas *c*. 1475–1530. English cleric and politician.

Father Abbot, I am come to lay my bones amongst you.
Cavendish, *Negotiations of Thomas Wolsey*

Had I but served God as diligently as I have served the king, he   2
would not have given me over in my gray hairs.
Cavendish, *Negotiations of Thomas Wolsey*

Woolf Virginia 1882–1941. English novelist and critic.

It is in our idleness, in our dreams, that the submerged truth sometimes comes to the top.

A Room of One's Own

We are nauseated by the sight of trivial personalities   2
decomposing in the eternity of print.
The Common Reader, 'The Modern Essay'

Women have served all these centuries as looking- glasses   3
possessing the magic and delicious power of reflecting the figure of a man at twice its natural size.

A Room of One's Own

Woollcott Alexander 1887–1943. US theatre critic and literary figure.

A broker is a man who takes your fortune and runs it into a shoestring.

S H Adams *Alexander Woollcott*

All the things I really like to do are either illegal, immoral, or   2
fattening.

R E Drennan *Wit's End*

Wordsworth 1840–1932. Principal of Lady Margaret Hall, Oxford.

If all the good people were clever, / And all clever people were good, / The world would be nicer than ever / We thought that it possibly could. / But somehow, 'tis seldom or never / The two hit it off as they should; / The good are so harsh to the clever, / The clever so rude to the good!

> *St Christopher and Other Poems,*

Wordsworth William 1770–1850. English Romantic poet.

For oft, when on my couch I lie / In vacant or in pensive mood, / They flash upon that inward eye / Which is the bliss of solitude; / And then my heart with pleasure fills, / And dances with the daffodils.

> 'Daffodils'

I wandered lonely as a cloud / That floats on high o'er vales and   2
hills, / When all at once I saw a crowd, / A host, of golden daffodils; / Beside the lake, beneath the trees, / Fluttering and dancing in the breeze.

> 'Daffodils'

Never to blend our pleasure or our pride / With sorrow of the   3
meanest thing that feels.

> 'Hart-leap Well'

I have learned / To look on nature not as in the hour / Of   4
thoughtless youth; but hearing often-times / The still, sad music of humanity, / Nor harsh nor grating, though of ample power / To chasten and subdue. And I have felt / A presence that disturbs me with the joy / Of elevated thoughts; a sense sublime / Of something far more deeply interfused, / Whose dwelling is the light of setting suns, / And the round ocean and the living air, / And the blue sky, and in the mind of man.

> 'Lines composed a few miles above Tintern Abbey'

That best portion of a good man's life, / His little, nameless,   5
unremembered acts / Of kindness and of love.

> 'Lines composed a few miles above Tintern Abbey'

And much it grieved my heart to think / What man has made of   6
man.
'Lines Written in Early Spring'

Milton! thou shouldst be living at this hour: / England hath   7
need of thee; she is a fen / Of stagnant waters.
'Milton! thou shouldst be living at this hour'

My heart leaps up when I behold / A rainbow in the sky.   8
'My Heart Leaps Up'

Nuns fret not at their convent's narrow room; / And hermits are   9
contented with their cells.
'Nuns Fret Not'

Our birth is but a sleep and a forgetting: / The Soul that rises 10
with us, our life's Star, / Hath had elsewhere its setting, /
And cometh from afar: / Not in entire forgetfulness, / And
not in utter nakedness, / But trailing clouds of glory do
we come / From God, who is our home: / Heaven lies about
us in our infancy! / Shades of the prison-house begin to close /
Upon the growing boy, / But he beholds the light, and whence it
flows, / He sees it in his joy; / The youth, who daily farther
from the east / Must travel, still is Nature's priest, / And by the
vision splendid / Is on his way attended; / At length the man
perceives it die away, / And fade into the light of common
day.
Ode. Intimations of Immortality

The rainbow comes and goes, / And lovely is the rose, / The   11
moon doth with delight / Look round her when the heavens are
bare, / Waters on a starry night / Are beautiful and fair; / The
sunshine is a glorious birth: / But yet I know, where'er I go, /
That there hath passed away a glory from the earth.
Ode. Intimations of Immortality

Thanks to the human heart by which we live, / Thanks to its   12
tenderness, its joys, and fears, / To me the meanest flower that
blows can give / Thoughts that do often lie too deep for tears.
Ode. Intimations of Immortality

There was a time when meadow, grove, and stream, / The earth, **13**
and every common sight, / To me did seem / Apparelled in
celestial light, / The glory and the freshness of a dream. / It is
not now as it hath been of yore; – / Turn whereso'er I may, / By
night or day, / The things which I have seen I now can see no
more.

Ode. Intimations of Immortality

Though nothing can bring back the hour / Of splendour in the **14**
grass, of glory in the flower; / We will grieve not, rather find /
Strength in what remains behind.

Ode. Intimations of Immortality

Whither is fled the visionary gleam? / Where is it now, the glory **15**
and the dream?

Ode. Intimations of Immortality

Once did she hold the gorgeous East in fee, / And was the **16**
safeguard of the West.

'On the Extinction of the Venetian Republic'

Sweet Spenser, moving through his clouded heaven / With the **17**
moon's beauty and the moon's soft pace.

The Prelude

Where the statue stood / Of Newton, with his prism and silent **18**
face, / The marble index of a mind for ever / Voyaging through
strange seas of thought alone.

The Prelude iii

Bliss was it in that dawn to be alive, / But to be young was very **19**
heaven!

The Prelude bk xi

I thought of Chatterton, the marvellous boy, / The sleepless **20**
soul, that perished in his pride.

'Resolution and Independence'

She dwelt among the untrodden ways / Beside the springs of **21**
Dove, / A maid whom there were none to praise / And very few
to love: / A violet by a mossy stone / Half hidden from the eye!

/ Fair as a star, when only one / Is shining in the sky. / She lived unknown, and few could know / When Lucy ceased to be; / But she is in her grave, and, oh, / The difference to me!

'She Dwelt Among the Untrodden Ways'

A slumber did my spirit seal; / I had no human fears: / She   **22**
seemed a thing that could not feel / The touch of earthly years.

'A Slumber did My Spirit Seal'

Behold her, single in the field, / Yon solitary Highland lass!   **23**

'The Solitary Reaper'

Perhaps the plaintive numbers flow / For old, unhappy, far-off   **24**
things, / And battles long ago.

'The Solitary Reaper'

One impulse from a vernal wood / May teach you more of man,   **25**
/ Of moral evil and of good, / Than all the sages can.

'The Tables Turned'

Two Voices are there; one is of the sea, / One of the mountains;   **26**
each a mighty Voice.

'Thought of a Briton on the Subjugation of Switzerland'

O Cuckoo! Shall I call thee bird, / Or but a wandering voice?   **27**

'To the Cuckoo'

The world is too much with us; late and soon, / Getting and   **28**
spending, we lay waste our powers.

'The World is Too Much with Us'

Plain living and high thinking are no more.   **29**

'Written in London. O Friend! I know Not'

Wotton Henry 1568–1639. English poet and diplomat.

How happy is he born and taught / That serveth not another's
will; / Whose armour is his honest thought / And simple truth
his utmost skill!

'The Character of a Happy Life'

Lord of himself, though not of lands, / And having nothing, yet   **2**
hath all.

'The Character of a Happy Life'

He first deceas'd; she for a little tri'd / To live without him: *3*
lik'd it not, and di'd.
                                   'Death of Sir Albertus Moreton's Wife'

You meaner beauties of the night, / That poorly satisfy our eyes,   *4*
/ More by your number, than your light; / You common people
of the skies, / What are you when the moon shall rise?
                                   'On His Mistress, the Queen of Bohemia'

An ambassador is an honest man sent to lie abroad for the good   *5*
of his country.
                                   Written in the Album of Christopher Fleckmore

Wren Christopher 1632–1723. English architect.

If you seek a moment, gaze around.
(Latin:) Si monumentum requiris, circumspice.
                                   Inscription in St Paul's Cathedral, London,
                                               attributed to Wren's son

Wright 1869–1959. US architect.

The physician can bury his mistakes, but the architect can only
advise his clients to plant vines.
                                                   New York Times Magazine

Wyatt Thomas *c.* 1503– . English poet.

They flee from me, that sometime did me seek.
                                                   'Remembrance'

X

Xenophon *c*. 430–   . Greek historian, philosopher, and soldier.

/ The sea! thesea!

> The cry of the Greek mercenaries on reaching
> safety at the Black Sea, after escaping from the
> Battle of Cunaxa, 401BC; *Anabasis* IV.vii

Y

Yeats W B 1865–1939. Irish poet and dramatist.

Down by the salley gardens my love and I did meet;/ She passed the salley gardens with little snow-white feet. / She bid me take love easy, as the leaves grow on the tree; / But I, being young and foolish, with her would not agree.

'Down by the Salley Gardens'

All changed, changed utterly: / A terrible beauty is born.
2
'Easter 1916'

When I play on my fiddle in Dooney / Folk dance like a wave
3
of the sea.

'The Fiddler of Dooney'

I have spread my dreams under your feet; / Tread softly,
4
because you tread on my dreams.

'He Wishes for the Cloths of Heaven'

Nor law, nor duty bade me fight, / Nor public men, nor cheering
5
crowds, / A lonely impulse of delight / Drove to this tumult in the clouds; / I balanced all, brought all to mind, / The years to come seemed waste of breath, / A waste of breath the years behind / In balance with this life, this death.

'An Irish Airman Foresees His Death'

I will arise and go now, and go to Innisfree, /And a small cabin
6
build there, of clay and wattles made: / Nine bean-rows will I have there, a hive for the honey-bee, / And live alone in the bee-loud glade.

'The Lake Isle of Innisfree'

Like a long-legged fly upon the stream / His mind
7
moves upon silence.

'Long-Legged Fly'

Hearts are not had as a gift but hearts are earned / By those that   **8**
are not entirely beautiful.

'Prayer for my Daughter'

Cast a cold eye / On life, on death. / Horseman pass by!   **9**

'Under Ben Bulben'

When you are old and gray and full of sleep, / And nodding   **10**
by the fire, take down this book, / And slowly read, and dream
of the soft look /Your eyes had once, and of their shadows
deep.

'When you are Old'

Yellen Jack 1892– . US lyricist.

I'm the Last of the Red-Hot Mamas.

Song title

Young Edward 1683–1765. English poet and dramatist.

You are so witty, profligate, and thin, / At once we think thee
Milton, Death, and Sin.

'Epigram on Voltaire'

Be wise with speed; / A fool at forty is a fool indeed.   **2**

Love of Fame

Procrastination is the thief of time.   **3**

Night Thoughts

Life is the desert, life the solitude; / Death joins us to thegreat **4**
majority.

The Revenge

Z

Zangwill Israel 1864–1926. English writer.

America is God's Crucible, the great Melting-Pot where all the races of Europe are melting and reforming! ... God is making the American.

The Melting Pot

Zanuck Darryl F 1902–1979. Hollywood film producer.

For God's sake don't say yes until I've finished talking.
Philip French *The Movie Moguls*

Zappa Frank (Francis Vincent) 1940–1993. US rock musician, bandleader, and composer.

Rock journalism is people who can't write interviewing people who can't talk for people who can't read.
quoted in L Botts *Loose Talk*

Zemeckis Robert 1952– . US film director.

Back to the Future.

Film title

Zia ul-Haq Mohammed 1924–1988. Pakistani general and president.

If the Court sentences the blighter to hang, then the blighter will hang.
Of the death sentence imposed on
former president Zulfikar Ali Bhutto 1979

Zola Émile 1804–1902. French novelist and social reformer

J'accuse. / I accuse.

Heading of an open letter to the President of
the Republic concerning the Dreyfus case 1898

THEME INDEX